Gerti Baldwin

The Other Heaven **Can Wait**

novum ▲ pro

www.novum-publishing.co.uk

© 2022 novum publishing

ISBN 978-3-99131-273-4
Editing: Phil Kelly
Cover photos: Kevin Carden,
Ints Vikmanis | Dreamstime.com
Cover design, layout & typesetting:
novum publishing

www.novum-publishing.co.uk

Climate neutral
Print product
ClimatePartner.com/16547-2201-1002

CHAPTER 1

WALES 1992

Slipping into my bathrobe after a lovely hot shower, all I wanted was a nice cup of tea. With a long evening ahead of me I could take my time, watch TV, and perhaps read for a while. Taking it easy was not only a pleasure after a lifetime of working; it had become a necessity since my car accident. I was still in a lot of pain and easily exhausted. But tonight I would ignore the muddle and leave everything as it was. Living alone had its advantages I told myself, but I missed my son who just came home during holidays now, since working in London.

Two weeks ago I had moved here to the Pembrokeshire coast, and though quite a few packing cases still stood around, I had what I needed. Tonight I'd relax in my recliner, placed strategically by the patio door, so I could look down the wooded hills leading to Amroth Beach, with its silvery sliver of sea in the distance. My house was close to the wood, the last in a row of small dwellings, right in the countryside. It was quiet here, almost deserted most of the time. People only came for weekends or holidays, as commuting to work was too far. For me it was ideal, I needed peace and quiet to help me heal, cope with my pain, to think, and perhaps find a different way of earning a living in case I couldn't return to my social work job.

Somehow, I'd have to start a new life.

It was a miracle I had survived. In my mind I was back on the motorway, overtaking an articulated lorry which suddenly changed lanes and went into the side of my car. I saw the giant wheel coming towards me through the metal of my car, heard this terrible grating and crashing noise, and knew nothing more for quite some time.

I have survived, I told myself again, and I will get better, and now I'll go downstairs and make myself a cup of tea. Chamomile would be good, or lemon-balm, to help me relax.

I tried opening the bathroom door, but it wouldn't budge. I pressed and I pushed, but try as I might, neither the door handle moved, nor the door. I checked the bolt, but it stood open as usual. I never bolted the door, living alone. Panic rose but I had to stay calm. I couldn't really be locked in. Again I tried, pressing the handle down and pushing the door, but in vain. I had to face it, I was locked in.

How was it possible – the door had no lock, the only bolt was here on my side, and it stood open?

Again and again I tried, pushing and pulling and shoving, but to no use. The door stayed shut. Now panic was really threatening to overcome and suffocate me. I had trouble breathing. There was no window – how long would I have enough air?

Somehow I swallowed my panic and fear; to get out of here I needed my brain, to think clearly.

There must be a way out. The door handle was stuck, there was no doubt in my mind anymore. Perhaps something inside had come apart, broken off. I pulled the handle very gently, pressed on it gingerly, and then shook it as hard as I could. But whatever I tried made no difference. I really was locked in.

Weakness overcame me, and I sat down on the floor. Not even a chair was in this room. Suddenly I was angry with myself about having put this small matter off for so long. Then the seriousness of my situation hit me. No one would hear my cries for help, the bathroom lay between two bedrooms – not that it mattered, no one went past anyway, as my house was the last in the row.

No one would hear me. My neighbors were away, even if they came at the weekend, they would not look for me, or hear my screams.

My son phoned rarely. Only last night I had called him, and told him how lovely it was here. For a week or two he would not think something was wrong if he couldn't reach me.

I had no friends here, and my old friends would not come looking soon enough. I could be locked in for days, even weeks, die here in the end. But not quickly, because I had water.

At least I had a toilet, I reflected, so when I was found – I pushed this frightening thought far away. This was not the direction I wanted my thoughts to meander, at least not now, when I had to find a way out of here.

But these thoughts were not so easily banished; they persisted, focusing on death and pain. It was not death I feared most, but pain. I had no medication here in this room, and knew from experience that my pains would get worse, especially with no comfortable chair to sit on and no bed. I'd have to sit on the toilet or the floor, where, eventually, I would die, going crazy with pain, or suffocating because no air came in.

Pull yourself together Gerti, I told myself. There has to be a way out, and you must find it.

Again I concentrated on the door, pushing carefully and gently at first, then with force, again and again, but I was just wasting my strength. I tried thinking of another way out of here, but couldn't find one. No window, the walls were thick, the ceiling solid, and all the tools at my disposal were my back-brush, the toilet-brush, a plastic beaker, and my toothbrush. None of it was any help, though I poked around a bit at walls and ceiling and tried pushing the brush-handle under the door to lever it, but it was no good. Defeated, I sat down on the floor again, exhausted, in pain, my brain switched off, my mind almost blank.

Suddenly, out of nowhere, a clear picture appeared in my mind. I saw another door, white painted wood like this one. I remembered seeing it, when I visited a couple who had problems with their boy. I was their social worker. As I entered, the husband stood in front of the living room door, blocking my way. When I looked at him, he stepped aside to let me pass, and I noticed a dent in the door.

Like a little boy found out in a misdemeanor, he grinned self-consciously. "I lost control," he admitted. "I hit the door with my fist – or I might have hit her."

Looking sideways at his wife, he added, but very quietly: "She deserved it."

The picture vanished as fast as it had come, but it gave me an idea. If he could make a dent in his door, I could do it in mine. And a dent can be the beginning of a hole.

I hit the door as hard as I could with the brush, but it broke, and the other brush followed suit. I too had to hit the door with my fist.

But I was no young and strong man, but a woman of fifty, and the accident had made me weak.

This is the way to get out of here, perhaps the only way. I have to do it, I told myself. Forget about weakness and pain, Gerti, and gather your strength.

I concentrated, took a deep breath in, and with all my power hit the middle of the door with my fist. The pain was enormous, engulfing me in a red cloud. But through the red, I saw a minute crack in the white of the paint. I hit this spot with my other fist, and then with the broken bits of the brushes, but it made little difference. I had to use my right fist again and then again, before the crack in the paint became a small dent.

Scraping minute bits of paint from the wood with my nails, eventually I succeeded in getting to the pressed wood underneath, carrying on, dislodging tiny pieces of wood with fingertips and nails. I did not stop until I had dug a small hole, just big enough to push a finger through. But a new problem confronted me: there were two panels to this door; I had only broken through the inner part. With my fingertip I could feel the space between the inner panel and the outer, which I also needed to break. But now I had hope. Somehow I would break through the second panel too.

But not yet. I was so exhausted, I collapsed on the floor, and for a while just lay there, unable to move. Eventually I did manage to get up, and drank some water. I longed to bathe my hands and wrap them in towels, the pain was hard to bear, especially where the splinters stuck under my nails.

Not now, I told myself. I have to carry on, however much I hurt.

So I forced my bleeding hands to continue their work. The hole grew slowly bigger, but very slowly.

Painful hours went by as I carried on in this way, but finally my hole was big enough to attack the outer panel with my fist. Eventually I broke through, and the broken handle of my brush went all the way through the door. I turned it around and around, angling it, to increase the hole, but it just removed some splinters. But now I could look through. I couldn't see anything, the hall was in darkness. It was already night.

I put my nose to the hole, breathing in, feeling fresh, cool air in my nostrils going down to my lungs. For a while I stayed like this, the deep breathing calming me down. I'd get out of here, everything would be all right.

I drank some water again, and lay down on the floor to rest for a while. I tried to recover a little, but the pain in my hands and in my whole body, did not allow it. Afraid of losing consciousness, I got up to carry on with my task. And finally, after what seemed a lifetime, my hole was big enough to squeeze my whole body through.

I collapsed on the other side of the door, totally exhausted, and totally happy. I had made it.

Much later when I had some control of my body again, I went down the stairs to the kitchen, put the kettle on, and sat down in my recliner. It was half past four in the morning, soon it would get light. Only ten hours had passed since going to the bathroom, but it seemed an eternity.

The kettle had long turned itself off, and still I sat here, my whole body shaking. The fear and the panic I had not allowed myself to feel, had me fully in its power, engulfing me now.

Finally I did get up and, with great difficulty, made the tea. Then I swallowed two Tramadol tablets to lessen the pain. My hands were so swollen and bloody, I couldn't hold the mug, but had to bring my head down to where it stood.

Again and again new waves of panic hit me. I couldn't get rid of the feeling of being locked in, never to breathe fresh air again.

It was over, it was in the past, I told myself. But somehow it was not. Suddenly I realized these terrible feelings were not new, they had been with me a long time, hidden so deeply within me and only rarely raising their head. I didn't know they were there. The trauma of being locked in had brought them back, re-awoken them fully.

I knew where I had felt like this. And though it was so long ago, in my mind I was there now. It was all happening now. I was split in two pieces, divided. The adult Gerti sat right here and the other Gerti, the small Gerti was here too, but somewhere else at the same time. And suddenly I was just this Gerti, the child.

I was small, lying close to my mother and holding her hand. It was dark, I was struggling to breathe, as so much dust was in the air. We lay buried in the cellar, this much I knew. The bomb had hit our building, and here we were, under a whole house of rubble and debris.

It was the last year of the war, and I was not quite three.

As I lived through it all again, I knew, that what I had buried a lifetime ago, was still somewhere inside of me, even now. And with it, came all the feelings, the emotions I had felt then. They were engulfing me now.

For a long time I just sat, overwhelmed. Only much later I thought: and what now?

Should I bury it all again? Could I keep it all for another time when I was stronger?

But I was stronger, I told myself, at least mentally. I had to face my past, and with it my emotions, which were alive again and threatening to engulf me and overcome me. I shivered, I was suddenly very afraid.

All my old feelings of panic and fear had erupted; they would not disappear, if I tried pushing them down – this much I knew.

I had to relive it, face what had happened. By transforming the trauma into memories, they'd lose their power over me.

For a long time I sat in silence – lost. I was totally in the past. But this past was alive, and I was in it, a little girl.

The pain in my hands and my whole body brought me back to the present. I would face my past; remember it all, because being bombed in the war was not the only trauma. There was so much more. And by remembering it, I'd come to terms with what happened. Writing it down might help.

I'd write about my childhood, my siblings and my mother and the people in Vienna, the panic and terror we felt, and how life carried on somehow.

For now, writing was impossible – my hands were too painful. They needed a week or two in order to heal. But I didn't need to wait – only yesterday I had unpacked my tape recorder, and the dictating gadget from work. If I switched to voice activation, it would only tape when I spoke.

But first, after soaking my hands in warm water laced with Dettol, I'd try to get some splinters and bits of wood from under my nails, hoping I didn't have to tell the doctor, who was bound to ask what had happened. And I was not yet ready to talk.

And I had to find someone to take the door off and replace it – I would not crawl through the hole again. For now, a bucket would have to do.

I knew a builder; he had looked over the property two days ago. It needed some minor changes. I would phone him.

With my plans in place, I soaked my hands, and then activated the recorder, ready to record.

I took another Tramadol, and as I felt the pain recede I began digging out the horrors in my hands, and then lay back in my recliner.

I began speaking, but didn't know what I said. It could all wait, I thought, as sleep finally overcame me.

CHAPTER 2

VIENNA 1944

At first, as I started to remember, I got lost in dark, horrible emotions. Mostly I experienced fear, a huge living presence which I knew only too well. To me fear was a terrifying 'She' who would lurk anywhere; waiting and ready to pounce. The cellar was her domain, where she was at her strongest. Silently, like a huge black cat would she creep from a dark corner, come ever closer, touching each one of us. Reaching me, she'd wrap herself around me, until the real Gerti disappeared. Only fear would be left, mingling with my family's fear, and the fear of other people sitting in the cellar, waiting like us. What we waited for, I did not know; until the bomb dropped. Then I knew, and every time thereafter I sat in a cellar, I too waited for the bomb.

And though no one ever talked of fear by her name, I knew that we all knew her well.

With my fresh emotions of panic still alive, mixing with similar feelings of the past, I remembered what it was like to lay buried in the cellar, in complete dark, with the rubble of a big building on top of us. Mama, next to me, was powerless, but holding her hand gave me some comfort.

Then, as this picture faded, there was nothing for a while. My mind was blank, until suddenly the next scene appeared where I saw us standing in the street, not knowing where to go or what to do, because our mother didn't know and just stood there, gathering us children close to her. Some people moved about, without any purpose so it seemed to me, others just stood like us. Everywhere was rubble and debris, and so much dust it was as if we were in a fog. I still had trouble breathing. On the opposite side of the street broken parts of a building rose steeply up into the sky. It must have been our building; I could see the staircase and half a bedroom with a bed, a wardrobe still in one piece. All this lay exposed for everyone to see. It seemed indecent to see the private parts of a house in such a way, the rooms where people had slept not so long ago – where we had slept.

The sound of the plane above us changed, but this time the bomb was not for us. Mama let out her breath and eased the painful hold on my hand. We had survived, all of us, she said, finally finding her voice. Not that I knew much about survival then, I was not even three. But in the next weeks and months, I should learn quickly.

My uncle, Onkel Karl, took us in. He was Mama's brother, a small very thin man, who needed to stay calm and not exert himself because of his heart. His wife, Tante Mali, was big, but we were not allowed to say so because it was rude and besides, she looked like this because she had a certain illness, my sister told me. But I just had to look at her again and again, because I had never seen anyone who was fat. She and Onkel Karl had a small flat, just a kitchen and living room serving also as their bedroom. We children and Mama slept in the kitchen on the floor, rolled into blankets with our coats on top, because it was so very cold.

Onkel Karl was nice to us, but Tante Mali did not want us there. We were constantly under her feet, she complained. So, when Mama heard about an empty flat up the street, we moved there.

Our new home was even smaller than Tante Mali's, just a kitchen and a small room called das Kabinett, which became our bedroom. We were five, Mama and four children. My two sisters,

Lilly and Christl, were fourteen and ten, and I was nearly three. My full name was Gertrude, but I was called Gerti, which I liked.

Willi, my brother, was five. At this time we still called him Pepi, until some years later he decided otherwise, answering only to Willi. This name stayed with my brother in spite of Lilly's protests. She found it stupid because her name and his were so alike. Mama also did not like to call him Willi; she loved the name Pepi, short for Joseph, which was also the name of our father.

Papa was no longer with us. I hardly remembered him, and did not want to, it hurt too much.

The fear followed us to this flat, perhaps it had already been there, waiting, or the people living here before us had left it behind. But although I could sense its presence as soon as we moved in, the real home of this monster was in the cellar, two stories under the ground, where it smelled of damp, decay and death – and of fear.

The fear of the bombs I now understood, but the fear of the Gestapo was new to me. Gestapo was just a strange word without any real meaning, like the black man, the bogey man. No one explained anything, all my questions were ignored. I only knew the Gestapo would take someone away, probably us, if we said something. What we shouldn't say Willi and I didn't know, or, what the Gestapo would do with us – only that it was terrible, worse than the bombs.

In the cellar, if we younger children talked, Mama stopped us with a 'ssh ...' or Lilly would try to get our attention with a story or a word game, and everyone around grew silent, aware of our presence. But if we sat quietly in a dark corner, the grownups forgot we were there and talked. In this way we found out that our Tante Rosa had gassed herself, because Rudi, her son and our cousin, had joined the SS and got shot. I did not understand about gassing, and Christl told me Tante Rosa had killed herself by putting her head in the oven, and she was dead. I tried to find out if she had killed herself because Rudi had been in the SS, or because he died, but Mama talked only about his age. He was eighteen, only three years older than Lilly, who took it very hard, having played with him before the war.

I could not find out, what the SS was, only that it was terrible.

When we were not in the cellar, Mama went out trying to buy food, leaving Willi and me in the flat, often on our own. Mama's main occupation was to get food, which wasn't easy, she said. Obtaining it seemed to worry her more than anything else, even more than the bombs. My sisters were allowed to go with Mama, or they visited friends living in one of the other flats in our building. Willi and I never went anywhere; we had no friends and had to stay in our flat.

I hated it. At least in the cellar were other people, even children, and one girl had a tortoise, which sometimes she let me stroke. In our flat were no animals, no plants, and no one visited. I could no longer see the sunlight, as in our old flat, and I never felt a breath of fresh air. The kitchen window led into a narrow shaft, called Lichthof, but no sunlight came in. Next to ours was the window of the toilet we shared with other people, and Mama opened our window only in emergencies, usually when something caught fire.

Our second window was in the small bedroom. Big, almost reaching the floor, this window overlooked the yard in the center of our building. A metal walkway in front of it led to other flats, and I could see the legs of people going past. I could have touched them when this window was open. I worried someone would step over the windowsill into our flat. But Mama said, we had nothing to steal, and needed fresh air. Though this fresh air smelled terrible on times, we lived on the first floor and the stink of the rubbish bins drifted up to us. They were full to overflowing, as no one collected any rubbish.

Although not much was thrown away, except a dead woman once, but she was left in our toilet. One morning, as Lilly opened the toilet door, this dead woman fell on her. Mama said someone must have put her there, because she was stiff, and if she had died in the toilet, she would have fallen over. Since then, Lilly refused to go to the toilet alone. What had happened to the dead woman I couldn't find out, but at least she was gone.

Our new flat was crammed full with the things we needed most. Four narrow beds stood in the bedroom, two by two, the space between so narrow, I had to squeeze through to get to the window. In the middle, between the two sets of beds and opposite the door stood a small chest of drawers.

I slept in the kitchen. For me there was no space in the Kabinett, and so each night our four chairs were pushed together, a folded blanket laid on top. This was my bed.

During the day, my chairs stood around the kitchen table, a small cupboard fitted into one corner of the kitchen. The stove stood in the other corner, next to the gas cooker. I often wondered how all this stuff came to be here. It was from our previous flat. Our father had a hand cart. He was a carpenter and needed it to deliver furniture, and to transport wood and other material. But if he had brought our stuff, surely he would have visited us?

All my efforts to find out why Papa was no longer with us were in vain. Mama only said we had been lucky, the bomb went only through part of our flat, so some of our things had been saved. But we had not enough space in our flat, so some pieces were left outside on the landing. And sometimes, especially if it was very cold, Mama would take the saw and a hammer to attack a piece of furniture, chopping the wood small enough to fit through the door of our stove. On these lucky days we would not freeze, but sit close to the stove enjoying the warmth.

Suddenly, from one day to the next, everything changed, even the fear. We were no longer afraid of the bombs, but of the Russians. The war had ended, someone said, and the Russians were coming. They were approaching Vienna and on their way to us.

And soon they reached our district, and then they were here.

I remember how we all sat in the cellar, on long wooden planks supported by rubble and bricks, two flights of stairs below the ground. I hated the cellar. Shut in so deeply below, I felt there was not enough air to breathe, and the horrible smell of damp and decay was worse than ever, especially as the cellar door was closed now. A single candle gave some light, but created huge frightening shadows, moving slowly as if they were alive. The fear around me was stronger than ever.

We waited; women, children, two very old men. Mama sat next to me, with Willi on her other side. Christl had dirt smeared over her face, an old shawl covered her head. She was told to stay in the corner where it was darkest, but didn't like it there and begun to complain. But she was ordered to stay there, not to move or speak. Not only Mama said so quite sharply, but also several of the women. Christl was not used to be treated in this way, but she did shut up and stay put.

I can't remember where Lilly sat, and why she didn't stay with us. Only many years later did I realize why I suppressed what happened to her during that night.

As we sat waiting, Mama remembered her rings. They were still on her fingers. She hid them under the makeshift bench, because the Russians would take anything of value, and whatever took their fancy, someone said.

Time seemed to stand still.

For a very long time nothing happened as we sat waiting silently in the semi-dark of the cellar. It was as if now there was nothing left to talk about anymore. Suddenly I heard the sound of many heavy footsteps coming down the cellar stairs, rough voices talking loudly, the door was pushed open with a rifle and they stood there, pointing their guns at us.

In spite of the guns I felt kind of disappointed, having expected terrible monsters. But these Russians were just a bunch of dirty men in strange clothes, talking loudly, yet I couldn't understand a word. They walked between the makeshift benches where we huddled together. One soldier shone a light into each of our faces in turn. They looked at us closely, one after the other, made remarks, and laughed. One man said something which must have been very funny to them, because their laughter grew louder. I knew they talked about us, and that their words were not really funny, because the fear around me grew even stronger. One of the men put his arm around the shoulders of a woman sitting across me, and tipped up her chin. Mama held her breath, holding my hand so tight, it hurt. But I made no sound, just held my breath like she did, until we both had to breathe out.

Later, most of the Russians left our cellar, their guns pointing at the girls and women walking in front of them. Some of the men stayed, one soldier stood directly in front of us, pointing his gun so closely at Mama, it almost touched her face.

After an eternity, one Russian gave a loud order, and they all left.

Slowly the people began talking again, at first in whispers; until two women got up and opened the cellar door to be sure all the Russians had left.

"They wrote: 'Stary Baba' on the door," said one.

"That means old women," the old man in the corner informed us.

Christl, who had first left the cellar with the other girls, but had been sent back when they were hardly out of the door, piped up now.

"I am not an old woman." Her voice sounded indignant.

"Be grateful," a harsh voice came from the dark. "Be grateful whatever they thought, and thank God that you are here with us."

I don't think Christl understood any more than I did.

No one said anything about Lilly, or the other girls and women who went with the Russians and had not come back. But I had no time to ask, because the next group of Russians came down the stairs. They stopped in front of our door. 'Stary Baba,' said a rough voice, followed by loud laughter and some remarks, perhaps a Russian oath. But they also came into the cellar. And, like their colleagues before them, they pointed their guns at us and shone their lights into our faces and made remarks I could not understand. But I knew they were nasty remarks. And the women they chose had to leave with them. So it went on. One group came after the other. Sometimes, they would just read Stary Baba, and go back up the cellar stairs. Others would enter, in spite of the message on the door. And so it went on and on, hour after hour, or was it days? To me it was a whole eternity. And each time they left, people sighed as though relieved.

But no one said a word about Lilly and the others who had not come back.

I lost all sense of time. We seemed to sit in the cellar forever. Mama did not care I was hungry, thirsty and tired, and going to the toilet behind a blanket used as a curtain was a great problem for all of us. And again and again I heard the footsteps ap-

21

proaching, pausing outside the cellar door; someone might curse reading the message, or there would be laughter. And each time the Russians departed, a little of our fear would go too.

Finally it seemed to be over.

The Russians had not found my mother's rings, but they were gone nevertheless. Mama shrugged her shoulders in resignation: at least we were alive, she said, and her younger children were unharmed. She said nothing about Lilly, and I was afraid to ask. Willi, on Mama's other side, had not said one word throughout the whole nightmare, except when he got up to go behind the curtain.

As we returned to our flat we found the door wide open, our rooms had been ransacked, with everything strewn all over the place. Mama looked terribly ill and exhausted, she just collapsed on a bed, and we children pushed things out of the way, found our blankets, and covered her. And then we all huddled together, and sleep overtook us.

I did see Lilly again, but she only came for a visit. She lived with Tante Paula now, who was Mama's sister. My big sister was not like she used to be. She was quiet and hardly talked. I missed her so much, and was not even glad to have her bed. Much rather would I have continued to sleep in the kitchen, if only she had been here with us.

Everything changed in our family, and always for the worst, and I could do nothing to stop it; first Papa, and now even Lilly.

Then some things did improve, because now, without the bombs falling from the sky, at least we didn't have to go into the cellar again. But the hunger grew worse, food was even harder to get and we were always hungry.

My memories about this time center mainly on food or rather the lack of it, and Mama's efforts to get something edible, something different from the usual dried beans and peas which was all we ever got. But apart from the few nettles Lilly had brought some time ago, there was nothing. Then I overheard people talking on the landing outside, about finding a fungus growing on a tree in the park. Apparently the tree-fungus took some cooking, but was not poisonous, as no one died. So now everyone looked for these fungi. I too would have liked to go looking for fungi, or nettles, but my siblings and I hardly ever left the building. Mama kept us home when she went out. This changed when the Gasthaus Wimberger, a large pub on the corner which had survived the bombing, offered a hot savory liquid from Maggi. But first we had to stand for a long time in a line with all the other hungry people, holding our cups. But this delicious soup was worth waiting for.

All too soon there was no soup anymore, and the dried beans and peas were not often obtainable. In desperation Mama decided to go to the Russians, to try bartering her golden wrist watch for food. The watch was the last thing of value from our life before the war, but what did it matter, she said, we couldn't eat it. She took me with her, which was very unusual.

We walked through the dirty streets where the rubble and debris from the bombed houses still lay around. Jagged walls reached up into the sky, carcasses of houses showing almost obscenely the intimacy of what had been a home. Other buildings remained strangely untouched, as if the destruction around everywhere had nothing to do with them. They carried on as we did, and the people going past, their heads bent low, without looking at anyone.

On a lone side wall was a huge picture of a shirt which seemed to blow in the wind. Underneath were letters. I wanted to know what was written there.

"Persil waescht weisser." Mama told me, the purpose of this picture was to make people buy washing powder. A strange thought to make people buy things. We all would have been glad to buy things, had it been possible.

Apparently it was different before the war. Mama said everyone could buy washing powder, even different brands, and all sorts of other things.

I looked at the shirt with renewed interest. It was gray now, but once it must have been white, or no one would have bought Persil. But then I forgot the shirt, because I remembered to look for nettles or a fungus, but saw only bits of concrete and rubble, and people hurrying quietly past. It was as if everyone was as silent as possible and made themselves small, not to attract any attention. Only the Russian soldiers strutting around talked in loud voices, mustering us as we hurried past. They did not bow their heads like we did, but looked straight at us, as if daring us to look back.

We found the building they were stationed in quite easily, because the soldiers tried to stop us from going near. But Mama defied them, and, with her face grim, pulling me along by my hand, she just carried on and to my surprise the men let us pass. Eventually we were in a room with a tall bearded Russian who sat behind a large desk. He looked up and mustered us silently.

"Child is hungry," Mama pointed at me. "Needs food."

The Russian looked me over. "Looks OK," he said eventually waving his hand to dismiss us.

As Mama did not move and we stood there, he added: "Does not need anything."

My mother stood her ground, took her golden wrist watch from her pocket and gave it to the man. He took it, held it to his ear, listening to the ticking. Nodding his head in satisfaction, he put the watch in his pocket, called something in a loud voice, and another man came and gave Mama a small bag of flour.

Now, the peas and beans were thickened with a thin floury paste, and tasted even worse. When cajoling did not work to make us eat, Mama threatened us with all kinds of disasters, even the destruction of our building. "Der liebe Gott lasst das Haus einfallen," she would threaten us. But Willi didn't believe Mama, he even said to her face, he hated this house and God could destroy it as far as he was concerned.

I was more concerned that Mama would lie to us. And I worried about God. Would a dear God we prayed to for help, be cruel enough to let houses fall on top of people if we didn't eat beans? That would be so unjust. But after all that had happened, one could never be sure. But perhaps Mama was just worried about us, especially about Willi, who frequently refused to eat even if there was something. He didn't seem so hungry anymore, and was thinner than me, and more often ill.

Mama went out every day, often for hours, to see if she could buy something to eat, but usually she came back empty-handed.

One day Willi and I heard loud voices, and we sneaked out to look down to the yard. We saw several Russians, which was nothing unusual. They were often here, seeing if there was anything they could take, so people said. Or perhaps they were bored. Normally everyone avoided them, but now they were surrounded by women, who were arguing with them. This was unheard off. No one ever dared to talk back to the Russians; it meant risking your life.

My brother and I crept down to the yard to see what was happening. The row was in full swing, with three Russians and many women gathering around them, close to the rubbish bins.

"Throw away," said a Russian. "Is bad." He pulled a face, holding his nose. "Throw away."

"Don't throw it away," a chorus of Viennese voices objected. "We eat it."

The commotion was about tins of contaminated sardines, and eventually the women succeeded in capturing their booty. The Russians shrugged their shoulders and walked off.

It was not only the first time that I saw a fish; I was able to taste it. Tins of sardines. Each time someone opened a tin, tiny white maggots crawled busily in and out and all over the headless small fish.

I, too, was given an open tin, and told to enjoy it.

"Eat it all up Gerti, it's only Thursday, not Friday," someone joked. "Today it's no sin to eat meat."

Everyone laughed, and I laughed too though I didn't know why, until Christl tried to explain, that the maggots were the meat which we were not allowed to eat on a Friday because it was a sin. But I still did not understand the sin, and I did not know what meat was. Christl tried her best, it seemed to have something to do with animals, but was so complicated I lost interest and concentrated on the fishes instead, and on the maggots. It all tasted heavenly. We ate here in the yard next to the rubbish, and did not care how bad the smell was. All the tins were shared out. Willi and I took several home and when Mama came empty handed from the shops, she had tears in her eyes. But when I asked her what was wrong, she said she was just happy we had food. And so were we all, and for several days we ate sardines.

And all of my life I would associate sardines with maggots and vice versa.

Then after days of starving, someone came to our door with a food parcel from the Caritas, containing hard cheese, salted butter and lots of cod liver oil. The butter and cheese were soon eaten, but the cod liver oil lasted a long, long time. I quite liked eating it from the spoon, especially if I could have a bite of bread with it, which was sometimes available now. But with the butter long gone, Mama had no fat for cooking, so she used cod liver oil, which smelled terrible as it got hot. Even after the cod liver oil was finished, the smell lingered on in our flat for a long time, covering the other bad smells I had almost got used to.

Days came when there was nothing to eat – nothing at all – not even beans or flour, or cod-liver oil, and although Mama kept going out to see if she could get something, she always returned empty-handed. Nothing was to be had in any shop or anywhere, and we had been hungry for so long. Mama was desperate, she didn't know what to do, and decided eventually to get away from Vienna, into the country where she said there was food, and if there was no transport, she would walk. Willi and I were too young to come along, and when Lilly came to visit, she had to stay with us. Mama left, taking Christl with her.

I didn't trust Lilly since the day she had left us, because she might leave us again. And I was right. After two terrible days without any food she was gone too, leaving Willi and me on our own.

Many years later Lilly talked to me about this day.

"Somehow I had to get something to eat for you both, and I hoped Tante Paula would be able to help," she told me. "I could not take you and Willi along; you would never have managed the long way."

"Can you imagine, Gerti, how I felt? Mama had already gone two days, and you had been starving even before. You were not yet four and Willi was six. You were so hungry, and I had nothing to give you."

My sister, my grown-up sister, looked at me with eyes, where the shadows of the past still lingered on.

"I was only fifteen," she continued. After so many years, she wanted to be sure that I finally understood.

"You were so hungry," she said again. "There was no help from anywhere – total chaos reigned. I didn't even know if our mother would ever come back. You never knew what would happen to a woman."

Even as a small child I knew that women got raped. And though I didn't know what this meant, I was aware it was terrible, worse than being shot. I also had heard, that the women who tried to defend themselves were brutally beaten, and some were killed. But in the end they were raped, and no one could do anything about it.

But now, as an adult, I finally wanted to know what had happened to Lilly when we were in the cellar. But even now I was afraid to ask and then the opportunity had gone. Lilly's thoughts had meandered on.

"Lillymama, don't go away, you cried, over and over again, Gerti," my sister continued. "You often called me Lillymama; I was like a second mother to you. Until I could no longer live in the Pelzgasse, because ..."

I thought she would at last tell me what had happened. Instead, she put a hand over her eyes, as if to shut out painful memories.

"It is so long ago," she finally said, and sighed deeply. "But do you understand now, why I had to leave you and Willi on your own? You did not understand then. And you never called me Lillymama again."

She stopped speaking, and we both seemed to go back in time. The distance that had been between us, and the resentment I had vaguely felt towards her for so long, melted away, as I begun to understand what she must have gone through. And love, the pure strong love I had felt for her as a child, was back.

"I had to go," my sister was still talking, unaware of what was going on inside of me. "Had I not gone, we might all have died. People died of starvation then."

Lilly had gone across the war-torn city, facing once more the dangers to a young and pretty girl, with the occupying soldiers around claiming anything they wanted. She had made her way to Tante Paula, returning with something to eat. And we survived.

Although the Russians were the first to enter Vienna, subsequently the city was split into four, each quarter occupied by either French, British, American or Russian forces. But none were as feared as the Russians. Yet Lilly found compassion for them now.

"When they first marched into Vienna, they were the same starving poor devils we all were," she told me. "The large horses pulling their wagons were no better off, they were also exhausted and starving. I saw one of the horses keel over, right there in the street, it could not get up and was dying. But the most terrible thing was that people didn't see a dying horse, they saw food. They came out into the street, and everyone, Russians and Viennese alike, cut chunks of meat from the dead horse. Fires were lit, pieces of meat held over it on whatever could be found in the debris, and right there on the street we all ate together, friends and enemies alike – our hunger was stronger even than our fear."

CHAPTER 3

ROGENDORF – VIENNA 1945

Mama and Christl did come back, and they brought food: thick slices of bread topped with creamy butter, boiled eggs, and an apple for each child, delicacies I didn't know existed. When we could eat no more, we had to pack. Next morning we would get up very early, Mama said, and travel to a farm where we'd have enough to eat. The farm belonged to Tante Hilda.

Lilly did not want to come and went back to Tante Paula.

I had never heard of Tante Hilda, and during our journey Christl told us the reason. Actually there were two reasons, one was shame, the other sin. All of it was a secret that we must not tell, Christl insisted, but as it was a family secret, we had to know at some time. But just in case our mother thought we were not old enough, we only talked about all this when she wasn't listening.

We had to walk a great deal on this journey. Mama would stride ahead and we children followed as best as we could. Twice a lorry stopped and gave us a lift, and once a horse-cart, but mostly we were walking. In between we'd rest in the grass by the side of the road, and Mama usually fell asleep. So we had plenty of opportunities to learn not only about Tante Hilda and the secret, but also about my grandparents, although I knew already a bit from Mama and from Lilly.

I loved my grandparents dearly, especially Oma. My grandfather was only a vague memory. He died when I was so young that I barely remembered him, but Oma I remembered well. I had always felt her love for me, and though I had not seen her for a long time, in my heart she was still with me.

But I remembered her as very old, and had to use all my imagination to picture her as a young country girl going into service, as my sister now described her.

Oma had lived in as small country village in Upper Austria, but she wanted better opportunities than she had there, and came to Vienna to go into service, finding a post with a rich family. One evening, going out with her friend Eva, she met the young man who would one day become our grandfather. He was a Kellermeister, a wine specialist, and socially far superior. Eva advised Oma not to become involved, it could only bring unhappiness, as there could be no marriage. But Oma was in love, and seemed to have been quite adventurous and determined, because she bet her friend that she would get him. She did, but it took some time until they married, and Tante Hilda was born too early. Which was a terrible sin, and very shameful on top of it, so it had to be kept secret.

I didn't care about the shame or the sin, I was proud of Oma marrying the man of her dreams. But it amazed me that such things had happened to these very old people, although I knew that once they had been young. I could not imagine them as young and fit, and in love. And they must have been strong to cope with poverty, as Opa lost his inheritance because he defied his mother.

His father was dead, and as the only son, our grandfather should have inherited a big farm with vineyards. He and his mother produced and sold a lot of wine, and to prepare him for his future as a wine merchant, Opa had come to Vienna to work as a Kellermeister; a wine expert, employed by top establishments, in charge of the wine they bought.

When my grandparents got married, he lost his inheritance as his mother disapproved of the marriage. But Opa kept his job in Vienna, and so they managed. What happened to the farm and the vineyards, Christl did not know. She only knew they were in Hungary, a separate country now, which had belonged to Austria then.

Because of all the shame and secrecy surrounding Tante Hilda's birth, she grew up with other people. Later she married a farmer. He had not returned from the war, so the farm belonged now to Tante Hilda.

After a long and tiring journey, we arrived at the farm. It was so beautiful in the country, with green grass everywhere, and flowers, and all sorts of trees. White and brown cows were dotted around here and there, and in a meadow sheep grazed peacefully.

I liked it here, although Tante Hilda was not friendly at all, not even to Willi or me. We were not allowed to call her Tante Hilda, but Bauerin, like all the people working here. It was a name for a woman-farmer. From the beginning it was clear that she wanted nothing to do with us. She said this was a large farm with many other workers, and we would have no special privileges. We were here to work for our food like everyone else. And our work was already waiting.

Mama was a tailoress. After the long years of war everyone on the farm needed clothes, and so all sorts of things were waiting to be mended. Tante Hilda had prepared huge piles of bedding. Some sheets or pillows could be patched, and what had gone too far, would be used as patches. An old sewing machine stood ready for Mama to use.

The next day, some of the farm workers came with their clothes to be mended, or new garments could be made out of the material.

Mama showed Christl how to take the clothes apart, the pieces would be washed and ironed and turned inside out. Avoiding any holes and threadbare places, Mama recut from what there was, to make into new skirts or blouses, even trousers. Whilst she did most of the cutting and machine sewing, Christl helped with all the rest. But she had to work around the house as well, and in the kitchen, and though she complained bitterly to Mama about the amount of washing up and cleaning, she had to do what she was told.

At first Willi looked after the goats, but he always got into trouble because they ran away from him. He told me that he did it on purpose, because he did not want to work. But I was not so sure. He seemed to try hard to bring the goats home from the meadow, but when they ran in the wrong direction, Willi ran after them to bring them back. This made them run faster, and eventually an adult would come to the rescue, shouting at Willi. After several more mishaps with other jobs my brother was left alone to do as he pleased.

I was given his job with the goats, which made me very happy. I loved animals, and they seemed to know what I wanted them to do. One small goat adopted me, and followed me all day long, as I went about all my chores, looking after the geese and hens and collecting the newly laid eggs in my apron to bring to the kitchen.

All day, as long as I was outside, my goat followed me. People stopped to watch, because the small creature jumped as I did, but if I skipped, she tried, and could not do it. Of course I didn't see this with the goat behind me, but everybody talked and laughed about it. I didn't mind their laughter, I was so happy. I loved my animal-friend. If I sat down in the grass, she would rub her head on my shoulder, or lay it in my lap so I could stroke her, or scratch her under the chin.

It was beautiful here on the farm, I could run and jump and my new friend shared my joy. In the evening our family went to the wooden hut, where we slept on the floor. The goat had to stay outside. But every morning when I woke, I'd hear her calling me. If she got impatient, we heard the clop-clop of her hooves on the wooden plank outside as she came right up to the door, and stomped with her hoofs. Her plaintive calls grew louder, and became so insistent, Mama would send me out to greet her.

Our hut had a partition in the middle with a door leading to a second room. Here, a group of Russian soldiers who were stationed on the farm, had their bedroom. They needed to go through our room each evening, and in the morning too. Mama had strictly forbidden us to speak with the men, or to have anything to do with them, especially outside, where she could not supervise us.

During the first few days I ran away if one of the Russians was anywhere near. But as they seemed to pose no threat, I soon stopped running, and just ignored them. They tried to speak to me, and to give me small brown squares, which they enjoyed, pulling faces to show how delicious this food was. But I heeded Mama's words and took nothing.

But I began to doubt these soldiers were evil. And each evening, as I listened to their beautiful songs drifting through the wooden partition, something touched my heart with longing. I missed my father so much. But he did not miss me, so I would not think about him anymore. But those men were here, and clearly liked me. Perhaps Mama was wrong, I thought, listening to their melancholy melodies lulling me to sleep.

They could not be all bad, if they sang like this. They never hurt me and had never been unkind as Tante Hilda was. They laughed when I ran away, but not nastily, like Willi when he teased me. Mama must be mistaken, I decided eventually. Perhaps there were good and bad Russians, and these were the good ones. Finally I was certain, and stopped running away.

I don't know how I came to be in their room for the first time, I just remember their sad, beautiful songs pulling me like magnets. Mama was very cross when I came back. She shouted at me and slapped my face. She might have hit me again, but the biggest of the Russians, their leader, came into our room and shouted at Mama.

She was so angry that she shouted back at him. But she had gone too far. He was furious. His throat got red, and then his face, his hands balled into fists, ready to attack. Just as I was beginning to be afraid for Mama, he took a deep breath in, put one hand on my head and pointed with his other at his chest:

"Ich, Kind in Russland," he said.

Then his hand moved from my head to my shoulder. "So gross. Drei Jahre."

I knew he told us he too had a child, she was three. I think Mama understood now that he would not harm me, and that I would be safe. I was, and Mama never stopped me from joining the Russians in their room again.

After we had finished work and eaten with the other farm workers, Willi and I went back to our hut together with Mama and Christl. Now came the best part of my day: my evening with the Russians. When they entered our hut, my big friend held out his hand to me, and together we followed the other soldiers to their room where we would settle comfortably on the floor, on blankets and pillows. Then we would sing. Sometimes I let them persuade me to sing for them, and was rewarded with grapes and chocolate, treats I had never even seen before. But I would just eat a little, and only because they wanted me to. The bigger part I'd bring back to Mama, who shared it justly between all of us.

Even without gifts I would have spent my free time with the soldiers, because I loved them. My favourite was their leader. I didn't know his name, so in my mind I called him 'my Russian.' I liked everything about him. His thick black hair and curly beard, and that he gave the orders which everyone obeyed. I'd curl up in his lap, with his strong arms around me, making me feel safe again. I could not remember having felt safe before, yet it felt familiar, like a wonderful feeling which I had lost.

Once 'my Russian,' told me in gestures more than words about his little girl at home. I could tell how much he missed her. She was very lucky, I thought, to have such a wonderful father. But I felt lucky too, as now he was with me.

In a world full of violence, uncertainty and fear I felt safe and protected in the arms of the big Russian soldier, listening to the sweet and yet so sad melodies, and soon I was joining in. I still remember some of the songs even now.

But suddenly, quite out of the blue, Mama told us we had to leave, and go back to Vienna. Her work was finished and we were no longer needed.

From freedom, from running through open fields, with trees and bushes all around, back to the airless prison that was my home. Worst of all, I would never see my Russians again, or my little goat.

Back in Vienna, it was worse than before, because now I knew what it was like to roll in the grass and touch a tree, and even climb it.

I almost gave up hope, I certainly gave up joy as I entered the semi-dark hallway of our building, and the heavy, dank smell of decay surrounded me again.

Willi also missed the freedom of the farm and especially the animals, so we asked Mama for a pet. There was no point in asking for a dog or cat, such a large animal would need a lot of food, and we still didn't have enough for us. And although we would gladly have shared our meals with a pet, we knew Mama would never agree. But a tortoise would make a great pet or perhaps a goldfish – it wouldn't need much and perhaps someone had a fish to spare – and we could give it a few crumbs of bread each day. We begged Mama again and again, but she stood firm.

"It would not be fair to the animal," she always said. "There is no light or fresh air in this flat, nothing can survive here."

"We have to," Willi retaliated. He was cheekier than I, and increasingly talked back to Mama.

I could not understand her. She must know that we needed something alive, something we could stroke or at least touch – though with a fish this was impossible, but at least we could watch it. It lived and moved. Perhaps there were no animals to be had after the war, and Mama knew it.

So we begged her to let us have a plant. A plant was alive, it was growing. Perhaps we could just dig out something green in the park, it would cost nothing.

"It would die," Mama said, "a plant needs light."

Eventually we did get a plant, because we visited Tante Mitzi. She was married to Onkel Fritz, another of Mama's brothers, who had not returned from the war, and perhaps would never come back.

This visit was a rare and special event, because we went by tram. They were running again now, but as we had little money to spare, this was my first journey. We all enjoyed it, though we were apprehensive when Mama had to show our pass to the soldiers, to get from one part of the city to another.

Tante Mitzi and my cousin Veronika had many plants in their big sunny flat. Because Willi and I were so fascinated and showed freely our admiration, Tante Mitzi gave us a beautiful plant with thick hairy leaves. We took it home, watered it, gave it the best place by the kitchen window and did exactly as Tante Mitzi had said. But the plant soon died, just as Mama had predicted. And we were on our own again.

Soon Willi started to go to school with Christl, and I had no one. Then something happened which was very strange; Mama would play with me. I was not used to her attention, and I was not used to playing.

Willi and I did not play, we drew if we had pencil and paper – on the farm we had drawn with sticks in the mud. We did talk and argue, and we fought. Mama would shout at us equally, as if we did it to upset her. She said we only fought when she was home – which was true, at least since we broke the glass in the bedroom door when Mama was out. We could not take the risk again. The flat was so small, if we fought, things broke, and one of us often got injured – usually it was me.

We had few toys. My brother had a small rubber horse that Papa had carved for him. He carried this horse around with him, and had always taken it with him when we went to the cellar. I did not care about the horse, but would have liked to shoot people with his toy pistol. But he would not let me touch it. I tried, but never managed to take it away from him, he was too strong. When he went to school he hid the gun, but sometimes I found it and stroked it, and shot my enemies, but quietly, so Mama would not notice, and tell me off.

Because I was a girl, I could not have a pistol. I had a rag doll called Claudia. She had been a Christmas present Lilly had made for me. But I didn't like playing with a doll, perhaps I did not know how, at least not by myself. But now Mama showed me.

I loved our games, playing with Mama made me feel warm and special, almost as if I were important. Mama made a black velvet cloak for Claudia and put it over her dress.

"Claudia is going now," she said, waving with the arm of my doll. "Goodbye, Gerti."

Mama talked often about going away, because Willi and I had to go to the country, as there was still not enough food in the city.

"You'll live with a foster-mother," Mama told me again and again. "And she'll love you just as much as your real mother does."

Never before had Mama told me that she loved me. It gave me a warm glow inside, and I felt special.

The day finally came when we had to say goodbye. The Westbahnhof, the railway station at the bottom of our street, was crowded with children and their families. Willi and I didn't know where we would go, or what was waiting for us. We had cardboard labels on strings round our necks, and were told to get ready.

When Mama put his rucksack on Willi's back, he fell over backwards. Everyone laughed, except my brother. He was so embarrassed, he had tears in his eyes. But he swallowed them, because boys did not cry – though on this day, many did.

Then it was time. A last hug and Willi and I were on a train with hundreds of children. We felt so alone in spite of all the others, as we started our journey into the unknown.

CHAPTER 4

PUPPING – 1945

It was a terrible journey. The train was overcrowded, and many children cried bitterly. I promised myself not to cry, because I was brave, and for a time I managed to swallow my tears. But then I needed to go to the toilet, I was getting more and more desperate, and no one had prepared me for this possibility. Afraid of disgracing myself, I finally burst into tears. A woman tried to comfort me, which made me cry even more. I could not tell her what was wrong, I felt too ashamed. Then Willi whispered something in her ear, and the lady took me to a toilet right here on the train.

Bringing me back, my rescuer looked at the label around my neck, then at my brother's label, shook her head and said we were on the wrong train; we should have changed trains somewhere. I don't think she knew what to do about it, but neither did we, so we stayed where we were. And when the other children left the train, we followed, and finally arrived in a farmhouse.

We could eat here, so we were told, and our new foster-parents would come and collect us.

The table in the big farmhouse kitchen was laden with food. Thick slices of dark bread with butter, hard boiled eggs and red apples. As we were eating, people came, names were called, and children left with their new foster-parents. But for us no one came.

"That's because we were on the wrong train," Willi whispered into my ear. Clearly, he was worried.

The lady from the train talked with the large man who was sitting opposite me, on the bench surrounding a huge range with green tiles. They were talking so quietly we could not understand what was said.

"They are talking about us," Willi hissed, which made me feel even worse.

Just then a huge cat jumped from the top of the range, and settled in the man's lap. He must be the farmer, I thought. He was very old – fifty at least – and tall and powerful. Straggling gray hair surrounded a deeply tanned face, and his arms, emerging from rolled up sleeves, were brown too. His strong large hands began stroking the cat which started to purr loudly as she settled herself comfortably.

My mind was made up: he would be my foster-father. Although Mama had said nothing about a foster-father, if a foster-mother would love me, so could a foster-father, and perhaps even better and more so.

I walked over to the farmer and stroked the cat, a big gray tabby, with a white patch under her chin. I lifted her up and she did not object. Neither did the farmer. I looked into his face where a red round nose emerged from a gray stubble of beard, and blue eyes with a merry twinkle, looked back at me. Now I was certain.

"I like your cat," I said to him. "I'll stay here with you."

Climbing into his lap was difficult at first because the cat was heavy and I would not let her go. Then his strong arms lifted me, and the cat and I settled with a sigh of pure bliss. It was going to be all right. Feeling safe, I began to show off my skills, counting the big shiny buttons on his waistcoat. I had found my home.

The cat's name was Minki and she accepted me as readily as all the family. I also had a foster-mother now, and several grown up foster-sisters. That night, and every night thereafter, I took Minki to bed with me, a large cot, which had been quickly put up in the bedroom behind the kitchen, where my foster-parents slept.

Willi also found a home, only a few houses away, at a farm which also was an inn. A huge St. Bernard barked ferociously each time I visited, but although I was very impressed, and would have liked a dog, I was too happy to want to change anything. I lived with family Hinterecker, and soon became the Hinterecker girl.

Pupping was only a three-hour train journey away from Vienna, but here I discovered a new enchanted world, so different from Tante Hilda's farm. And coming from the hell called Pelzgasse I was in heaven. For the first time in my life I lived within a happy family.

My new home was part of the village and small by comparison to Tante Hilda's place, but the house was very much to my liking. With the cowshed next to the kitchen I could visit these fascinating animals several times each day. The pigsties were adjacent to the cowshed, with the hay loft above it all, so the hay could be thrown down through a trapdoor as fodder for the cows.

Behind the house the pigs wallowed in the mud in their own fenced-off garden. And on the side of the house, next to the dirt road leading to the village center, lay a vegetable and flower garden.

A big tree stood in front of the house, with a trestle table and benches beneath. Hens and a rooster with shining beautifully colored tail-feathers, roamed freely during the day, walking up the wooden plank every evening into their little house, one hen after the other, and the rooster in between.

Ten or twelve farmhouses lined the dirt road which led to the center of the village. Twice a day the bus stopped in front of the inn where Willi lived. Next was a tiny shop and one more farmhouse. Another inn with a big garden came next. The post office where one of my foster-sisters worked was opposite and a very big impressive church dedicated to St. Wolfgang, dominated the village center.

Around the village lay farmland, parcels of land belonging to different farms. It was illogical how the land was divided up, but it didn't seem to matter. The village children played where they pleased, and were welcome in most of the farms, and at least tolerated in two or three others.

I spent every day with my brother, but still he wanted to go home, he was missing Mama. On Tante Hilda's farm Mama had been there, and so he could enjoy himself, but here he had only me. People said Willi was homesick, which made no sense to me. But I did wonder if I had this illness too, and it was the pain I felt in my side if I ran very fast. But nothing and no illness would stop me from running, just for the sheer joy of it, because I was so happy.

My brother returned to Vienna with the other children, but I stayed on. I knew I had to return at some time, because Mama loved me, and would not let me go altogether. I loved her too, but did not miss her, because she was in our flat in the Pelzgasse, and I never wanted to go there again. So I pushed everything connected with Vienna and the Pelzgasse firmly out of my mind, refusing to think about it. I knew, if I pushed a thought away quickly enough, or a feeling, it lost its power to hurt me.

Occasionally a letter from Mama arrived, and Nandl read it out to me. Mama always wrote she missed me and looked forward to me coming home. Luckily, she never said when that would be, because I wanted everything to remain as it was. I wanted to belong here, and was almost certain I did. So I adopted the same dialect and the way everyone spoke and acted, and lived for the moment.

No one hushed me if I wanted to talk, quite the opposite. For the first time in my life people were interested in what I said, and told me how clever and pretty I was. I began to blossom, I talked, laughed, sang songs and told jokes, an art which I learned from foster-father, my Pflegevater, as I called him. He was my hero and I loved him with all my heart, and never doubted his love for me.

It made me happy to know that I was good for him too, as I found out, listening to the grown-ups talk. It seemed when Franzl, the only son, was killed in the war, Pflegevater had withdrawn from life, hardly spoke, just did his chores. He even refused to take a child into the family. But when I told him I wanted to stay, he opened not only his arms to me, but his whole heart, and became the man he used to be, outgoing, and living his life more fully again, so people said.

And I was quite certain, not only I had fun, but he too enjoyed my company and the games we played.

We were firm friends and allies, although he teased me a lot. His sense of humor was new to me, but I soon got used to his ways. And I loved the tricks he would play, even though at times they were directed at me.

The village boys were scared of him. When they came to stare at me, he would look fierce, scowl at them, and brandish the big knife he used to kill pigs.

"Come closer if you dare, boys, and I'll cut off your heads," he'd shout. The boys would run away screaming. But I knew he'd never hurt anyone.

"Go on, do it on me," I'd challenge him, walking right up to him. "Cut my head off, Pflegevater."

He wouldn't give in so easily, but grab me, making terrible threats in a frightening voice, and pretend to cut my neck, but with the blunt side of the knife. I knew it was just a game, a game called prisoner of war, and I was under torture.

So I'd wait patiently, until he laughed and gave up.

I was again the winner.

And if it got too much for me, I only needed to call: "Pflegemama" and she'd come to my rescue.

"Leave the girl alone," she'd say, swiping him across the head, but lovingly and gently. "You silly old fool you."

Perhaps my foster-father tried teaching me how to be a child again, to play and be naughty, and disobey. In this he succeeded, as I was a willing pupil, who followed his lead with enthusiasm. I especially liked playing tricks on Pflegemama. Fingers on our lips to stop me from giggling, we would creep silently behind her when she went to feed the pigs. Once she was in the sty, we'd bolt the door, and stand there grinning, rubbing our hands in glee. She was bound to call for help when she found herself locked in with the pigs.

But foster-mother never got flustered. "You silly old fool," she would shout, "open the door."

He always did, just as he always did what she said. He was the boss and decided what work had to be done and when, and it was rare his wife disagreed. But if she did he listened, and they would discuss the issue. Their daughters would also give their opinions, especially Mirzl, as one day she would have to take over the farm.

Occasionally I too got locked in with the pigs; sometimes together with foster-mother and once or twice alone when I looked at the piglets. But I just climbed over the top and beamed at my hero; I'd won again.

I liked my five foster-sisters, but not equally so, because they were very different. Mirzl, the oldest, and in her late twenties, was always busy and took little notice of me. But then, she took little notice of anyone, and only spoke to discuss a job, or in answer to a question. She had to get married soon, so I heard, because the farm needed an heir. And nearing thirty, she had left it late.

But Mirzl once told me there were hardly any young men about; most had not come back from the war. And she had not known that marriage and children would become so important. Her brother, Franzl should have been the farmer.

A big framed photograph of Franzl in uniform hung on the wall, and I always put the prettiest flowers I could find on the shelf underneath. They were for foster-father too, because I knew he was still hurting so much.

The next sister in age, Agnes, lived in Linz and worked for the post. She visited often, and always came home to help with the harvest during the busiest times.

Nandl also worked for the post, but in the village. She liked to talk, and would tell me about faraway countries. From the very beginning she took on the supervision of my hygiene. She'd check that I washed every day, and put my feet in a bowl of warm water to scrub them thoroughly, because of walking in bare feet. And every Saturday, in the back room where the onions were stored and all sorts of interesting foods and equipment as well as barrels of fat, a tub was filled with hot water. Here I had a bath. Later, as the weather got warm, Loisl and Nandl would take me down to the river, to a beautiful spot, deep enough to swim. And after we washed, they would teach me to swim.

During my first few months in Pupping, Liesl, another daughter, still lived at home. But she took a job in a hotel by a beautiful lake, the Attersee. When she left, I was allowed to sleep in her bed, sharing the bedroom with Loisl, which was marvelous.

Loisl was the youngest and only eighteen, and she was my favorite.

She always had time for me, and in the evening with the light out and the moon and stars shining through the window next to my bed, Loisl would tell me stories, or we talked. If she had been quiet for too long, I'd ask her something, but usually I got no reply, and from her deep even breathing I knew she was asleep.

The last snow still lay on the fields when I arrived in Pupping, but as it melted, there was much to do. By the time I woke, everyone had already left for the fields, but Nandl always told me the night before, where they would work, and if I wanted, I could join them. For emergencies, the old grandmother next door was at home, looking after their baby. But I never had an emergency.

I'd get up, dress and have breakfast. A cup of warm milk waited in the oven for me, and a slice of white bread on a covered plate on the table. The day was mine to do as I pleased, provided I was here for meals. Nandl had taught me the time by the clock on the church tower. After the evening meal I had to remain near the house. There were a few other rules but they made sense, such as not to go near the bull next door, because he was dangerous. As I was eager to please, I did my best to stick to the rules, especially as the bull did look fierce and on occasion bellowed ferociously.

But perhaps I was too obedient, as Pflegevater encouraged me to disobey especially when Nandl got ready to wash my hair. He would scowl, and growl at his daughter: "Hair-washing again? Leave the girl alone."

When she ignored him, he'd turn to me: "Don't let her do it, Gerti. Tell her your hair is clean. It doesn't need washing."

Now I was in a dilemma, and didn't know what to do. So I looked to my leader for further instructions. "Scream," he would say. And if I still hesitated, he would advise me: "Go on Gerti; defend yourself, resist, and scream."

This would never have occurred to me. I had learned long ago resisting was pointless, whatever was to come would happen anyway, and would hurt even more then. I didn't even mind having my hair washed. But my foster-father insisted. "Go on, Gerti," he repeated, "scream."

Only to please him I started screaming, but to my surprise I began to enjoy it, especially as Nandl was not cross, and only laughed, as if to indulge us. But she still washed my hair, and I enjoyed it so much, I forgot to scream. Nandl rubbed a whole egg into my scalp to keep my hair blonde and healthy, and put cider vinegar into the rinsing water. "To make your hair shine," she said, noticing my astonishment.

I always had to think of Mama then. What would she say, wasting so much food on my hair?

Because of the screaming and all the attention, hair-washing became a ritual, which I always looked forward to. I enjoyed all of it, especially the screaming. It felt so good, to defend myself, and to say no, and to scream as loud as I could.

My hero missed no opportunity to get me to scream, to say no, I won't, and shan't, supporting me against any form of authority, which usually came in the shape of Nandl towards me. But with my ally on my side, I learned to refuse, dared to say no, and screamed. If the situation got out of hand, foster-mother stepped in.

"You silly old fool," she would scold her husband." Leave the girl alone."

Enjoying my life to the full, I learned to have fun, never mind the consequences. But I would never have believed, the whole family could go over the top, and have so much real fun, until this special day I when we had apricot-dumplings for supper.

Having dumplings for supper was nothing unusual, we had them often, filled with savory meat, or sweet fruit. On this memorable day, our dumplings were filled with apricots.

I was competing with Pflegevater who could eat the most dumplings, and was almost certain to win this competition, when Nandl said I should not play in the mud, where the pigs rooted, because of the smell.

"Leave the girl alone," my hero defended me. "If she wants to roll with the pigs, there is no harm, they're clean animals."

"Give over, father," said Nandl.

"Don't let her tell you what to do, Gerti." He turned to me. "You tell her, Gerti. Pigs keep themselves clean. And a little smell has never hurt anyone."

But I noticed now, a peculiar smell was clinging to me, and I began to worry.

Whilst I was still occupied with worrying, foster-father defended his opinion regarding pigs and my right to roll in the mud. But all the family joined in now, and it seemed I had caused the first serious quarrel I had experienced in Pupping.

"Into battle, comrades," foster-father suddenly shouted. "Get ready to fire. Aim, come on Gerti, get ready to fire, and aim."

To my astonishment he took a dumpling, aiming it at Nandl, and motioned me to do the same. So I took a dumpling too, joining in the game, and aimed at Loisl. It was only for fun; after all, we would not really throw our dumplings.

But it should come otherwise.

"Aim and fire," our leader ordered.

I don't know what would have happened, had not Loisl, quick as lightning, thrown the first dumpling. It hit her father on the cheek, the dumpling burst, and the soft orange filling clung to the gray stubble of his beard, and slowly dropped over his shirt.

I caught my breath, really afraid now, but he only roared with laughter, retaliated, throwing his dumpling at Loisl. Then we were all at it. We threw dumplings at each other, and we laughed, and when there were no dumplings left, our leader made a long speech about losing the war, because we had run out of ammunition.

Never had I enjoyed anything as much in all my life. To think that grown-up people would throw food around – just for fun. If I told Mama she would never believe me. She had always insisted that food must never be wasted.

I must have said something about Mama and not wasting food, as we all cleared up the mess and put the bits into the big bin where all the leftovers went for the pigs.

"But Gerti, we don't waste our food," foster-mother said in her quiet pragmatic way. "The pigs eat the dumplings, and we eat the pigs. So in the end we'll eat everything; it's just gone round the circle one more time before we eat the pork on a Sunday for dinner".

I had never before thought about it like that, but it did make sense. And though I loved the pigs, and played with them, I enjoyed the roast pork on a Sunday too much, and the smoked bacon, to worry about their eventual fate. And after all, they did have a good life.

But from that day on, if I played with the pigs, I made sure I had a good wash straight after, not wanting to cause a quarrel again.

Most evenings, foster-father would stride around the fields to see how the crops were doing. I'd run beside him, and he would talk about how well the potatoes grew, or the lettuces, and what kind of weather we needed. He showed me the difference between rye, wheat, oats and barley, and explained what the different grains were used for.

Occasionally on a Sunday evening, we'd visit one of the outlying farms. Foster-father would lay a wooden plank across the wagon as seat, put our ox Maxl into harness, and we were off. A gentle slap of the reins and the big white ox walked steadily on. Occasionally foster-father would let the whip play over Maxl's back, but our ox took little notice. He was probably glad to have the horseflies chased away, which settled on him in clusters, and plagued us too.

Once we were on our way, we would sing. First all the songs we both knew, then Pflegevater taught me his songs, and then it was my turn to teach him. And so on each outing we could sing more songs together. And if our journey took very long, we had time for jokes and riddles, an art I was acquiring from my idol.

Reasons for visiting varied. The growing crops had to be discussed, the weather and how it affected the lettuces and carrots. The potatoes were in danger, because of the Kartoffelkaefer, a small beetle threatening to destroy the potato crop. I had seen a picture of this innocent-looking insect, but as it destroyed the potato plants it had to be killed. Even a reward was paid for each beetle handed in to the gendarme, who occasionally rode his bike through the village and always had time to stop at our farm, ready for 'a drop'.

This meant the cider jug would be filled from the barrel in the cellar – which was my job – and everyone sat round the table, talking, enjoying the visit.

Just as everyone enjoyed our visits and the cider came out for us. Information was exchanged, people asked me questions, and when foster-father said I was a great singer, I was asked for a song. I obliged happily, sure of everyone's approval and foster-father's pride in me. Soon most people in and around Pupping knew me, and I felt at home everywhere.

One evening, Nandl talked about her day at the post office. I hardly listened, until she said: "Bursts of loud laughter came from the pub." She looked at me meaningfully, as she continued. "For a while it was quiet and I started working again, but as I heard loud laughter again and again, I got up and looked out of the window."

I began to feel very uncomfortable, when she said: "And there was our Gerti, sitting in the Gasthausgarten, surrounded by soldiers from the camp, telling jokes."

Everyone laughed, and I let out a sigh of relief. I had done nothing wrong after all. I often wandered around the village, and each time I went past one of the pubs, if the landlord saw me, he would call me in. "Let's hear a song, Gerti," he'd say, and I was always happy to oblige. Then I would get Frankfurter sausages with mustard, and a Semmel, a white crusty roll, and a Kracherl, delicious soda pop. I could even choose the color. I had never known anything as good, before coming to Pupping, but so many things were new here, and all were wonderful.

The men from the prisoner-of-war camp would sit in the garden, enjoying the sunshine and the beer. No longer prisoners, but victors, having won the war, they were just waiting to go home, or be stationed somewhere else. The villagers and the soldiers were on good terms. Sitting together in the garden under the chestnut trees, drinking cider or beer, they laughed and told stories. It seemed, the village people had helped many of the prisoners, and even stories of escape were told. I loved those adventure stories. Most of the men were from England, and though their German was patchy, I could understand them, and they understood me.

The fear I had felt in Vienna was not present here. Perhaps it had never reached Pupping. Or perhaps here people were the same, wherever they came from and despite of a war. They'd sit together and drink and talk, because when it came right down to it, people were just people, especially now, all this killing was over.

When I had arrived in Pupping, the winter was drawing to an end. It was a magical time, forever changing, with catkins floating in the breeze. Snowdrops flowered down by the stream, primroses appeared, hesitatingly at first because the snow was slow to melt, and patches still covered the grass. The buds on the bushes and trees turned into leaves and flowers, or into pussy-willows, velvety soft to my touch. The air felt milder, the most wonderful smells were in the air, and the pale-brown grass changed miraculously to a wonderful green.

Each morning I went outside to the big tree in front of our house where foster-father had tied a rope to a thick branch and put a seat on it, as a swing for me. I loved to swing, higher and higher.

One morning a boy stood under my tree, looking at me. He did not speak, so, for a while we just stood, looking at each other in silence. He was a little taller than I, in bare feet, and his big toe trailed a pattern in the mud, beside a last bit of snow. I looked at him, waiting. Between us was a huge puddle from the recent rain. The boy dropped his gaze to concentrate on his toe for a while, ignoring me. Suddenly he seemed to make up his mind.

"Do you want to see my Christmas tree?" he asked and smiled, revealing two missing teeth.

He lived close to us, next to our neighbor, in the pretty white house with the red roof I had often admired. I was impressed by the Christmas tree, never having seen one before.

"It should have come down long ago," my host informed me, "but Mariandl cries if we go to take it down."

The tree was almost bare, with a thick carpet of needles spread out underneath. But to me it was a beautiful tree and I admired it. The boy's name was Poldi. His father worked for the railway and was also the village cobbler. He was at work now, with the trains, Poldi informed me, quite chatty now. Just then, his mother and his sister Mariandl came to join us; she was a little younger than I and became my best friend.

Never before had I had a best friend, at least not a girl my age, and it was marvelous. We were soul mates, and soon we spent all our free time together, parting only for meals. We talked, we played, and if I had chores to do my friend helped me. Occasionally her brother was around, but he usually played with the village boys. They didn't usually allow us to join them because we were girls – unless they needed us for their games, where we had to take the inferior roles, like being the congregation in church when they were priests. Or we had to be horses, pulling their wagon. A small cart was used for this purpose, which was not easy to pull, especially with two or three heavy boys in it, using their whips to make us run faster. This was not the way we wanted to play, so usually Mariandl and I played on our own.

Every morning, if my friend was not already waiting on my swing, I would go to her home. Like all children here, I too was allowed to walk in bare feet, now the spring had come. It was wonderful to enjoy the fresh morning dew on my skin as I walked through the grass or the soft earth after rain. And the puddles, the mud, there could be no better feeling, so wonderfully wet and cold between my toes, and squishy.

If the weather was dry and we wanted to squelch in the mud, we'd join the pigs in their garden. In the beginning, they took little notice of us, or squealed and ran away. So at first we just let them be. But they soon came to be stroked, and to enjoy a scratch on their heads and backs, and before long they joined in our games. We all liked mud.

Afterwards we needed a wash. In front of the house was the water-pump, with a big stone trough underneath. This trough was ideal, not only to get clean, but also to splash and to play. First, all the drowning wasps and other insects had to be rescued, in case we fell in and got stung. Feeling sorry for the tiny creatures, I would perform this rescue mission most days, using long stems of grass or dandelion stalks. Some wasps were dead, and could not be helped. But the live ones crawled up on the stems, to be dropped on the ground to recover and dry their wings, before they flew off. The dead wasps had to be scooped out too, because we knew from painful experience, they were still able to sting. Now, we could safely splash, or play with dandelions. If we split the stems, they'd curl into ringlets, and form pretty patterns in the water.

All of nature, everything around was here for us, to explore and to enjoy.

On rainy days we hunted for snails to have a race, letting them creep up on our arms. Then we would celebrate the winner. Ants too were wonderful to observe. We gave them granules of sugar, which they busily carried away – a sin Mama would never have allowed. But in Pupping, sins didn't seem to exist. And food was always available, we just helped ourselves. Everything was a constant source of delight, especially together with Mariandl.

Playing families was our favorite. With only two players, this game had limits. But as long as I could be the naughty boy, I did not mind if we were just a small family. Mariandl usually played the mother, although sometimes we had to switch roles, because she got fed up with being the sensible grown-up with a very naughty child. Everything I had never done and never even thought of doing, I did now, as a naughty boy. I screamed, I kicked, and hit out at my mother Mariandl who rose to the occasion as well as she was able. At first she tried to persuade me to be good, but as this method wasn't successful, she too had to use force. This could lead to a serious fight, and in this way we became good fighters – which was just as well, because when the village boys made threatening noises at us, we stood our ground, and it would be the boys who retreated.

But occasionally my friend and I got so caught up in our fights, we fell out. We were both stubborn and neither gave in easily, so we went our separate ways. But I missed my Mariandl so much; all I could do was sit around moping. Usually Nandl would notice, or foster-father.

"Where is Mariandl then?" they'd ask.

"We've had a fight," was all I could reply. "We are no longer friends."

"Never mind, you'll soon be friends again," came always the same answer.

And this was true, because the longest we ever managed to be apart, was three days. Then either my friend would come, or I'd seek her out, and we talked as if nothing had happened.

Seven boys lived in Pupping, but only one other girl. Her name was Monika. She lived at the far end of the village and it had taken us a while to get to know her. To our delight we discovered, she not only liked playing family, but preferred being the mother. Mariandl could now take the much more interesting role of the father, or better still, be another naughty child like me. We could even be twins.

But to cope with two bad boys proved too much a challenge for Monika. One day, when the game went out of hand, Monika got kicked in the stomach. She did not believe it was an accident, and ran home crying.

"She is a coward," Mariandl said.

"She is a sissy," I agreed.

Now, as this friendship had ended, the animals played bigger roles in our games. The pigs were no use as family members, because of the mud. Minki the cat accepted her role as the baby with patience and grace, but to play the mother was beyond her capacities. So we stopped playing family, and looked elsewhere for our entertainment. We stroked the cows and tried to milk them, but without much success. Now and again there was a new calf to admire, or piglets. Our ox Maxl became my best animal friend, although he was a working animal, pulling the plough autumn and spring, and the wagon at harvest time.

One of my duties was to lead Maxl when foster-father was ploughing. Mariandl got bored after an hour or two just walking beside me, and she was too small to lead the ox, so she went home. I stayed, because I liked helping foster-father. He always said I was the best oxen-leader he ever had.

Maxl was a huge white animal with long, curved horns. He loved me talking to him, scratching the thick curly fur between his horns, or when I chased the horseflies off, which plagued us equally. His large soulful eyes with their long lashes fascinated me, and gently, so as not to hurt him, I'd take the lashes between my fingers to pull his eyelid close – and open and shut again, and so on. Patiently, the big white ox would indulge me, just occasionally, when he'd had enough of this game he would shake his head as a warning. I'd stop and move back, out of reach of his horns, in case he shook his head again, and this time harder.

Autumn came, and with it harvest time. The wagon would be loaded high, a large beam put on top, and secured with a rope. Mariandl and I climbed up on the rope, and foster-father walked home, leading Maxl. When we passed a farmhouse with walnut or fruit trees overhanging the road, he'd stop under the tree. The farmer would come out with a jug of cider, and while the men talked, we plucked the ripe fruit from the tree, or walnuts, which we loved even more.

All children were allowed to take as much as they could eat; whatever it was. Carrots, radishes, tomatoes, I loved the cobs of corn, and especially the poppies with their sweet juicy seeds. "Just make sure, Gerti, the poppies are ripe," Nandl always reminded me.

But Sundays were different and extra special. The preparations started on Saturday evening, when we took turns in the back room to wash. Sacks of grain were stored around the walls, as well as flour, onions and sauerkraut, small barrels with fat, and all sorts of edible treasures. This magical room was also our bathroom.

A round tin bath would be filled with hot water. With Nandl supervising me, I washed properly and with plenty of soap. At first I did not like using soap, because in Vienna, sitting in the cellar, I had overheard, after the Jews were gassed, soap was made from their bones. But Nandl assured me that Pflegemama made her own and it was not made from people. And so I lost my fear of soap, and enjoyed my bath.

Prior to his bath, my foster-father would sharpen his shaving knife with the leather-strap hanging underneath the mirror. Then he lathered his face. Like a miracle, all the gray stubble disappeared as he shaved, I could see all of his face, and his skin felt smooth and soft to my touch.

In the morning we all dressed in our Sunday clothes, and went to church. I too had Sunday clothes now, and sandals, which Mariandl's father had made for me.

In church we all sang together during Mass, and afterwards everyone stood around in groups and talked. Many of the men went to the inn, but foster-father always came home with us. Here we changed back into our normal clothes, and I'd kick off my shoes. Even on a Sunday we children walked in bare feet, except perhaps in the fields, after the grains were cut, or in the woods because of snakes.

The woods were a source of pure delight, of mystery and magic. Pupping was almost surrounded by wooded deep-green hills. It felt so good to be within this magic circle, I often wished that I could always live like this. Once, when I had this thought again, I turned to Mirzl, who just came from the cowshed, carrying a bucket full milk.

"What is it like, Mirzl," I wanted to know, "living in this beautiful place all the time, seeing the forests and hills as soon as you open your eyes in the morning, and knowing all this is always here for you?"

She put the bucket down, and milk slopped over its side, making a white puddle on the ground, which slowly disappeared into the earth. Clearly I had taken her by surprise.

"You know, Gerti, I never really thought about it," she said.

Mirzl paused, her forehead puckered, as she gave the matter some serious thought. She looked around her; she really looked, as if she saw the beauty surrounding us for the very first time.

"I guess if it's always been here, you don't see it anymore," she finally said.

Her words made me feel sad. How could she not see the beauty around her, be aware of it, every minute of the day?

I was sure Loisl felt this special magic when she took me and Mariandl deep into the forest on Sunday afternoons. But then Loisl was young. Perhaps as you got older, you changed. I promised myself, I would not change this way, but always feel the beauty that was nature, my whole life long.

Occasionally, Nandl also came with us to the woods. Then we would go to my favorite destination, an old ruined castle, the Schaumburg, where noble knights had lived, long ago. But to get into the castle, we had to cross the drawbridge, which was dangerous. I could see so far down, and with pieces of the bridge missing, one false move, and I would lie down there. But we made it each time.

It was worth the risk, because now Mariandl and I could climb down to the dungeons to save the prisoners. Or we would be the noble knights, defending our castle from the enemy. Later, getting tired, we'd sit in the soft moss as Loisl told us stories. And we'd look down, where in between the fields, which looked like stripes in every shade of green and gold, Pupping lay.

On our way home we'd stop at a small inn, right in the middle of the woods, to drink a Kracherl, red soda pop, which we all liked best. Our Sundays in Pupping were always very special.

CHAPTER 5

PUPPING

I had always felt safe and protected in Pupping, but one day I had to find out that bad things could happen here too.

It began on the morning Mariandl couldn't come out straight away, as her father was going to measure her feet for new shoes. As I waited, her brother Poldi offered to show me something, and when I asked what it was, he just smiled mysteriously.

"It's a surprise," he said, "but you have to come now, Gerti. It's not far, just behind the barn. We'll be back before Mariandl is ready."

Perhaps he had found a wild cat and her kittens, I thought, or a hedgehog – or even a nest of snakes. I loved snakes.

I saw nothing unusual behind the barn, just tangles of weed and flowers, bushes, broken-off twigs, and a big log with bits of moss on it.

"Where is it Poldi?" I asked, looking around again.

But while I was still trying to see whatever it was, he lifted my dress and tried to pull my knickers down. It happened so quickly, and I was so surprised, that he was touching my belly before I could pull myself free.

"Your turn," he said.

"Never," I shouted, already running. I ran home as fast as I could and straight into the cowshed.

Putting my arms around Maxl, I pressed my face into his warm smooth neck, behind the ears and his horns. I felt so awful. What Poldi had done was terrible, and I felt so ashamed.

Worst of all, I had committed a sin, the capital sin Mama had warned me about. It was a long time ago when she told me, and I had not understood at the time. But now I did.

In my mind I was back in Vienna, sitting in the round bathtub in the kitchen. The water was so warm; I did not need to rush my bath. I felt relaxed and enjoyed the sensation of warm water on my skin, listening to Mama talking. I didn't realize, or think anything of it, when my hand slid down my belly. But Mama saw, and told me that I must never touch my body there. I was bewildered, because she had just insisted I wash all over, and everywhere. So I reminded her.

"You can wash Gerti," she said, "but do not touch." And then as an afterthought, she added in her sternest voice: "and don't ever let anyone else touch you there."

Her words had made no sense at all. Who would want to touch me there? But the tone of her voice had been so final, I hesitated to ask. And then it was too late.

"It's a sin," she only said to my unspoken question, and I knew better than to ask any further.

Now I had committed this sin. Poldi had been too quick for me. But that made no difference to my sin. And he had only touched my belly – but he would have touched more, had I not run away, of this I was certain.

It gave no excuse. He had touched me, and I had committed this terrible sin, Mama had warned me about.

I could tell no one, not even Mariandl – with Poldi being her brother, she would feel terrible too, and perhaps want to tell someone.

I stayed for a long time with Maxl, not knowing what else to do. But I couldn't remain forever in the cowshed, someone would find me. I needed to hide.

In the passage Minki came to meet me, and I took her with me to the hayloft, and climbed up the bales of hay to the highest spot, right under the rafters. It was a difficult climb because of holding the large heavy cat to my chest. Eventually I found the right spot and dug myself into the hay, with Minki settling on top of me, purring louder than usual, as if she was telling me that she loved me, whatever I had done.

We stayed like this for a long time. I forgot the time; I forgot that I had to go to the kitchen for lunch. It started to rain, and the sound of the heavy drops drumming on the tiles of the roof right above me, comforted me, and lulled me to sleep.

When I woke I went down to the farmhouse kitchen, not knowing what else I could do. I was late for our meal. Everyone was sitting at the table, eating. They all looked at me as I entered, their eyes sad and full of reproach, but no one said even one word to reprimand me. This made me feel even worse.

I wanted someone to tell me off, shout at me – but they just looked at me, and stayed silent. I felt terrible. Not much was asked of me, only to be on time for meals, and even that I had failed to do.

"I fell asleep in the hayloft," I said, to interrupt the painful silence.

"Don't be late again, Gerti," Nandl answered. And that was all.

I was never late again, and I never told anyone what Poldi had done.

The shame about Poldi, and having let my family down, lay heavy on my mind. But every day this load seemed to get lighter, and gradually I forgot to think about it. But I never played with Poldi again. If I met him, I ignored him.

Mariandl and I remained inseparable. Usually we played outside, surrounded by nature with its changing seasons. Spring had become summer, and then it was harvest time. The potatoes were dug, sorted and collected, and Mariandl and I helped Pflegemama collecting the last heaps, the smallest potatoes, which had been left for us.

The grains had been harvested and were waiting for threshing in the big barn, which lay away from the farm in a meadow. Many apple trees grew there with deep red apples, rodlers, they were called, Loisl said. We always took a good supply of apples with us when we played in the barn.

But suddenly we were not allowed to play there, because a machine would arrive for the threshing, and many people would come to help.

The next morning, a huge monster of a machine was pulled to the barn by the two enormous Pinzgauer horses belonging to our neighbor, and it looked as if half of the people from the village had turned out to help. The threshing machine made so much noise we could hardly hear anything else and as the work progressed everything and everyone was covered in a layer of gray dust. Mariandl and I had to stay out of the way, but we were allowed to help foster-mother with the food. And we brought jugs of cider to the helpers, who stopped working as we approached, wiped the dirt and sweat from their mouths with a sleeve, and took a long swig of cider from the jug.

The weeks went by, November came. Now, as wild flowers became scarce, I picked twigs with pretty coloured leaves or red berries for the house. And I still put the prettiest bunch under Franzl's picture.

Foster-father had ploughed most of the fields, so the winter with its frost and snow would break up the clods of earth, ready for sowing next spring.

Gradually our life got slower, and with the first flakes of snow, work ceased in the fields.

Soon the countryside was covered with a mantle of crisp white snow. Some work had still to be done. The animals had to be cared for, foster-mother needed to cook, but she had it easier now, with Loisl helping. On a Saturday morning the whole house was cleaned as usual, but more thoroughly now. In the kitchen, the wooden floorboards were scrubbed with a hard brush, and fresh sawdust put on the floor, so any dirt could be swept away with the sawdust.

Loisl told me stories more often, and we sang. A new song, a special song, had been made up about me, and the whole family would sing it. The first lines were about a little girl from Vienna, who was nice, beautiful and charming. I was embarrassed to be called beautiful and charming, yet basked in the warm glow of being appreciated, but in this song I would not join in, remembering Mama's insistence that one must not praise oneself.

Foster-father mended his tools and sharpened every scythe, and all the knives. And during the long dark evenings he taught me to play cards. We played Schnapsen; a game for two people, and once I could play it, he explained the more complicated version for more players and the whole family would join in.

On Christmas Eve, as it got dark, the Christkindl brought a tree with real candles on its branches, and after Nandl lit them, we had to sing carols before opening the presents under the tree. I had new shoes, two pairs of thick stockings, mittens, and a warm coat with a bobble hat, so I could play in the snow.

Mariandl and I loved the snow. In spite of the cold, we still played outside, building giant snowmen and all sorts of animals. And when the village boys came past, we engaged in snowball fights. But our hands would get so cold they'd tingle and go numb. We'd rub them and put our mittens on, and in the end go to the kitchen. Sitting on the bench surrounding the range, with our backs against the warmth of the tiles, we soon got warm.

At times we'd play in one of the outbuildings, or the barn, or best of all, in the hayloft. Here we could play many games, make elaborate nests, or play circus and jump somersaulting from the highest level, down to the cushion of hay on the bottom.

One day, a warm and gentle wind blew, then it rained, and a few days later, snowdrops opened their petals down by the stream, amid the last patches of snow. Then catkins and pussywillows appeared as if by magic, and finally the last bits of snow melted away. The year had run its circle. Mariandl and I took our shoes off, to run barefoot through the grass, moist with the morning dew. And we splashed in the puddles, enjoying the soft squelching mud between our toes.

Then came the letter Nandl still had in her hand, as she told me that Mama had written that I had to return to Vienna, to get used to being home again before starting school in September.

My world, the world I loved so much, came to an end. It fell, collapsing inwards like a house of cards. It did not help that Nandl assured me; I could come back every summer. I could only think, I had to go back to the Pelzgasse – I would not call it my home.

Deep down inside I had always known that one day I would have to go back, but always refused to think about it, because it hurt. But now I could no longer do this, because it was fact, and would soon happen.

At least I did not have to go immediately, which helped me to get accustomed to my fate. But everything changed for me. I changed.

I still enjoyed each minute, and the days were still golden and blue. But the blue of the sky was not quite as bright, and the golden light of the sun had lost some of its sheen. I loved my foster-father as much as ever and knew that he loved me, but now a huge shadow hung over me. And when I thought about leaving, a heavy weight, like a big stone, pressed on my chest. Even foster-father, who was so powerful, could not help me now. He did not say, I shouldn't allow this terrible thing to happen, but kick and scream. Because he knew as well as I did, nothing would be any use against Mama. He was as powerless against her as I was.

The dreaded day arrived. Nandl gave me a brand new leather school bag, which Mariandl's father had made for me. I loved the bag, it was a proper grown-up school bag like the older children carried, but it did not make me feel any better.

Then my sister Lilly came with Tante Paula. They stayed for the day, and I showed them around. But my heart was not in it, because they had come to take me back to Vienna.

CHAPTER 6

VIENNA 1946–47

On the train journey home, Lilly folded a square piece of paper to make a game she called heaven and hell. With great care I painted the two so very different sides. Then, depending which direction you chose when you opened it, you would either be in the blue colored heaven with the white fluffy clouds and the golden sun, or in hell: which was deep red with yellow and orange flames. Black devils lived there, with horns and tails, holding pitchforks to stick into you, to torment you, and hurt you as much as they could.

My life turned into this game. Only it was no game, but reality, and I could not choose my direction. I was powerless. Pupping was a memory, of blue skies and a golden sun, the moon by night and the stars; of flowers, trees, animals, and of people who not only loved me, but approved of me. I could be who I was.

Mariandl and my foster-family were only memories too now – my most treasured memories. Everything I had done in Pupping, was not only OK, I had been praised, even admired. I had freedom to run and to jump, to talk and to laugh. It was enough to be me.

Now, freedom and laughter were things of the past.

As I entered the building which housed our flat, and the almost forgotten smell of damp and decay engulfed me, hopelessness was engulfing me too.

Our flat was the same, but Mama had changed. There was a distance between us. She didn't hug and kiss me, or play with my doll like she used to. Not that I wanted to play with Claudia, but Mama had been close to me then, had touched me and hugged me sometimes. This was gone, like most physical contact. The only time we touched with affection, was in bed with the light out. Sometimes in the dark, Mama's hand would bridge the narrow gap between our beds, and she'd touch my face or my shoulder. My hand would be waiting to take hers, and hold it. I'd feel close to her again, she was here for me, just as she had been in the dark of the cellar. So Mama's hand would be comfortable, I'd put my pillow underneath her arm, on top of the hard edges of the narrow metal beds. Then I'd cover her arm with my duvet, to keep her warm. Now I could go to sleep, feeling better, until I woke in the morning.

I hardly saw Christl, she was an apprentice, and would be a tailoress in three years. In her free time she went out, either straight from work or as soon as she had eaten. When she came home I was asleep. Even on Sundays she was hardly ever here. But then, I would have gone too, if I could have.

Willi was not here anymore. Mama said he was in Holland. When I asked about Holland, she only replied: "Just like you were in Pupping."

And when I wanted to know more, her face closed and she paused as if she were considering something important. Then she said: "And you'll go to kindergarten, Gerti."

But first we had to visit the school, so I could start a year earlier. Mama told the lady who was the director that I was very intelligent, and to prove it, she had brought several old locks and keys, which were left from the furniture we had burned during the war.

The director appeared not impressed with the locks or my abilities to open them, and pushed it all aside. Instead she talked with me, asking all sorts of questions and finally agreed that I could start school in September.

At home I didn't know what to do with myself. In this, Mama was right. I felt locked in. I missed Pupping so much, and I was so lonely, I even missed my brother. Mama didn't tell me anything. When I asked again about Willi, she said: "Until school starts, you can go to the kindergarten, where you have children to talk to."

When she told me what a kindergarten was, it sounded so terrible I refused to go there. But Mama was adamant.

"You'll have children to talk with, a big yard to run around in, and fresh air," she said. "You need fresh air, Gerti."

I did not care about the air or the children, but whatever I said Mama would not change her mind.

My worst fears came true on the very first day. I hated the kindergarten. It was run by the church and in the same building we had gone for handouts as the war ended. I had been deeply ashamed then, and I felt ashamed again now.

The woman in charge was called Tante. Why, I didn't know, she seemed nobody's aunt in the kindergarten. After Mama had left, she introduced me to the other children. But I could not respond, and stayed silent. All the children knew each other and played in small groups, and each morning they'd grab all the toys as their own. Once I managed to get hold of a bear which lay unloved on the floor, but as soon as I started playing with him, one of the bossy girls snatched him off me.

During the first days the Tante tried to help me. Perhaps Mama had said I could sing, so the Tante stood me between her knees with her arm around my shoulders, and made me sing. I couldn't cope with her arms round my shoulders, or her legs on each side of me. I just could not cope with her being so close and wanted to get away from her.

And my singing didn't help in the least. The other children didn't like me any better, and I felt terrible, being the center of attention. I hated everything here. I wanted to crawl into a hole in the wall which would open for me, and once I was in, it would close. Perhaps I could die in this hole, or at least be left alone.

Eventually I was left alone, apart from being teased about my country dialect. I quickly shed this beloved way of speaking, and became Viennese again.

Occasionally a boy sat by me. He was different too, had dark skin and black curly hair, which stood up around his head like a halo. We would sit in silence. There was nothing to say.

I attempted again to convince Mama to let me stay home, but without any success. "You are better off in kindergarten," she insisted. "You have other children to play with, and fresh air. You need fresh air, Gerti."

So I tried other tactics, foster-father's teachings were not totally forgotten. "Don't let them do this to you," I heard his voice in my head. "Scream, Gerti, come on, do it, and scream."

I followed his advice and I screamed, right here on the street, on the way to the kindergarten.

It was no use. Mama just dragged me along, ignoring my screams.

But Pflegevater's voice was still in my head, and I knew I had to defend myself and use force. So I screamed louder, digging my heels in, making my feet grow roots going deep into the earth, like the roots of a tree. And I refused to move even one step. But Mama's grip just became firmer; she moved even faster and pulled me along with her. She would have pulled me off my feet, had I not run. But she could not stop me from screaming.

People stared at us, and a man stopped, wagging his finger at me, he said: "I'll take you with me, if you don't shut up."

I kept screaming, I was less afraid of him than of the kindergarten, but he just mumbled something and shaking his head he walked on.

There was no escape from Mama, or the kindergarten. Eventually I stopped screaming, because it was no use. I had learned once again, it was no use to resist and defend myself; this method did not work here in Vienna, at least not with Mama.

Then suddenly Willi came home – Mama had not even told me he was coming. She was in the kitchen making jam from apricots which Lilly had brought from Tante Paula's allotment garden, when I heard a knock on the door. Mama ignored the knocking, but the door opened, and my brother stood there, holding the hand of a strange woman. He cried bitterly, and remained standing at the door, as if this wasn't his home. I knew he felt terrible, and I felt terrible too.

Mama carried on stirring the apricots, ignoring Willi, not saying one word.

The woman broke the painful silence, and said she was from social services. She wanted to know why Mama had not come to the Westbahnhof to collect Willi; the railway station was only at the bottom of our street.

Mama stopped stirring the apricot mixture, to point with the wooden spoon at the boiling fruit on the stove. "I had to finish making the jam," she said, as if that was a good enough reason.

The woman shrugged her shoulders, and without another word turned to leave, shaking her head as she went.

My brother entered the flat, and finally I could talk to him, as our mother wordlessly carried on with the jam.

Now Willi was home, life was better, because we had each other. I talked about Pupping and he told me about Holland. He had stayed with a family who lived in a flat above their shop. They had been nice to him, and he had plenty to eat. But he had hated being away from home and from Mama, and said he would never leave her again.

My brother had brought brand new clothes with him, and small red dwarfs with little hooks on their heads. He told me they were for a Christmas tree, but we played with them, making up games as we went along. He also had a book with many small pictures on each page, with writing under each picture. Willi explained it was written in Dutch and he could not only understand and speak this language now, he could read it as well. I was proud of my brother. He translated the words for me, and wrote them in German under each picture so I could read the whole story myself, once I was in school. I looked forward to school, because then I could leave the hated kindergarten.

On the whole, if not for us, in Vienna, life had become better. A greater variety of food appeared in the shops. I liked shopping with Mama, to look at the vegetables I remembered from Pupping. Even different kinds of fruit were for sale, apples and pears, and sometimes plums, as the summer was drawing to its end.

On the fifth of November, for my sixth birthday, I had a sausage as a present. I told no one, that in Pupping I only needed to go to the inn and sing a song, and I would not only get one, but two Frankfurters. But these things belonged in the past. And I could not have told anyway, because Mama would have been horrified that I sang in a pub.

Because of my birthday Christl stayed home and Lilly came visiting. Everyone was so excited about the sausage, I didn't want to spoil their fun, and then I got excited too. As it was my present, I could decide what to do with the sausage; so I cut it into five equal pieces and we all had a bite. It was the first time since the war that Mama had tasted meat, but I still remembered only too well the roast chicken and the black smoked bacon I had eaten in Pupping.

Meat was still rare in the shops, and very expensive. We couldn't afford it. The money Papa sent each month wasn't enough to live on. There were times when Mama put only food for us children on the table.

"Mama, where is yours?" I remember asking.

"I've eaten," she always replied.

Strange, I would think, how could I have missed it? But I never really thought about it until I was older.

Much seemed to change during this time. Willi was already eight years old and very tall and whatever I did, he was stronger and also more clever than I. But at least I could read Willi's book now, because in September I had started school.

Lilly had already taught me the alphabet, so reading came easy. But I did not like school. I had become shy and withdrawn, and found it difficult to relate to other children. But school was better than kindergarten, and because everyone had to learn, I made the best of it. As the teacher and the other children left me alone, I accepted school as a necessary part of my life. I learned easily, and liked drawing and painting and singing. Because of my voice, our teacher, Frau Schiller, took an interest in me. She would invite me and Ursula, who also had a good voice, to her home and we would sing in harmony: I would sing high and Ursula low, and our teacher accompanied us on the piano. Afterwards we played with a fabulous doll's house, whilst Frau Schiller prepared something special to eat, before taking us home.

I liked these visits, but could not feel the joy which had always been a part of me in Pupping, where I had felt so alive, so full of joy and happiness, that I had to shout and sing, to run and to jump. Now, I got a glimpse of a happier life occasionally. Sometimes I skipped on the way to Frau Schiller – just once or twice – before returning to the Pelzgasse. I never called it my home.

For Mama, the Pelzgasse was also bad. She had changed out of all proportion, and got progressively worse, shouting more, telling us off constantly, and she nagged, a terrible process which could last for hours. Mama called me names, horribly insulting names, much worse than anything she called Willi. I couldn't shake off what she said, and was deeply hurt.

Sometimes her anger was not directed at us, but our father, at least at the initial part of this terrible process of shouting, ranting and raving. No words can describe what went on, I have never since seen anyone behaving this way. And once Mama was in this state, it could take several hours until she finally stopped.

Soon her talking became a monologue, because Willi and I learned quickly, if we said something, anything at all, it would take her attention off Papa, to bring her scorn down upon our heads. Then she would shout even longer, because she was angrier. It was all about us now, and our misdeeds.

So we stayed quiet, as Mama talked on, and on, hour after hour after hour. It was not wise to read or to draw, or go to the other room. It made Mama angrier if we sneaked away behind her back. She seemed to need our presence, but only to be there and to listen in silence.

As weeks and months passed, Mama's 'talks' became more and more frequent. Nearly every day we heard the story of the divorce. Papa was the villain, and as I totally agreed, I said so once. This was a grave mistake. Mama turned on me, and suddenly it was no longer Papa's fault, but Mina Worrell's, who was the other woman, and had lured him away. And then my misdeeds were brought into the light, and her wrath and frustration erupted on me. It seemed I had committed so many crimes just to spite her, and make her life even more difficult.

And all of my badness and cheekiness, it all came from 'Him.' "Just like your father", was her worst judgement. And I was much worse than Willi, because she never said these words to him.

If I was upset and tears came to my eyes, Mama would threaten to hit me, saying it would give me something to cry about. I knew from experience this was no idle threat. Now I finally realized, that crying was not only bad, it was stupid.

Crying only made things worse. Willi didn't cry anymore, and neither would I, ever again. And slowly I succeeded in this.

Willi told me about the Red Indians; how brave they were. Even under severe torture they would not show how they felt, and never gave their enemies the satisfaction of seeing their pain.

These brave men became my heroes. If I closed my eyes I could see them running across the open country, with the tall grasses waving in the breeze. At night, they would sleep in their tents, made from the skin of the animals they had hunted for food.

They looked at the moon and the stars, here for everyone to admire. Only I couldn't see them anymore here in Vienna.

The Red Indians were tough and brave, as Mariandl and I had been in Pupping. And as I, the real Gerti, still was, deep down inside, where Mama could not get to. I knew she wanted to get there, turn me inside out. And if she succeeded, I would break into hundreds of pieces, and the real me would cease to exist. Only a shell would remain.

But she would not succeed; I would not let her do it. I was brave like an Indian warrior, and would never again show how I felt, so Mama could not get to the real me.

This was very important, because even if I had lost everything, I still had myself.

When I asked my teacher about the Red Indians, she lent me a book. I loved reading. Forgetting about Mama and the Pelzgasse, in my mind I was a warrior, running free. I felt a kinship with these brave people. They were my real relatives, because they thought as I did. And I too was angry at the white man, the enemy. He took their land, killing their food just for fun. And then he killed the Native Americans too.

I hated the white man, our enemy. And I would be like my warrior friends. Not a muscle would move in my face under pain, torture, or threat. However much I suffered, I would never again show how I felt.

So I pushed my pain, sorrow and anger, and everything else, just to be sure, deep down, somewhere inside me, and showed nothing. Willi already acted this way. It was safer.

But sometimes I forgot my intentions, because Mama was not always the same. She could change almost instantly. Without any apparent reason, the old Mama came suddenly back. And everything was as it had been before I left Vienna for Pupping. Mama cared for me again. She would show me how to cook, and to sew, and she'd praise my work. And the light in her eyes was back, as if she loved me.

I could not help myself but respond, and open my heart to her. My guard would come down, and for a while, a few minutes, or hours – sometimes even a day or two – it was so nice between us, so peaceful. Then I'd say something – anything – it didn't seem to matter what I said, and suddenly the frightening mother was back, who shouted at me for no reason. The nasty Mama was in charge again.

Slowly I realized Mama's behavior had nothing to do with my words, though they seemed to initiate her change. It was a mistake to let her come close. I must be on guard, and never say anything ever again, except what she wanted to hear.

I tried to anticipate what she wanted to hear, and began to lie. This worked marginally better, but didn't help much. Everything was still my fault, especially if I became ill.

I was ill often now. First, I had measles; so seriously, I had to stay in hospital for two weeks. Then came the flu. I always had colds, and was prone to throat and chest infections. I tried my best to avoid getting ill, or to hide it at least, because Mama would blame me.

'You wouldn't be bad Gerti, if you had put your scarf across your throat properly,' she'd say.

Or, had I kept my mouth shut on the street when it was cold, or because my hat had not been far enough over my forehead. And so it went on, and on, and every illness was my fault.

In Pupping I had never been ill, though I wore no shawl at all, and only put on my hat if it was very cold. But here in Vienna, my hat was of the greatest importance. I had to pull it well over my forehead and ears, which looked ridiculous.

I hated this hat. It came from the clothes parcel we had to collect from church when the war ended. Mama had made Willi and me go there alone, and we had felt like beggars. Every time I wore this hat, it reminded me of this humiliation.

Made of thick gray felt, it had bits on each side which turned up. No one here wore such a hat, and the children at school made fun of me. On one occasion a boy had pulled this horrible thing off my head and thrown it to another child. Trying to grab my possession, if necessary by force, I was preparing for battle. But the children formed a circle round me, throwing the hat to each other. They were laughing, and teasing me. It was pointless chasing my hat, especially as I had enough trouble holding my tears back.

Realizing how I felt, one girl gave me the hat, and said she was sorry. She had not wanted to upset me, and was sure the other children felt the same – but the hat was so funny.

Afterwards I took it off on the staircase when I left home for school.

Then fate stepped in, and I lost this horrible headgear. Mama punished me, but it was worth it. I had to wear a Pullman cap now, which other girls wore too, so it caused no problem. I left it on my head, but it made no difference, I still got ill.

Mama behaved as if I got ill to annoy her, to make her life even harder because she had to look after me. But after she had ranted for a while, she would sigh, calm down, and tell me to go to bed. She'd take my temperature, and if my fever was high she would panic, and start shouting again, but not for long. Then Willi or Christl were sent for the doctor who lived round the corner, and if no one else was at home, Mama herself would go.

Now she would turn into the good, quiet and kind mother, making tea with sugar for me, and tempting me to eat, with food I liked best. She looked after me well, until I was better.

But afraid of her first reaction, I tried to hide any illness or accident. Yet Mama could always tell, just by looking at me.

One day I cut my thumb and it was bleeding. I hid my hand behind my back. But Mama knew instantly something was wrong.

"What is it Gerti?" she asked, and I could tell she was ready to shout.

I couldn't answer, and avoided her gaze by looking down. To my horror I saw large tell-tale drops of blood hitting the linoleum floor. Mama saw it too. She looked so frightened; I reluctantly showed her my thumb.

Relief spread over her face, and she hugged me, which she had not done for a long time.

"I was so afraid it was something serious," she admitted, relief on her face.

This was the only time I was not shouted at, or blamed for an illness or accident. And this time, it had really been my fault.

Although my brother was ill even more often than I was, he never seemed to be at fault.

Mama was ill too, permanently and quite seriously, because of her heart, and the doctor was a frequent visitor. If Mama could

81

no longer get out of bed, Willi or I went for the doctor, and Mama would be given an injection and had to stay in bed for a few days until she was better. Christl would bring groceries home after work, and I shopped for milk or anything else we might need in the meantime. Then I cooked under Mama's direction. Willi had no chores to do, being a boy.

Mama was always nice when she was very ill, and she'd praise me for helping, especially if I cooked a good soup using bones and whatever vegetables we had. But as long as she could Mama just carried on without making any fuss.

At thirteen, she'd had tuberculosis in her bones, and stayed in hospital for a year. On her chest was a deep scarred dent where the bone had been open and weeping. The doctor had told her it was important we children had fresh air and good food; otherwise we might get this illness too.

Perhaps the problem with her back had its source in the tuberculosis, or in the war and the way we had to live, I didn't know, but it was obvious being in pain made Mama more irritable. If she had to go to school to see my teacher for whatever reason, good or bad, Mama would get angry, because going up three flights of stairs made her back worse, and it would take days to recover.

Perhaps this was also a reason we stayed in our flat in the Pelzgasse, which was on the first floor.

CHAPTER 7

VIENNA 1946–47

In Vienna, fear had begun stalking me again, but it was a different kind of fear than the one I knew from the cellar. This time the monster attacking me showed a side new to me, which had to do with God, the devil, and hell. God was the worst, as he created everything and made sure it could happen, at least until the devil took over in hell, or perhaps he even took over here on earth on time.

In Pupping, I had almost forgotten about hell and fear had vanished altogether somehow. But here in Vienna, this tactile beast was again part of my life. As Mama talked constantly about sinning and hell, because of what happened in Pupping with Poldi, her words took on a new and much greater meaning. And to make matters worse I committed new sins all of the time because of the lies I told Mama.

One evening I saw the flames of hell. Opening the bedroom door, I didn't see our beds as I usually did but I saw hell. It was waiting for me with its hairy devils; some red like the flames but there were black devils too; their pitchforks ready to poke, so I'd hurt even more; and there was no way out, ever, from hell.

Luckily, I saw the devils of hell only once. But the good beings I saw often, and always on the way to church, as they lived in the scrubland and the allotments next to our path.

Taking the shortcut through the allotments to church, there on the left, lived friendly and happy little men and women and children too. They were much shorter than people, about my size or even smaller, but more square looking, as if someone had pushed each one down from the top, squashing their bodies slightly and their faces. They wore brightly coloured clothes, much red and green and were happy and cheerful; often laughing when they talked to each other.

I wanted to go over and talk to them. But Mama wouldn't let go of my hand because the first time I saw them, I had told her. She just said that that these small beings did not exist.

But I saw them as clearly as everything else and they saw me too, wanting me to come over and join them. I tried, but Mama held on to me. So I could only smile and wave with my free hand. I think they understood, because they always smiled and waved back.

One day big machines flattened the whole area; a paddling pool was built and later a sports center; die Stadthalle. The grass, trees and bushes where the small people had their homes gave way to concrete. I never saw them again, though I kept looking when we went to church.

Church and prayer ruled our lives more and more. Apart from Sunday Mass and various services during the week, we prayed the rosary before going to bed. The light was switched off, and we sat at the kitchen table, repeating the same words and sentences, over and over, again and again.

I had a problem with praying, because of God, who would send me to hell. And I couldn't accept everything it said in the Bible, especially God telling Abraham to murder his son. That God had stopped this crime before the deed was done made no difference to how I felt. He should not have asked this murder of Abraham in the first place.

How could I love a God who asked a father to kill his own son? As for Abraham, I had no patience or understanding at all. How could he even consider this horrible murder? Fathers should protect their children, no matter what.

Whatever anyone, even God, ever said or did to me, I would never hurt my children, when I had them one day. But how could I love such a cruel God? And if I didn't love him, I had sinned again. I could not escape this circle of sins. I found no solution for this dilemma, and so I pushed all thoughts about this subject from me, deep down somewhere. How else was I to cope with it?

With the Ten Commandments I had problems as well, especially the third, which said I had to honor my father and mother. With my mother I just about managed it, at least most of the time. But to honor my father? who didn't care what happened to me, and who never bothered at all? How could I honor him? I didn't even know him.

I wanted to forget about it all, but Mama wouldn't let me, because I had to keep praying. But what difference would my prayers make, if I went to hell anyway?

To pray the rosary took half an hour. To sit still in the dark for so long, mumbling the right words, was difficult and boring. If I made a mistake or faltered, I'd feel Mama's elbow in my ribs and though it was dark I knew she looked at me reproachfully. But with daily practice, I soon managed to mumble the right words, and give my imagination free reign. And so my black panther came into my life.

Soon he visited me every night to take me to his island. Here I was safe, because my new friend would let no one come to our island, only me. I knew he loved and protected me.

Now, sitting down to pray, I was no longer bored, knowing marvelous adventures awaited me. Exploring the island's dense jungles or the rocky shoreline with my powerful friend was exciting and wonderful. His fur was black as the night, taking on a blue-silvery sheen in the moonlight. His eyes glinted yellow or green, but turned golden when he smiled. We'd fight, but just for fun, and he would push me between his huge paws, always pulling his claws in, not to hurt me. Then we'd cuddle and I was surrounded by velvety fur, and pure love.

He stayed with me during the day, and it helped, knowing I could turn to him for comfort. But he couldn't change my life in the Pelzgasse, and I had to keep him secret from Mama, because she would tell me that he did not exist.

According to Mama, what she couldn't see did not exist, except God, Jesus and the Holy Ghost, and the devils and demons of hell. Everything else was superstition. Just once she admitted it gave angels too, when I pointed them out on the stained-glass windows in our church. But perhaps even with angels you had to be careful, because one of them, Lucifer, had turned into the devil.

Apart from angels, Mama remained firm about superstition. I overheard Lilly tell Christl, Tante Paula was superstitious, but felt not close enough to confide in her. I had no one to confide in. Once I had told Willi how I felt about Pupping. He had encouraged me, and it felt nice to talk. But later he teased me, and told Mama everything. My brother had a good memory, at every opportunity he repeated my words to humiliate me and for his amusement.

It was not safe to tell anyone what I thought and felt, except my black panther – though he always knew already.

The more restricted and hemmed in I felt during the day, the better my nights became, especially when my black panther taught me to influence my dreams. If I got my timing right, and pictured a tunnel of light in shades of color, I could direct what happened, as I drifted into sleep.

Now, I enjoyed lying in bed in the dark, planning my adventure. Once the decision was made where to go, I only had to wait for the right moment, which came between being awake and asleep, just as I started drifting. Visualizing the light-tunnel, I'd walk through it – or rather I floated, holding the hand of my companion, if I took someone with me. I had to keep focused, or I'd drift too soon into sleep, and could not direct what happened. And if I let go of my companion's hand in the tunnel, I'd lose him.

Once in the tunnel, if I didn't concentrate I'd feel a thump in my body, as if I had fallen from somewhere high up. I would wake, and had to start all over again. But with daily practice I soon became proficient.

At the tunnel's end, I could let the dream take me where it would, and if I didn't like what was happening, I took charge and changed it. Eventually, I would drift into deep sleep. When I woke, I remembered, and could continue my journey on the next evening, if I wanted.

I made new friends in my dreams. My best friend was a Red Indian chief, who wore a beautiful headdress of eagle feathers. We would ride over the prairie, on horses fast as the wind, to stop and watch as the buffalo herd approached. There would be more than enough, to feed our people.

Anything was possible in my dreams; there were no restrictions at all.

But on some nights, after the light was switched off, I forgot about my dream journeys, because Mama started to sing, and we all joined in. These were the golden times we had as a family, perhaps the only really good times. Christl had a beautiful voice. She sang *Ave Maria* at church weddings. But we all were musical and had good voices. Our mother loved music and in the old life, we had a gramophone and records of many operas.

Mama was proud of my musical talents. She often told us, that I sang Humperdinck's opera *Hansel and Gretel*, standing in my cot, when I was only two. Such a funny name, I always thought when she talked about it. But though I could not remember the cot, I could still sing the whole opera. It was one of the few things Mama liked about me, and for a short while I would bask in her approval and pride, perhaps even her love.

In the joy of singing together, I'd forget where I was, and everything else. We'd sing for what seemed hours, until drifting into sleep, one by one. Our voices carried, and sometimes I worried because everyone in our building would hear us and probably in the street too when our window stood open. But nobody ever complained.

Next morning, the closeness and beauty and love we had shared, was a dream. It was an illusion and better forgotten – until the next time we sang.

Lilly's visits also brought a little joy into the monotony of our lives, especially since she had Blackie, a collie, who had come as a war mascot to Vienna with a Scottish regiment. A soldier gave Lilly the dog, as the army could no longer keep him.

It was love at first sight for my brother and me, and Blackie took to us too. But he liked everyone. He even got round Mama, and she allowed us to keep him with us overnight, sometimes even for days. Blackie was good for Mama too, she was much calmer when he was here, and stopped her long monotonous talks and endless shouting for a while. Willi and I took it in turns on whose bed Blackie slept, and it was marvelous to feel his furry warm body close to mine.

We had to speak English with Blackie, and Lilly taught us the necessary commands. He fitted in well, but if he decided to leave, nothing could stand in his way. When we took him for a walk, sometimes he just disappeared when we stopped to cross the street. Only his collar would hang on the lead, and we'd find his muzzle close by. But Blackie always found his way back to Lilly though even from my sister he would sneak away, but only for a few hours. Eventually Tante Paula was told where he went.

Blackie had discovered the cinema, which had opened again after the war. The entrance hall was always full, although not everyone sitting there could afford the price of the ticket, but people, mostly older women, came to get warm. Here, surrounded by an adoring audience, Blackie gave his performance. He'd offer his paw, walk on hind legs and dance, and he would sing. Blackie always sang if he heard music, he would sing on command or if he wanted attention. This little dog had an ear for music, and if he was singing with someone else, his howls would follow the melody. When he'd had enough, Blackie ended his show by rolling over to play dead, and then he made his round, shaking hands and collecting his reward. People gave him whatever they could; they saved it from their rations especially for Blackie. Tante Paula maintained their dog ate much better than we all did.

"That's why he turned his nose up at the beans in the black pudding skin," Lilly said.

She had managed to buy a black pudding, and stuffed the empty skin with beans, so Blackie would eat the beans too, like we all had to. But he had bitten into the fake black pudding, carefully shaken out all the beans and just eaten the skin.

I just wished I had a black pudding, and that I could leave my beans too.

Lilly had a better life with Tante Paula, and sometimes she took me to spend a day with them. But she took Willi more often, because she liked him better. And I had no one now.

I had lost all the confidence I had gained in Pupping, and hated to be noticed, or worse, be the center of attention. When I was out with Lilly, especially on the tram, people looked at me, and said how pretty I was with my big eyes and long lashes. I was so embarrassed. I hated to be stared at by strangers; I hated people talking about me as if I was not there or couldn't hear. One day, when I saw Mama's tailoring scissors lying on the table, I knew what I had to do. I put the scissors into my pocket as I left for school, and on the staircase I cut off my lashes. Now people would leave me in peace.

Mama was appalled when she saw me. "What on earth possessed you to cut your lashes off?" she shouted. "You could have poked your eyes out, Gerti."

I couldn't tell her the reason, I couldn't explain anything to my mother, but Lilly knew as soon as she saw me. Mama never understood me, and often I was angry with her, or upset, but I also felt sorry for her. She never laughed or smiled, she was so unhappy. The war, the loss of Papa and of her home, and the pain she was in, it all had been too much for her. She also missed our garden. Our mother had lost everything she had loved; only her children were left. And we were too much responsibility, because of her illnesses, and because there was not enough money, and because of the awful way we had to live in this terrible flat in the Pelzgasse.

The light in her eyes, the golden spark, seemed to have gone, together with the love she once had. But not everything of her old self had totally vanished, but lay, deeply buried, under layers of rubble and debris and ashes. And because her light was so strong, sometimes it would shine through the rubble and emerge again. Then my old Mama was back, the mother who loved me, and whom I loved deeply. But as time passed these moments got rare, and I too became more and more burdened with rubble, and my own light too was in danger of disappearing under the debris of everyday life.

Mama's monologues got even longer and more frequent. Willi and I had heard her stories so often, we knew what came next. My brother had more courage than I, and less compassion for Mama, so behind her back, he would mouth the story as it unfolded, almost word for word, to make me laugh. But he too found nothing funny about the situation; it was just his way to cope with it all.

Mama would pace up and down – three steps turn, three steps turn – there was not enough room in our kitchen to walk more than three steps without turning. When she paced in this way, it could take hours until Mama was finally so worn out, that she stopped. And as we heard about the past so many times, Willi and I began to put the disjointed bits together, to form a picture which made sense to us. And so finally I begun to understand how it all happened, why we were poor and without our father, and why we had to live in this horrible flat.

Mama was twenty, when she met our father. They fell in love, married, and were very happy.

I often tried to imagine Mama in love and happy, but always failed. Probably, because I had never seen her happy. I knew it was because Papa had left her.

Though hard to believe now, we seemed to have been a normal and happy family once, and had everything we needed and more. Our father's business was doing well and we lived in a big flat with seven rooms. I could not imagine living in such a huge flat, although I'd lived in it too until the bomb had destroyed it. At the time we had all been in the cellar, except Papa, who had already left, because of Mina.

To interrupt Mama now was particularly dangerous. If she spoke about Mina, her fury increased tenfold.

Mina Worell had once threatened our mother with a revolver, which she carried hidden in her muff. She said if Mama didn't let Papa go, she would report us. And then, so Willi said, the Gestapo would have taken us away and we would have been gassed, which meant we would be dead now.

In spite of this threat, I was certain Mama would not have let Papa go, if she could have helped it. But he went anyway, and started divorce proceedings. Mama couldn't stop it, though she tried. They were divorced, and our father had to pay alimony, but with inflation this got worth less, and Mama could not manage anymore.

She said terrible things about our father, but if we agreed, she'd defend him. Suddenly the fault lay with the other woman, who had lured him away.

I failed to understand how anyone could lure our father away, if he had wanted to stay with us. And what did Mina lure him with? And he had not left only Mama, but his children too, letting us live here in the Pelzgasse.

I felt so resentful and angry about Papa. I could have forgiven him for leaving Mama, but I could not understand or forgive, that he left us in this terrible flat. Not once had he come to visit us. If he had seen how we lived, surely he would have taken us away from here.

Willi felt even worse towards our father than I. He hated him. He didn't need to tell me, I knew.

Only many years later, when Lilly and I were grown up, and women with our own families, did I learn more about our past. I lived abroad then, and though Lilly and I met when I came on holiday, the distance between us which had developed during my childhood, lasted a long time. But after Papa died, I heard her side of the story, and a very different picture gradually emerged.

CHAPTER 8

30 YEARS LATER IN WALES
GOING FORWARD, LOOKING BACK

When I was twenty-five, I left Austria and came to Britain, more than thirty years ago now. There had been little contact with my father throughout the years and I rarely thought of him. Then one day Christl phoned. Our father had been in an accident, and was in a coma. He couldn't move or speak and was not expected to recover.

I felt nothing at first, I was totally numb. It must have been the shock, because as the numbness left, I felt great sorrow and pain. At the same time a separate part of me could not understand why I was so upset, why I should hurt so much. I had not seen my father for many years, we exchanged letters or a postcard just on occasion. We had never been close, I couldn't talk to him about the things that mattered to me, we had never built a real father-daughter relationship.

When I was fifteen, I went to live with him – a mistake, I should soon regret deeply. It turned out a disaster for both of us, and after six months I returned to my mother. We had no contact at all until I wrote to my father, many years later, when I already lived in Wales. Since then, when I was on holiday in Vienna, I visited a few times, but we never talked about the past. He'd said he would come and see me. It was too late now. It was sad, but why was I hurting so much, as if I loved him?

I booked a flight ticket, arranged for the journey, packed, and finally went to bed. But sleep avoided me. I cried, missing my father. But how could I miss him? In all of the many years of my life I could not remember missing him like I did now. It was too late – too late for what? There was nothing between us, never had been, the father I needed had never been there for me.

Finally, I must have dozed off, because I heard him talking to me. I woke, but Papa was still with me. He knew that he was dying and wanted something from me before it was too late. "Will you give it to me, Gerti?" he asked.

Still half asleep, I didn't understand what he wanted, why he was so in need, so insistent, why it was so important to him …

"Anerkennung," he said. He wanted recognition, but I didn't know what he meant.

"Anerkennung, I want you to recognize me as your father." His words were clear, but still I didn't understand. There was no doubt he was my father. No one had ever denied or even doubted it. Why did he want me to recognize him as my father? But he insisted, asking me again if I was willing.

"Yes," I just said. I was willing, but found it most odd, having believed all of my life that he never really cared about me. But now that he was dying, suddenly all of the past was swept clean. I felt love, deep love for him, and some understanding, having made my own mistakes in the process of life. So I gave him my love freely and told him yes, I would give him what he wanted, what he needed, the recognition that he was a good father.

"Not a good father," I could feel him smile, but it was a sad smile. "Just a father. It's enough that you recognize me as your father, Gerti."

And so I did. I just said the words he wanted to hear, I said that I recognized him as my father.

His spirit was with me all night, and I felt so much love coming from him, for the first time that I could remember. Sometimes he talked to me, and as dawn broke, he asked me to sing the song he had wanted me to sing for him, when I was a child. I had refused, because things were already bad between us then.

Lilli Palmer had sung this song, it was popular during the time I was in his care. Then, I wouldn't sing this song for him, but now, thirty years later, as my father was dying, I sang it and was glad to, and I meant every word.

'Oh mein Papa, war eine wunderbare Clown, oh mein Papa war eine grosse Kuenstler.'

As it said in the song, my father, he was a great artist, a clown, and a great man.

When I finished singing, I knew his spirit had gone, my father was dead.

Getting ready for the journey, I sang the song again. And as I was singing, memories came, and suddenly I knew why he had needed to be recognized as my father.

When I went to stay with him, Papa was married to Mina. I couldn't share their flat, it was too small. So he rented a room for me close by, with a family. I looked forward so much to have my own space and privacy.

But the couple I lodged with, had other ideas. They treated me as their servant. When I was not at work, I had to help with housework and look after the children. And then the events started, which would bring the relationship with my father to an end.

It was a few days before Easter. I told Frau Hammer, my landlady, I would be visiting Mama on my first day off. She didn't answer, and I thought I'd escaped my chores on that day, and went to bed, not realizing something was wrong. Next morning Papa burst into my room, telling me to come to the kitchen. Frau Hammer had told him, I had refused to help with the housework.

My father was furious. As I entered the kitchen, without any warning or explanation, he hit me, punched me in my face. They were strong, heavy blows, lifting me into the air, sending me reeling to the other side of the kitchen where I landed in a heap. But Papa had not finished with me, until I lay on the floor, bleeding and unable to move.

I couldn't understand what was happening, and why. Blood came from my mouth, dripping down on to the brown linoleum floor. Suddenly there was quiet, no one talked anymore. The whole family stood around, staring at me, including the children.

I looked at Papa, but I couldn't speak. He said something but I couldn't take it in. His voice sounded as if it came from a long way away.

At last I managed to get up. I left the kitchen, went to my room and shut the door.

I sat there, feeling totally numb. In spite of the pain, I was totally empty, feeling nothing. I never wanted to speak with him again. He was worse than Mama. She had slapped me in temper, but this had been an assault. Not only had he hurt me physically, what hurt more was the injustice. He believed strangers, and had not even given me an opportunity to speak and to defend myself. I could never trust him again.

I had nowhere to turn to, no one to speak with. What could I do? The Court had given my father full authority over me. I had to live where he decided. This last incident was just a link in a chain of terrible events, which made me see clearly what I had known deep down for a while: it was worse here with my father than it had been with my mother, and I would not have thought this possible before coming here.

In three years I'll be eighteen, I thought. Then I can live on my own and be free. I shall try to survive these years. But three years seemed an eternity.

And what if I can't manage anymore? A voice from deep within me asked. What then?

For a long time, there was silence in me, until the answer came: there is only death.

But death frightened me. Not because of dying, but because if I killed myself, I would go to hell.

I pushed these thoughts far away from me, because now, I was in hell already. Now, I was more afraid of living than of dying. I couldn't live this way. Not for three years. If I found no other way out, death would be my only escape.

Then doubts arose. Would I be able to kill myself, was I brave enough? How would I do it?

The easiest way would be to cut the artery above my wrist. It would be a slow and gentle death, as my life-blood flowed away.

But not yet, I told myself. Only if I can survive no longer, and don't find another way out.

But did I have the courage to kill myself? I had to be certain, and make a deep cut on the other side of my wrist, where I knew it was not dangerous.

I found a razor blade and started to cut, but felt a strange reluctance, which I had to overcome. But once I continued to cut into my flesh, it became remarkably easy, and eventually blood ran all over the gash.

I felt stronger, more in charge of my life. And suddenly I knew what to do. I would make an oath – a blood-oath. And so I swore by my blood, that I would never again recognize Papa as my father, as long as the scar showed on my arm. He would no longer be my father – he would get no recognition from me as my father anymore.

Recognize was the precise word I used then, and the word recognition. These were the same words my father said a life time later, when he was dying.

I had never told Papa, or anyone else, of my oath. Yet as he was dying he knew, and he needed me to take back the oath and dissolve it. He needed recognition as my father, he needed my love. Perhaps we both had to undo what had happened that day, I don't know. But I do know when he died, we were united in love.

CHAPTER 9

LATER IN VIENNA
LOOKING BACK

Our father's death brought Lilly and me together again. His flat, and all his possessions had to be sorted. We, his four children, were the inheritors.

Lilly, Christl and I were in Papa's flat, only Willi was absent. He had not come to the funeral, and his solicitor had sent a formal letter, informing us our brother refused his inheritance.

He had always said that he would never have anything to do with our father, and he had kept his word. Even his money he refused.

Later, when Lilly and I were alone, we came to talk about the war, and about the day Mama went to the country with Christl, leaving us younger children in Lilly's care.

"As two days passed without Mama returning, I didn't know what to do," my sister confessed. "You and Willi were starving, you had not eaten for days. I had to do something. I didn't know when our mother would be back – if she would come back. Unspeakable things happened to women, it wasn't safe to be on the road. And although in the end everything turned out all right, I've always felt guilty, leaving you both on your own. Tante Paula was the only one who would help, but I couldn't take you with me, it was too far to walk. We had no public transport, everything was in chaos. Willi was only six, and you were not even four."

Only now did I realize how my sister must have felt. At the time I was too young. But even in the many years since, I had not given it any thought. And now, as Lilly finally got it all off her chest, she added, that living with Tante Paula had made her feel even worse; she had it much better there than we did. She had carried this guilt with her, all her life.

"But you know how small the flat was. You couldn't even put two small children into one of the camp beds, they were not stable enough," she said. "For a fifth bed was no space anywhere. Until I left, you slept on four chairs. Someone had to go, and I was the oldest."

"This flat was a terrible place. I knew how you all were suffering and I tried to help, taking Willi with me when I could, usually to Tante Paula, especially to her allotment. You seemed to cope better than he did, Gerti. I think your holidays in Pupping sustained you. But Willi had nothing, and we were the only ones to help."

My belief, that Lilly had preferred Willi to me, became shaky. And this old feeling of not being good enough, of being second best to my brother – this ancient feeling of inferiority which had accompanied me for so long – began to shake. And then, as my sister's words really sank in, these old, negative feelings dissolved, like smoke mixing with fresh air, turning to nothing.

My childhood suddenly appeared in a different light, as Lilly continued to explain why she and Tante Paula took Willi out so often, and me, hardly at all.

"We tried to help Willi," she said again. "Get him away from Mama as much as we could. He was tied to her apron strings, it wasn't good for him." She sighed deeply, remembering. "I was only fifteen, and it was much easier to take him. Every time we took you on a bus, you were sick."

I remembered only too well, in every bus, even in the tram I threw up if I couldn't get out in time. Taking me anywhere was no pleasure for anyone, not even me. No wonder Lilly took our brother, who was never sick.

The invisible wall between us had been my doing, I had constructed it as a protection against getting hurt – I had been hurt too often. The pain of loss was still with me even now. Not only my father had left, his whole family had disappeared out of my life, and both sets of my grandparents. I had lost my home, the garden with the hens and rabbits. And then my big sister went, the only one still here for me. My wall of protection had gone up, and stayed, at least partly until now.

But now it was crumbling fast, as I realized, my sister had continued to love me, had done what she could for me. She did her best for us all, but also needed to find a way to survive herself. She was so young, only fifteen, with her own problems.

During the next few days we were often together, talking of the past, and Lilly gradually realized how little I knew about our family history. Now, so many years later, I found out that so much was quite wrong. What I knew about our family came from Mama's 'talks.' It had come in disjointed pieces, which my brother and I had fitted together as best as we could. But our interpretation was one-sided, it was skewed, and entirely from our mother's viewpoint. My sister saw things differently.

She talked about her childhood, the time before I was born, and about later, when I was too small to remember. Then Lilly got an album out, and we looked at old photos. A picture showed Mama, young, pretty, happy. On the next photo she was high up in a tree, laughing.

I couldn't imagine Mama climbing a tree, or laughing like that. And I had never seen her happy. The woman on the pictures was a totally different person than the mother I remembered.

But the greatest surprise came, when Lilly told me it broke Papa's heart not to see Willi and me anymore.

"Didn't you know how much he loved you?" she asked, seeing the astonishment on my face.

I could only shake my head.

"Can't you remember how he used to play with you?"

I still could do no more than shake my head again, silently, in disbelief.

"I suppose you were too young to remember." Lilly mused. "For you it must be hard to believe we were a normal family, when I grew up. Papa loved all his children. Naturally, Willi had a special place in his heart as the only son, who would inherit the business. But he adored you. He took you with him everywhere, and walked for hours pushing your pram. In these years, you wouldn't often see a man with a pram, but Papa didn't care about people's opinions, or if they stared at him."

"To me he was always a good father," emphasized Lilly. And after the divorce she had continued visiting Papa, and they stayed in close contact until his death.

But why had he not cared about my brother and me? Why had he not come to see us, taken us out, to our grandparents and other relatives?

"He couldn't see you and Willi," Lilly answered my unspoken question. "Mama wouldn't allow it, you know what she was like. Christl and I visited him secretly."

Now, as I thought about it, I knew she was right. If Mama would not allow something, it became impossible, because she would make life impossible for everyone, especially Willi and me.

Now, so many years later, with both my parents dead, I heard another, a very different story, about the marriage of my parents, and what had led to their divorce.

It was 1927. Our father was twenty-four and Mama two years younger, when they married and rented a place which doubled as workshop and living quarters. Papa started his own business as a cabinet maker, just with his tools and a hand cart.

Lilly was born, and Christl came four years later. The business was already thriving. Our father had become a well-known expert in antiques, and an active member of the master cabinet-maker's guild.

Our family moved to a seven-room flat, just round the corner from his new big workshop. These were happy times for our family, and Mama wanted everything to continue just as it was. When they bought a garden with a small wooden bungalow, her life was complete. She loved the garden with its walnut and fruit trees. We kept a few chickens and rabbits, and later, when food became scarce because of the war, our father grew vegetables.

Now that he could afford it, Papa was able to devote more time and money to his other interests. From childhood on he had been fascinated by foreign countries, their culture and art. And although he was still too occupied expanding his business, he began to prepare for travelling in years to come, by reading books, and learning languages. He also studied yoga, different religions, and psychology – Freud had published some of his work during this period.

He began practicing sport, especially weightlifting, and loved the mountains.

Mama refused to go to the mountains with him. She resented all his outside interests, especially weightlifting. But Papa ignored her objections and carried on, and soon won competitions. And though Mama hated every sport and tried to make him stop, she was always proud of his looks and achievements.

"She was proud of him," Lilly confirmed what I thought. "But she tried to stop him, especially if his interests took him away from home."

"Papa did his best to include Mama, to wake her interest in something new. He wanted to hire a maid, so Mama could share his hobbies, and help him at work, in the office and with customers. He had a big business then, with nearly hundred people working for him. He needed Mama's help and support. But she preferred to stay home with the children."

"Their arguments got worse, and we all suffered. Mama got bitter and nagged constantly, and Papa spent more time away. He belonged to a group of fitness fanatics who went into the Danube each day, even in the winter when the river was frozen so solid, they had to hack holes in the ice to get in."

No small feat, I thought. The Danube has a strong current, it was a dangerous river, and Papa had never learned to swim.

"He became interested in psychology, in Freud, and began to study his writings and methods," Lilly continued. "Our mother resented Freud and all he stood for. To her it was rubbish, a waste of time, which Papa should spend with her. The only interests they shared were the garden, and music. We had records of all the big operas, and we all sang."

"If Mama had just let things be, perhaps it would have worked out in the end." Lilly sighed, sounding and looking so sad, having lived through it all with her parents, she had suffered with them. "But Mama nagged all the time, nothing he did was good enough."

"Willi was born. I was ten, Christl six. Mama loved babies. But with the arrival of each new child, the last one was pushed out of the nest, and she only had time for the new baby. This time it was Christl who suffered. But she never suffered in silence, someone always had to do something to pacify her, give her something or make a fuss, just to shut her up. This became my task."

"I felt sorry for Christl, remembering when our mother had brought her home from hospital. I had gone up to Mama and the new baby." Lilly's eyes looked into the past again, to the time when she was a little girl who had missed her mother.

"Go away, Mama said," she continued. "I have the baby to see to."

This pattern repeated itself, and Lilly was given responsibilities far above her age. She became our substitute mother, helping to look after us.

"At this time, the marriage was very rocky already, and our father didn't want more children. But when you came, he loved you, as he loved all of us."

I knew the story of my conception, Mama had told me once. It seems, she had been determined to have another child, though Papa planned otherwise.

He had wanted no more children, as he already thought of leaving. But to obtain a divorce, proof of infidelity was needed, or there had to be other serious reasons. Our mother relied on this, thinking she was safe in her marriage. But our father wanted out whatever it took, even if he had to lie and cheat.

One day, Papa took the children with him to visit his mother, and Mama stayed home. Helmut, Papa's friend, came by. As if by accident, they got locked into the flat, something seemed wrong with the lock. Mama couldn't open the door and was locked in with Helmut for hours. Later, she came to the conclusion, this situation had been arranged between Papa and his friend, to provide proof she was unfaithful.

Helmut did his best to seduce Mama, but she rebuffed him, reminding him he was her husband's friend, and owed him his loyalty. And she would not betray her husband anyway.

When Papa came back and realized his plan had failed, my parents reconciled, at least briefly, and nine months later I was born.

This was in 1941, in the middle of the war. "Why didn't our father enlist?" I asked Lilly. Even as a child, this had puzzled me. Every man below a certain age had to fight.

"He was against the Hitler regime – and against all war. But he had to keep his beliefs and convictions to himself, or he would have been shot. And we all knew what would have happened to us."

Lilly paused and we both got lost in our thoughts. We would have been one of the families taken away to unimaginable horrors.

"But our father was determined not to fight and kill people," she finally went on. "Through yoga, he had learned to control his body, even his heart rhythm. But to be sure, each time Papa had to go for a medical," Lilly smiled, remembering, "he drank gallons of strong coffee so his heart would play up. On medical grounds he was exempt from active service, but he had to build bridges. He hated to contribute to the war in this way, but to avoid serious consequences to all of us, he had to do it."

"After your birth, the home situation got worse. Our parents not only argued, they fought physically now. Both had violent tempers. We were in the kitchen one day, you in your pram, when Papa lost his temper and threw a knife. It narrowly missed you, and the knife buried itself in the pillow next to your eyes. I'll never forget it, you could have been killed, or blinded. It was then Papa knew he had to get out."

And now he met Mina Worrell, the other woman, who took an interest not only in our father, but in his interests and hobbies too.

"Das Luder, the bitch," my sister called her, and though her voice hardly changed and stayed calm, this word seemed to come from deep within her. I had to smile, never before had I heard my big sister swear.

The rest of the story I knew from Mama. Even as a child I could understand that our father found it impossible to live with her. But I did not understand or forgive, that he took no interest in us children; that he didn't make sure we were all right – that he never came to see Willi and me.

When I started to voice my thoughts, my sister stopped me.

"You've got it all wrong, Gerti, you have no idea," she said. "You don't know what you are talking about. Papa spent hours, waiting, to see you come out from school – just to see you. But you walked right past him, you didn't know your own father anymore. Once he called your name, and you turned your head. You looked through him, you didn't recognize your own father. It broke his heart, but he thought it was better for you, to let things be."

It was a strange feeling, that my father had loved me enough to wait for hours just to see me. And I had walked past him, without knowing.

But I still found it hard to let my old convictions go, which had accompanied me all of my life.

"If he waited for me, why didn't he talk to me? Why didn't he tell me he was my father?"

"Don't you remember what Mama was like?

I remembered only too well. She was bitter, and could be revengeful. Had she found out I had talked to Papa, I would have been punished, in one way or another.

Nothing could shift her, once she made up her mind. And she hardly ever changed her opinion.

On the one side, this was her strength. She had brought us up on her own, in spite of enormous difficulties. But her inability to accept change, and to make the best of a situation, had made everything more difficult. Mama's strength had been like the strength of an oak, carrying the heavy burdens of snow and ice, but she lacked the ability of the willow, to shake things off, and carry on with a lighter load.

It was this inability to adjust, and to accept change, which was a main reason we had nothing at all, after the divorce.

It seemed, at first Papa just wanted out, whatever the cost to him. He intended to give Mama everything, and start from scratch for himself. He'd train a manager to run the workshop, Mama would own it, and we'd live from the profit.

If she would let him go, she could have what she wanted, he told our mother. The garden would be signed over to her, so the children could grow up having plenty of vegetables and fruit. The chickens and rabbits would provide meat and eggs – an increasing consideration now, as food was scarce during the war.

"He really wanted to keep all his children," Lilly said. "But he knew Mama would never agree. And the court always kept children with their mother. Papa knew if he left, he would lose us, at least Willi and you. Christl and I were old enough to visit him in secret."

Our father had tried to talk to Mama about the arrangements he wanted to make, but she refused to discuss anything. He was her husband, she said, they were married, and nothing could change it. They had married in church, which was binding for life. She would not even hear him out, whatever he said or did.

"In the end our father left, got himself a solicitor and instigated divorce proceedings. Now he became stubborn too, and would only pay what the court decided. I am quite sure, his girlfriend Mina had much to do with this decision."

A bitter divorce followed. Strangely, Mina did not play any part in the proceedings, and Lilly knew why.

"Papa was careful, there was no evidence against him," she said. "But he had no evidence against Mama either. And no divorce could be granted without sufficient grounds. Our mother knew this, and counted on it. She was convinced that Papa could not divorce her."

But our father arranged the grounds. His workers said in court, Mama had not looked after him, that she had not cooked, or seen to his clothes, and buttons were missing on his shirts.

"We all knew they were lying," Lilly confirmed my opinion; Mama would never have behaved in this way.

"Mama always cooked and sewed," she said. "She looked after him well, after all of us. But she was her own worst enemy. Hearing these accusations in court, she got so angry, she antagonized the judge. I know, I was there, because I was a witness for Mama."

"She was so furious about the lies," she turned on the judge. "What about you?" she shouted at him. "A button is missing on your shirt, your honor. Does your wife neglect you too?"

I could imagine the scene in court. Mama had never been intimidated by any authority, and feeling cornered, had turned to attack. But her behavior had lost her any sympathy the court might have had.

I felt so sorry for Mama. She had indeed been her own worst enemy, losing her temper in this way.

The divorce was granted, and both parties were given equal share of the fault. Papa had to pay alimony for the children, but not for Mama. One-hundred Austrian Shillings per child every month. What might have been adequate at that time, became a pittance with rising inflation. And as the alimony was never increased, we lived in poverty.

Our big lovely flat was bombed and we ended up in the Pelzgasse, where we stayed.

Lilly stopped talking, and we sat in silence for a while. Now, as I knew so much about my parents, I felt sorry for both. We all could have had a much better life, had they been able to work things out, and if Mama had been able to accept that her life with Papa had ended. So much pain could have been avoided, had she eased her fixation on Papa, and started to live again. But she couldn't jump over her shadow – but then, who can?

Now, decades later, looking with new eyes at our past, it seemed to change. Like in a jigsaw puzzle where some pieces had been missing, and others were in the wrong place and didn't fit, the picture had been warped. But now the pieces were shifting, until suddenly they were in the right place. And I realized our past was not dead, it still had a life of its own, different for all the players involved.

Nothing had changed, and nothing could change, the parts were the same. They were just patterns, with their life force gone long ago. Both our parents were dead. But the way I viewed our past, had altered. Papa was no longer the villain and Mama the victim. But whichever way I turned all the pieces, between them they had not only caused all this misery to each other, but also to their children, and especially Willi and me. But though it had been their doing, it was not their fault.

Though my parents created this hell, I couldn't blame my father anymore, or my mother. Perhaps both our parents had done their best, or what they were able to during the time they lived, the conditioning they had received from their parents and from what was happening, at a time which had a violence of its own, with each individual battling for survival.

My father remained an enigma for me. Lilly had known a completely different father. Where lay the truth? Perhaps somewhere in between, skewed, dim, unclear, like in a fog, ever changing, depending who looked at the truth, from which side and angle, and when. And the life experience each of us had counted too. It gave no real, absolute truth for us, just memories, and they were different for each of us. Lilly and I knew a different father, although he was the same man.

I began to wonder, if my relationship with Papa would have turned out differently, had I not been so brainwashed by Mama. And Tante Paula continued were Mama left off – warning me not to trust Papa. She dressed it up, saying: "You can't trust any man, not even your own father," and though the warning was obscure, I knew what she meant, especially after she gave me a booklet about sexual diseases.

At fifteen, when I lived with Papa for a time, I worked for my aunt. She'd keep me in the shop after hours, knowing I'd get into trouble.

I scarcely saw Lilly then, she was married and had her first child, living an hour's tram-ride away.

I said something about all this now, finding it odd that Tante Paula was undermining my relationship with Papa.

Lilly laughed. "I can imagine she would. Didn't you know she held a grudge against him? In the early years she was in love with him, and propositioned him. Not only did he refuse her, he told Mama."

It was as if blinkers had fallen from my eyes. It explained the strange relationship between the two sisters, my mother and my aunt. Tante Paula did so much for Mama, for all of us, but it was never appreciated. Our mother always acted as if her sister owed her.

All these complex emotional entanglements, perhaps never completely resolved until death. Even then, the energies of it seemed to live on.

Only yesterday I had gone to the cemetery with Lilly. Rows of graves lay between our parents' last resting grounds. We lit a candle on Papa's grave which was still fresh, and put flowers there, saying a prayer. Then we went on to do the same where Mama lay buried. It was an old grave. Our mother had been dead more than twenty years.

Lilly's mother-in-law was our next stop, before we went on to Tante Paula.

It was all long in the past. But was it really over? If I wanted to admit it or not, our past had helped to fashion us, one way or another. The bitterness our mother had felt, had cast its dark shadows over our childhood, and each of us had absorbed some of it. At least I've had Pupping, but Willi had no such escape. I had always admired his brilliant mind, and in spite of our disagreements and fights, I had always loved my brother, and still did.

"I remember how Willi made up this story about our ancestors, living in a castle in Czechoslovakia," I told Lilly now. "He worked it all out, right to the last detail, and –"

Lilly looked stunned. "But it's true," she interrupted me. "Didn't you know it is true?"

I shook my head. "It can't be." There had to be a mistake. "I always thought it was wishful thinking – Willi's imagination."

Lilly laughed, but it was a bitter laugh. "Willi's imagination was never allowed to run free. Can you remember him imagining something, that he ever pretended?"

She was right. It was me who went off into realms of fantasy while Willi always stuck to hard facts. He might twist them to suit him, or to hurt me, but underneath, were always facts.

"No, the story about the castle is true." Lilly's surprise that I hadn't known, was still in her voice, and on her face.

114

"I always knew" she said," from Papa and Oma, his mother. I thought everyone in the family knew. Did Mama never talk about it?"

I shook my head. Mama only ever talked about herself. Even when she had talked about Papa or Lilly or Tante Paula, it had really been only about herself.

"We've been to Viscnegraz, to the castle of our forebears. It still stands. Peter wanted to see it, when he was about fourteen. He had his picture taken in the throne room, sitting on the throne. The owners allowed it when they heard he was a descendant."

I could imagine Peter, playing the knight in his castle. I too would have liked to visit, and I was sure, so would my son Sean.

"I'll take you one day, and show you the castle." Lilly must have read my thoughts. "We could still use the title. It is carried in the female line too. You could be Gertrude von Stary." She paused for a while, looking into the past, before adding: "I have no interest. Who needs a title? It makes no difference, one way or another."

I agreed with her. A title would make no difference to me, or to my son, I knew him well enough to be certain.

"And you never knew," Lilly mused. She clearly had problems coming to terms with this. I too was feeling stunned. We all had a title and I was the only one who had not known about it for forty-odd years. But as Lilly had said, it didn't matter, one way or another.

Still, it was a strange thought. Throughout my childhood I had felt a social outcast, inferior to my friends, because of our terrible flat and because of Mama, and because we were so poor.

I had felt so ashamed of my background, inadequate, lower than other children. And now it turned out I had a title, not a big one, but nevertheless I was the equivalent to a Lady, and always had been.

"The proof was in the Ahnenpass," Lilly told me, unaware what went on in me. She didn't realize how I had felt, because she had a different, a 'normal' childhood.

"During the Hitler regime, we had to prove who our ancestors were, not just our parents and grandparents," she said. "The Ahnenpass was a document we all had to have, to show not a drop of Jewish blood runs in our veins. It was in the Ahnenpass, about the castle and the title."

"What happened to the Ahnenpass?"

"When the Russians marched in, no one knew what they might do. Houses were ransacked, and our mother was afraid. If they found an official paper with a swastika, there was no telling what would happen. We might have been killed. Not wanting to take the risk, Mama burnt all the papers with a swastika on. But if you are interested, it wouldn't be difficult to find any relevant papers even now. And if you or Sean wanted to use the title, you could."

I shook my head. A title made no difference to me either, but knowing about my ancestors did.

"Do you know how our father's side of the family came from Czechoslovakia to Vienna?" Lilly wanted to make sure no other important event remained untold.

I nodded, because Papa had told me, when he spoke about his mother.

My grandmother Rosa, a pretty girl, sixteen at this time, had lived in Prachatitz, as the daughter of the town's mayor. The Graf, the local Count, had his eye on Rosa, and asked her father for her hand in marriage. The mayor was only too pleased to say yes. But he doubted Rosa would agree, because she had a boyfriend, an apprentice carpenter, two years younger than her.

Her father tried to stop this relationship, a carpenter was not good enough for his daughter, especially now, when a Count wanted her for his wife. To make it impossible for Rosa to refuse, her father and the Count hatched out a plan.

During a time of local celebrations, with the most important people on the podium, the mayor told the townspeople he had a happy announcement to make. Taking his daughter's hand, and the hand of the Count, he announced their engagement and the oncoming wedding.

But Rosa was quick, knowing no time should be lost. She pulled herself free, shouting: "Me marry him? Never!" and slapped the Count across the face, before she ran off the stage.

Having humiliated the Count, the girl was in disgrace. As a punishment, her father locked her in, until arrangements were made to send her to Vienna, where she had to go into service – a lowly job for her station in life.

Her parents washed their hands of her, and told no one where she was. Her boyfriend had no idea where to look for her. But she got a message to him, and after finishing his apprenticeship he followed her to Vienna. They married, and he started his carpentry business a few years later. They had eleven children and when he was old enough, Papa learned his trade from his father.

I had always been proud of my grandmother.

"Papa often said, I was like her," I confided in Lilly. I had thought he had meant I was stubborn and wilful, and didn't do as he said. But when I voiced these thoughts, my sister shook her head.

"He gave you the highest praise he could give you," she said, looking at me with love in her eyes. "Take it from me, Gerti, it was a compliment. Our father loved his mother deeply, and he thought she was the most wonderful and courageous woman on earth. He always took you with him when he visited her. She adored you. But then everyone did, you were so pretty, and such a happy, contented baby."

"You could have had a big loving family, Gerti, if Mama had allowed us to visit our grandparents. Christl and I used to go on the quiet, but you and Willi were too small. We couldn't take you, Mama would have found out."

Lilly sighed deeply once more. Then she smiled again, but her voice sounded resigned, as she added: "It would have been better for all of us had our mother not prevented us having contact with Papa. We would have had the support of his whole family. And our mother would have had it much easier, because she too would have had help and support."

Again my sister sighed. "As it was, she not only made everything harder for us children, but for herself too".

CHAPTER 10

VIENNA, SOME YEARS LATER
LOOKING BACK

I was sure I knew all the family secrets by now. The pieces of the jigsaw puzzle seemed to fit neatly together. That was until a few years later, when I found another piece belonging to the puzzle of our family. And though this piece was quite small, it not only belonged and completed the picture, but was of importance.

Years later I was back in Vienna, this time, for Lilly's funeral.

Later, Christl and I were alone, and came to talk about the war, and the time we were in the cellar waiting for the Russians. I remembered the sound of their steps and their voices, as they came down the cellar stairs in groups, again and again. I remembered it all so well. But was I wrong? Was my memory faulty? It seemed to have gone on for days and for weeks. It couldn't have been like that.

"They can't have kept coming into our cellar," I said to Christl. "My memory must be playing tricks. I know the Russians were the first to march into Vienna, before the city was divided into four, each part occupied by one of the four allied forces. But I don't remember any of the other soldiers coming to our building. And our district wasn't even occupied by the Russians."

"When the Russians entered Vienna, they got only so far." Christl remembered it all better than me. "They were stationed at the Guertel, round the corner from us. They came into the houses and cellars to see what they could find – and they could always find girls." My sister paused for a while, looking at me, before she asked: "Don't you remember, Gerti?"

I hesitated. What should I remember? I was afraid to ask, because I was afraid what the answer might be.

Did I really want to know? Something in me had always refused to remember it all. But now, after so many years, I couldn't hide any longer from the truth. I had to know.

My sister must have felt it, because she said: "How they came into our cellar and rounded up the girls."

I looked at her, the question in my eyes I didn't dare ask. Had she been one of these girls?

She shook her head. "I was only eleven and though they rounded me up at first with the others, they left me alone and I could go back to Mama. But Lilly –" Her voice broke, she couldn't go on.

Icy fingers seemed to clutch my heart. A part of me had always known that something terrible had happened, something to do with Lilly. A shiver ran down my spine.

I never had the courage to ask Lilly, because this question was too terrible to ask, and I wasn't sure if I wanted to know, if I could cope with the truth. And I didn't know if Lilly wanted to talk about it.

It was too late to ask her now. My beloved sister had died.

But my other sister wanted to talk – it had been too long for her to carry these memories in silence.

"They pointed their guns at us," she continued, as calmly as if this was an everyday event. But then – at the time – it had been.

"Every girl they pointed at had to go with them."

Her voice was still quiet and calm, as if she was talking about nothing unusual. But then, how did one speak about this? There was no easy way.

I could see the pain in her eyes, even now it was still here, after so many years without finding expression. But maybe this was the reason her pain was still so alive.

Perhaps I had seen too much. When my sister spoke again, she looked past me, to the wall.

"They led us away, girls and young women. Two Russians stayed in the cellar, to stand guard. Our people could do nothing. No one could help us. The Russians would shoot anyone who tried. We all knew it."

"The men looked us over, handling us roughly, touching us any way they wanted. Two girls resisted and were shot. With their bodies right in front of us, no girl tried anymore."

"I think I was too young for them. I was eleven, but looked younger, and had not yet started to develop. They sent me back to the cellar. But Lilly was fifteen, old enough."

"They raped all the girls and women – again and again."

Christl's voice broke. Trying to swallow her tears, she stayed silent, remembering the horror. And now, this horror was with me too.

Now she had opened up, my sister could no longer remain silent.

"I went back to the cellar, and stayed there," she continued. "We heard their screams, heard the girls begging for mercy – I can still hear their voices. And we heard the men's voices too and their laughter. Well, after that I wouldn't call them men. They enjoyed the fear and desperation of the girls – and especially their pain."

"Our mother sat rigid like a stone statue, her face without any expression. A Russian was pointing his gun at her face. You sat next to her, with Willi on her other side. She could do nothing, was completely helpless, as she listened to the screams of her daughter, who was raped, again and again." Icy-cold hate was in Christl's voice. Then she was silent for a time. We both stayed quiet, trying to get ourselves together again. Eventually my sister sighed deeply. Her hate seemed to dissolve, like a wave reaching shore and gradually petering out. And when she spoke her voice was calm.

"It was a long time ago – it was war. These things happened every day – they happen now where there is war. Lilly was lucky to survive. Many did not."

"What happened then?"

"When Lilly finally arrived in the flat, she was hysterical, and refused to stay. She begged Mama to take her away. Mama didn't know what to do, where to go to. So she took us all, and we started to walk. We walked away from the Guertel, away from the Russians, up the Maerzstrasse, towards the outskirts of the city. She didn't know where to go. We just walked and walked. Eventually Mama was desperate. You and Willi couldn't walk any further. She asked a woman we passed on the street if she knew where we could go. This woman took us home with her. 'I have room,' she just said. 'My husband has not come home from the front.'

"People were like that then, they helped each other. We stayed for a few weeks with this woman. Don't you remember, Gerti? In the yard was a tree. You always stood by this tree, sometimes for hours."

As she was talking about the tree, vague memories stirred, I dimly remembered the tree, and standing alone in a paved yard.

"What happened then?"

"Lilly refused to go back to the Pelzgasse, and went to Tante Paula."

So it was this I had felt all the time. Deep inside me, I had known there was something too terrible to remember, too frightening to know: the screams of my sister, as she was brutally raped and beaten. These screams were in my head now. How had our mother endured hearing them? She had to, because of her children – because of us.

She had no choice, having to think of her other children too. And somehow she had to help Lilly to survive, to deal with it all.

But how did one deal with something like this? How did Lilly deal with it once it was over? But then, was it ever over? No wonder so many people had hated the Russians.

"It's a lifetime ago now," Christl sighed. "We had to live with it, to survive. What else could we do?"

For a long time, my sister and I just sat there, in silence. The pain of those years was present now, though the events were in the distant past. Somehow, we had to put all of this back into the past again, where it had its place. We had to turn it into memories, to visit at will if we wanted to. But to do this wasn't so easy. Perhaps we should find a different subject.

Christl must have had the same idea, because she asked me: "Can you remember, Gerti, how our Pepi turned into Willi?"

"Yes," I answered, because I still remembered. "When we were small, he was called Pepi. But when he came back from Holland, he refused to be called by this name. We had to call him Willi, or he wouldn't react."

I had always thought Wilhelm was his second name, but now I found out this was wrong, as my sister told me more of his story.

"In 1939, when Willi was born, chaos reigned in Vienna, and in the hospital, where Mama gave birth. Willi was exchanged in hospital. At first, Mama believed she had a little boy, but the doctor and the nurses assured her and Papa, they had a daughter. And so they brought this girl home."

I knew the hospital had made a mistake, but was unaware of the details.

"Three days later, an angry woman stood at our door, pressed a bundle into our mother's arms with the words: here is your boy, I want my daughter back."

It turned out the babies had really been exchanged in hospital. Luckily this came to light before Willi – or rather the girl – was baptized. Our father was just on the way to church to make the arrangements, as this woman knocked at our door.

"Was Willi really baptized as Joseph?" I asked, remembering Mama telling me about it. She loved the name Joseph, which was the name of our father. She had called both her husband and her son Pepi, a short name for Joseph.

Christl nodded. "That's true," she confirmed. "After the christening, Papa went to register the birth. The registrar refused to write Josef on the birth certificate. He said it was a Jewish name, and Jewish names were not allowed."

"Then put Wilhelm down," said our father, not wanting any trouble.

And so it was, on one certificate our brother was named Joseph, and Wilhelm on the other. And as he got older he chose to be Willi, and could not be persuaded otherwise.

"Our Lilly did not like it at all," Christl said. "She was really annoyed, and tried to get Willi to change his mind. Lilly and Willi, it sounded stupid, she said. I agreed. But our brother was so determined, nothing and no one could make him keep his old name."

Perhaps it had also to do with Papa. At this time, Willi had decided to have nothing to do with Papa. It could be the reason he refused to be called by the same name.

"Mama took it hard," Christl said. "She loved the name Pepi – just as she continued loving our father, who always remained her Pepi. Mina, his second wife, called him by his second name Thomas. What his third wife called him, I don't even remember."

"But our brother remained our Willi. He always achieved what he wanted to."

Although he had been exchanged in hospital, we never had any doubt, Willi was our brother. He was the image of our father, and the resemblance only got stronger through the years. About this, Willi was powerless.

But I need to go back now to time when I was a young child, just six-years-old, and to the years that followed, in Pupping and in Wien – in Vienna. I have to go back in my mind, to Heaven and Hell.

Many years were yet to pass until this conversation with Christl took place, and much was yet to happen which is important to remember. But whatever happened, our life in the Pelzgasse only got worse during the aftermath of the war.

CHAPTER 11

1947–1952, FIVE TO ELEVEN – MAINLY VIENNA
THE AFTER WAR YEARS

Remembering my childhood, the years when I was about six until I reached ten, I lived in two very different worlds: one in Pupping and the other in Vienna. In each place I was a different child. And though I vividly remember the seesaw of emotions when I left one location for the other, somehow I managed to continue in each place where I'd left off the year before. And so, in retrospect, my childhood in Pupping seems ongoing, it was bright, happy, and full of joy. In Vienna my life also continued, somehow I managed. But it was always hell.

Each summer, when I arrived in Pupping, I took my shoes off to walk barefoot, glad to feel the earth beneath my feet. I was myself again. With the beauty of nature all around, and the people who loved me, I had everything I needed and much more. My shyness and insecurity left, my dialect changed. I could be who I was. I was OK just as I was. I could be me.

I felt that I belonged, and spoke and behaved like everyone here in Pupping.

Returning home, Mama's disapproving look was enough to make me shed the country dialect, and become a well-spoken Viennese girl once again. But though outwardly I fitted in, inwardly I did not, and I never accepted my life in the Pelzgasse. What made things worse: Willi resented my coming home, having got used to having Mama to himself.

Winters in Vienna seemed always endless, but the first winter after Pupping was particularly hard and long. The falling snow was still beautiful. With its white sparkling mantle it covered everything – even the ugly remnants of bombed-out houses looked almost pretty. Building work was now going on, but even that had to be abandoned until the weather improved.

As soon as the snow settled, people shovelled it from the pavements, and big machines cleared the roads. Only at the edge of pavements remained some snow, but in big ugly mounds. Mama wouldn't let me play in the snow, in case I got ill. She took me to school, but as I came home by myself, she couldn't prevent me making the best of the snow. Unfortunately only the big mounds were left, dirty and gray from the traffic, with yellow patches the dogs left behind.

I would stomp through the ice and snow, often sinking in to my knees or even further, or kick at the hard icy crust, just for the sake of it. When I came home I always got told off. Mama could tell what I'd been doing. But it was worth it, at least I was told off for something I enjoyed.

One day the air got milder, a warm wind blew, and the snow started to melt. It was dangerous to walk close to the buildings now, because big lumps of ice fell from the roofs. But the rain came, cleaning the roofs and dirty streets, and as the sun broke finally through the clouds, getting stronger each day, Mama took us to the park.

"To get fresh air," she'd say.

She liked sitting in the park, turning her face to the rays of the sun, watching the grass turning green and the spring flowers waking from their sleep.

I hated the park. The flowers and trees reminded me too much of Pupping, and I didn't want to be reminded. Here in Vienna I could not even touch a tree. They stood in the lawn, and it was forbidden to step into the grass. The wonders of nature were fenced in, even the grass. Nature was in prison, like I was. I longed to run to a tree, put my arms around it, and press my face on its bark. I wanted to walk barefoot on the new grass, roll in it. The dogs must have felt the same. They often escaped and rolled in the grass. For me there was no such escape. Little girls did not do this.

There was a sandpit, but only very small children played in the sand. Older children played on the big concrete square in the center of the park, surrounded by benches where people sat. I had only to stand and watch, and one of the children would ask: "do you want to play?"

A few times I tried it, but I didn't like the games. There was always a loser, and the others would chant and point at the child. I felt sorry for him or for her, but it was worse if I was the loser.

Willi refused to take part in any games, no matter what Mama said. He'd walk around for a while, then sit on the bench with her. Our mother tried to persuade him to play, or at least run around, but gave up eventually. They would talk for a while, then sit in silence.

One day I discovered a game I enjoyed. At the other side of the park, hidden behind bushes and trees, were a few rails, perhaps left from a building destroyed in the war. These rails were ideal for all sorts of gymnastics. Children hung upside down, or turned over, backwards and forwards, over and over again. These were my kind of games, and soon I managed to turn over forwards, then backwards, and then hang upside down. Just as I became proficient, Mama found me. She grabbed me, marching me back to her bench, where Willi still sat.

"Don't ever do that again, Gerti," she said.

I didn't know what I'd done wrong. Seeing how upset and baffled I was, Mama relented, and explained I must never do anything that would show my underwear.

"But the other girls show their knickers too," I pointed out.

Mama said that had nothing to do with her or me. I was not to show mine.

I begged her to let me wear Willi's old pants, but she would not allow it.

And though I didn't play on the rails anymore, my knickers became of the utmost importance. From this day on, Mama watched me like a hawk.

"Don't bend, showing everything, Gerti." She seemed to be aware of each one of my movements. "Bend in the knees and crouch down, like me." And she'd show me.

One day in May and out of the blue, Mama told me I could skip school for a few weeks, and return to Pupping quite soon. From then on the emphasis on my underwear increased.

"Keep your legs together Gerti," I heard, if I was sitting, or: "pull your skirt over your knees."

And constantly: "You are going to be six in the autumn, and turning into a young lady. Ladies don't do that."

I began to wish I were a boy, so Mama would leave me in peace. Boys could hang upside down. And it was bad enough being a girl, I didn't want to turn into a lady. Willi had none of my problems, as a boy. Mama would have let him hang upside down, if he had wanted to. But he was too shy and self-conscious, and afraid to show himself up in front of other children. He was much more withdrawn than I, and didn't mix with other children at all, except in school, where he had to.

Although it would be better to be a boy, I would not have liked being Willi. He had no fun at all, not even in the snow. But because my brother was not stubborn like I was, and more obedient, he got on better with Mama. She listened to him now as he got older, even took his advice sometimes. Though Willi was only eight, he began taking on the role of the man in our family, repairing fuses and changing light bulbs. He had fewer restrictions, and didn't have to help with the house work.

One morning, as I was drying the dishes, with my brother just sitting there smirking, I asked Mama: "What about Willi?"

"He is a boy," Mama said, her voice full of pride.

Lilly and Tante Paula also preferred Willi. Yes, I thought, I would rather be a boy. But not Willi, because he stayed with Mama, and I was going to Pupping.

But Mama was doing her best to spoil Pupping for me. She kept on that I was growing into a young lady and must behave like one, especially in Pupping, where she could not keep her eye on me. Apart from not showing my knickers, or anything else that was private, no one could touch me. And I must not hug or kiss anyone, without exception.

"And don't sit on anyone's lap, Gerti, that goes without saying," Mama usually ended her sermon this way, staring into my eyes, and holding on to my arms so I couldn't escape. Then she gave me a last shake to make sure I remembered.

Finally the big day arrived, and Lilly and Tante Paula took me to Pupping. It was a beautiful moment as I stepped off the bus, right in the village square. Nothing had changed, even the smells were the same: The heavy clean smell of earth after rain, the strong scent of the last blooms of lilac, the smell from the cowshed. Mirzl had once said this smell was healthy, when I wrinkled my nose.

Foster-father still loved me, but when he opened his arms to me, Mama's words popped straight into my head. I wanted to run to him as I always had done, but Mama's words stopped me.

"Where is my kiss then?" he asked.

"I am growing into a young lady, and ladies don't kiss," I had to say.

I felt pompous and a complete idiot. And I felt so sad for my Pflegevater, and even sadder for myself. I was hurting, as if I had a hole in my heart, which only could get better in his arms.

Years later I understood that my mother had tried to protect me. But if she'd only had explained, it might not have been the end of all physical closeness, which lasted throughout my childhood.

My new behaviour was accepted, although foster-mother or Nandl sometimes casually remarked how hurt my Pflegevater was not to get a hug anymore, and how they all missed the old Gerti. I didn't know how to respond, and remained silent. So the matter was left, except now and again I was teased, but so gently it didn't hurt. Quite the opposite. Making fun of this delicate subject took the edge off it. If we could laugh, it couldn't be so important. A new verse was added to my song, about Pflegevater missing his hugs and his kisses, but at least I still sang with him and teased him, and then the matter was closed.

In every other way, foster-father and I were as close as ever. We still went visiting, and I led Maxl the ox. Everything was the same as it had been, only my spontaneity had gone, and all physical closeness.

Mariandl and I continued our friendship as if we'd never been apart. Each morning we walked barefoot in the grass, feeling the morning dew cool and wet on our feet. We still liked the mud, and often went among the rooting pigs to cover our legs with mud, pretending we wore Wellington boots. One day we found a long wooden plank and put it across the fence of the pigs' enclosure to make a seesaw. With much heaving and grunting we managed to put the plank in the right place for balance, and successfully seesawed up and down for a while. Suddenly the plank slipped, hit the mud with a thump on my side, and Mariandl who was lighter in weight, catapulted over the fence, landing beside me on a pig, which escaped with a squeal. We looked at each other. Mariandl started to laugh and I joined in, relieved she had not hurt herself. She was covered in sticky gray mud and looked hilarious, but so did I.

Getting out of the mud, we got covered even more, looking like two funny gray ghosts, dripping with mud.

"Let's go and wash," Mariandl said, giggling again. "No one's home at my house."

A tall, thick privet hedge surrounded Mariandl's house, so no one could see us. The water pump was in front of the house. We took everything off, washed all over, then we washed our clothes. But we couldn't stay here, Mariandl's mother was due home from work, so we sneaked round the back to the barn of her neighbor. Here we were safe in the open grassland and if by chance someone came by, we would see from the distance and hide. We spread our clothes out to dry, lay down in the sun, watching the flowers and tall grasses move in the summer breeze. When we got bored, we picked the most beautiful flowers and made chains to hang round our necks and wrists, and to crown our heads. When our clothes were finally dry, we were adorned from head to foot with pretty flowers. In all the excitement, Mama's words about being a lady had been washed away with the mud and the water and the fun that we had.

In spite of the pretty flowers I still wore as I sat down for dinner, everyone wrinkled their noses.

"Where ever have you been, Gerti?" Nandl said. "You must have a bath. Better still, we'll go to the river."

After our meal, Nandl found towels and soap. Loisl and Mariandl came too, and we went to the river. At first I washed thoroughly, then Nandl held me round the waist and Loisl held Mariandl, and we practiced swimming like frogs. Then, as my foster-sisters swam, my friend and I built a pool with pebbles and sand and watched as shoals of tiny fish swam into it before closing them in with a dam. When it was time to go home, we opened our pools and watched our fishes swim away.

No one shouted in Pupping at me, whatever I did. It was bliss.

No one shouted at me throughout the summer. Only Mariandl and I shouted or screamed, but just for fun. I was happy again. Perhaps not totally happy as last year, because I knew what to expect when autumn came. But I pushed this thought far, far away, to enjoy every minute of every day.

But autumn did come, and next day I was leaving.

Pflegevater said: "Go next door, Gerti, and say thank you for all the grapes and the apples and everything else you have stolen."

Saying thank you before I left became a ritual. I would walk into the big farmhouse kitchen next door, sure I was welcome. "Thank you very much for the grapes and everything else I have stolen," I'd say.

"That's all right, Gerti," our neighbors smiled. "Are you off then tomorrow?"

I would nod, afraid to talk, in case the tears behind my eyes would spill over.

"Never mind," they always said. "Next summer you'll be here again. Come on, Gerti, give us a song."

So I'd sing, and then we all sang together. As a going-away present I'd get whatever extra special they had, sometimes even money. But my heart was as heavy as one of the big river boulders, because next morning I was leaving.

Vienna changed fast during these years, and things improved. My family changed too. But nothing got better for us. Mama became even more unpredictable, her solitary 'talks' increased, and her treatment of me became harsher.

In spite of it all I began to cope better, because I made friends in school. My first friendship turned into a disaster, because I made friends with a boy, with Martin. He had his appendix taken out during the holidays, and told the whole class about his stay in hospital. We were all very impressed hearing about this adventure, even the teacher. Everyone wanted to be his best friend, and I was so proud that he chose me.

He walked me home after school, and because we had so much fun talking, I walked with him to his home. Then he walked back with me again. This time I did go in, but I was late.

"Where have you been?" Mama asked and I could see she was angry. I should have been careful and lied, but I had such a nice time with Martin, I was still happy, and not on my guard.

"I was with my friend," I said, "I was talking with Martin."

The slap hit my face before I finished speaking. "That'll teach you," Mama shouted. "You are not to make friends with boys."

My head hurt, and I didn't understand why a boy couldn't be my friend. But Mama wouldn't explain, and I didn't dare to ask. And although in class I remained friendly with Martin, I could no longer let him walk me home, in case Mama found out. Under this pressure, our budding friendship dwindled away. But I began making friends with girls, and to my surprise I became quite popular and soon had several friends, who I kept, as best as I could, from Mama.

After four years in primary school, at nine I started high-school, and Helga, who was also very unhappy at home, became my best friend. Some months later Hilde was transferred from the second stream. She did not know anyone in our class, so Helga and I looked after her, and she became our friend. Hilde came from a good home, her mother was a teacher, but she had to study hard in her free time, to stay in our class. I couldn't understand it. I never studied, and my grades were better than hers.

I had decided to make no effort in school, because my mother insisted I must become a tailoress like her. That I hated sewing made no difference. Mama remained adamant. Sewing had helped her to survive the war, and it would help me too.

If I'd had a choice, I would have liked to be a doctor, and once I understood what they did, a psychiatrist. What went on in people's minds fascinated me. But it was pointless even to think about studying for anything. I had to leave school as soon as possible to earn money.

CHAPTER 12

MAINLY VIENNA

A special motive established itself in my life during these years, like a golden silk-thread in plain fabric, disappearing at times in the pattern of life, only to re-emerge and shine through again. When the Native American warriors became my heroes, certain energies woke, taking on a life of their own. What I thought of myself counted more than the opinion of others, and to have courage was part of this new pattern too.

Facing the dentist was a good way to practice being courageous, or when needles were stuck into me at the hospital. Even my everyday life offered enough opportunity to conquer my fear.

I was about six or seven, when Mama went out one evening, leaving me home on my own. Willi was in hospital, and Christl was out. I was already in bed when Mama turned off the light and left.

All was quiet as I lay in the dark, but suddenly I heard a sound. Something terrible was hiding under my bed. I wanted to jump up and run – or at least turn on the light – the switch was just over my bed. But I stayed where I was and said to myself: 'no one is here.' And when this didn't sufficiently alleviate my fears, I added: 'I am not afraid". But there was a distinct wobble in my voice I couldn't suppress.

But I still heard the noise, this time even louder, and although the room was dark, black shadows came to life, moving towards me, coming closer and closer. To turn on the light would get rid of the shadow-ghosts. I nearly jumped out of bed, but a voice inside my head said firmly: "Stay where you are, Gerti. If you stay in the dark now, next time you won't be afraid."

And what the voice said was true. Next time Mama left me alone, I really wasn't frightened as much. And I had proved my courage, and could be certain I was no coward – which was of great importance to me, though I never asked myself why.

But once this attitude got me into serious trouble. Mama had allowed me to go to the indoor pool with Helga and Hilde, a rare event which was never repeated, though she didn't find out what happened that day.

My friends were still in the changing room, but I was already in the pool, practicing my strokes in the shallow side, when two girls challenged me to swim to the deep end. And although I told them I could only swim three strokes, they wouldn't let me be.

"Swim near the edge," one girl said. "Just grab the bar if you can't swim any further."

It seemed a dubious venture to me and I refused, but when the girl called me a coward, and her friends joined in, common sense was forgotten. I swam along the side of the pool, but when I started sinking, my arm was too short to reach the bar. I went down and came up again, struggling for air.

Three floors above me, a man shouted, "hold on," as he pulled his shirt off. I saw him, between going under and coming up again. He dived in and pulled me out. Later, after I got dressed, I had to go to his office and he told me off, and made me promise never to swim into the deep, until I could swim properly.

I was only too glad to give him this promise, and I promised myself something too: I would never again be persuaded to do something against my better judgement, even if I was called a coward. It didn't matter what others thought of me, only what I thought of myself counted. My black panther encouraged me not to forget it. He was still with me, and accompanied me in my dreams.

But into my dreams came a nightmare, a dream I could not control. And in this dream I was always completely and utterly alone.

I was on a small island, completely surrounded by muddy gray water. The whole dream was in shades of gray. This island was just a big mud-heap, with a tree in the middle, a dead tree, its broken branches sticking jaggedly into the gray sky. All the small twigs had been broken off or worn away, only those few jagged branches remained. From the lowest branch hung a swing. There was nothing else on the island, and no sign of life.

I would go to the swing, sit down and start swinging. It was difficult at first, but as I persevered, the dreadful feeling I felt began lifting as I flew higher and higher into the sky. The higher I flew the better I felt, but just as I was really high up I'd slide off the seat, I couldn't help it, my hands couldn't hold on to the rope any longer, and opened against my will. I'd slip into the watery mud, sinking right into it, deeper and deeper. Just as the mud came up to my mouth and my nose, choking me, I'd wake up.

This dream haunted me for years, but only in Vienna, and the feeling of despair, of sliding deeper and deeper into the thick gray mud, would linger on.

Here in Vienna my life only ever got worse, and God and religion remained the biggest problems. For my mother it was very different. Her belief in God sustained her. For her, life meant suffering, and because of God and religion there was meaning and purpose to it all, and so her pain and suffering had purpose and meaning too; and so had her life.

I saw things differently. In my experience, most suffering was created by people, and could have been avoided. I didn't suffer in Pupping, and neither did anyone else, except for my foster-family's sorrow of losing Franzl – but his death was caused by people, too.

Even in the Pelzgasse, much of our suffering could have been avoided, had we hurt each other less.

Most of Mama's suffering had to do with our father. In the eyes of God and the church, he was still married to her. What was more, she was still married to him, and this was what counted. She never looked at another man again. And the endless 'talks' – the awful monologues, where Mama's frustration erupted– went on, affecting Willi and me so badly, we didn't know how to endure it.

My problems with God also continued. Apart from my other sins, I still struggled with the commandments, especially, that I should honor my father. But how could I? There was nothing between my father and me. We had no relationship and he didn't care one iota about me.

But if I did not honor him, I was committing another sin.

And so many things I wanted to do were also sins, like mountain climbing. Our father risked his life in this way, Mama said, which was inviting suicide – a capital sin. I loved climbing trees – which likely was a sin too.

But I wanted to climb trees, and mountains, too. And as soon as I could, I would do both.

There was no end to my sinning.

But worse was to come. In school we were preparing for our first confession and holy communion. In theory this should have got rid of my sins, but it didn't work out in this way. Not only would I have to tell each sin to the priest in confession, and be sorry for what I had done. To be forgiven, I had to have the firm intention, never to do it again. But how could I? I couldn't wait to climb trees in Pupping, and if I ever came close to a mountain, I would climb it as well.

In spite of it all, I might still have managed to make a proper confession, but for the sin with Poldi and my knickers. My mouth refused to bring out the words about such a shameful sin, to a priest who knew me. It was difficult enough to say I had lied, but I managed it. But the other sin? I didn't know how to say it, I was too ashamed. And before I knew, the confession was over and I had added another sin, this time the worst sin of all: I had made a false confession.

Sunday was my first Holy Communion, and I lived in a nightmare. I had to go to communion, Mama was in church, proudly watching me. I had no choice but to go up with the other children and receive the 'Body of Christ' in the form of the wafer, for me, the ticket to hell.

My fear of dying and hell took on a new meaning, because we had been told the most despicable sin of all was a wrong confession. And to take communion whilst in this state of sin, was even worse, if that was possible. I would be sentenced to hell everlasting, when I died.

And death was no longer far away in a distant future, but very close. I was often ill, and so seriously at times, I had to stay in hospital. My throat and chest infections became more frequent, I had pneumonia, and eventually was diagnosed with a bad heart, a defect of the heart muscle. My septic tonsils were said to be the cause, and I had them removed. But even without tonsils, my heart got worse, and my throat didn't get any better.

The shortness of breath and the intense stabbing pains in my chest frightened me. Fearful of Mama's reaction, I tried to hide how I felt, which was easier during the night, but more frightening. I could not breathe, and would sit in bed in the dark, asking God to let me live through this night. I was sorry for my sins, and would make a proper confession tomorrow – if he would just let me live that long. He always did. The pains would eventually subside, and with the pain going, my determination to face the priest also diminished, especially after I had slept a few hours.

In the morning, death seemed so far away, I couldn't even think about it. My fear of the priest was once again stronger than my fear of death. And I had to go to school, or Mama found out. How could I go to confession? So I put off going to church. My confession could surely wait for a better opportunity.

This terrible circle repeated itself, over and over, and for years to come. I had to go to confession as Mama accompanied me, but I never managed a true confession, and my conscience grew more and more burdened with the increase of my sins. There was no escape anymore.

Then, as if I hadn't got enough sins on my conscience already, I turned into a thief. I had never before stolen anything – in Pupping, what we called stealing was allowed. All children could take food from the fields and the trees. But this was different, and I knew it was wrong.

Our mother often left her purse on the table, and one morning it was open. Mama was making the beds. She had her back to me and couldn't see me, so I took a coin. I don't know why, perhaps because I was feeling angry and resentful. On the way to school I bought a packet of chewing gum, with pictures of film stars inside the wrapper. All the girls at school collected these pictures, swapping them with each other. Only I never had money for chewing gum.

My theft wasn't discovered, and I repeated this crime a few times, until one day, when I was just about to put my fingers into Mama's purse, I saw her eyes on me, watching. She knew.

I expected the most terrible punishment. But Mama just looked at me reproachfully, her eyes sad and full of disappointment in me. But she didn't say one word. This was far worse, than if she had hit me. How could I have done such a terrible thing? To my own mother, who gave us children whatever she could, and had gone without herself in the past.

Not one word was ever said about my stealing, I was not punished, yet I never took anything from my mother again.

I couldn't understand Mama. When I had done something really bad, I was not punished. Yet other times, when I did nothing wrong, she would not only shout at me, but punish me severely. Like the time when Nandl gave me money to buy a new bag for school.

Until then, what money I got, I gave to Mama, knowing she needed it. But the summer I was nine, when I left Pupping, Nandl said that I must not give the money to anyone, not even Mama. She made me promise to buy a new school bag because I started high school, and had to carry more books.

When Mama asked for my money, I told her about my promise, and that I could only lend it to her. Mama agreed, but when Papa's alimony came, she didn't give me any money. And when I reminded her, she got angry, demanding I should tell her to keep it.

For me, it wasn't about the money, but my promise – and Mama's promise to me.

"I promised Nandl, to buy a school bag with it," I reminded her.

I was apprehensive because Mama was so angry; but I had promised, so I insisted: "You promised you would give it back, Mama."

My mother was furious. She called me such horrible, vulgar names she never used for anyone else but me. I felt so bad, so humiliated. I wished I could crawl into a corner, where a hole would open, so I could disappear forever.

Then I got angry too, wanted to shout back, tell Mama she was wrong about me. But I knew from experience, my punishment would be severe if I answered back.

By now, I would have abandoned the whole matter, because I knew I would not get my money back, whatever I said. But Mama kept shouting: "You are not going to bed Gerti until you say, you don't want the money back."

And because of my promise, I could only repeat: "I promised Nandl, and I do want the money – not now, if you don't have it, but at some time."

Mama slapped me across the face. "Get in this corner, Gerti," she said, "face the wall and kneel down."

I did as I was told, but promised myself, that nothing would make me retract my words.

"You'll kneel here Gerti, until you say what I told you."

This was just the beginning. Mama ranted on and on. She seemed unable to stop.

I didn't know what to do, but suddenly my Red Indian friends were in my mind. They only said what they thought was right. No threat could break them. Turning my head, to look into my mother's eyes I repeated: "I have to keep my promise to Nandl, so when you have it, I want my money back. It is my money."

"You stay on your knees, Gerti, until you come to your senses and finally say what I want to hear."

I stayed on my knees, but the words she demanded, she could not get from me.

Mama said no more, ignoring me completely as if I didn't exist. She turned to Willi, speaking calmly, as if everything was as it should be. My brother, who had been silent until now, responded in kind, as they both prepared for the night.

"Are you ready to speak, Gerti?" Mama addressed me one last time, as she climbed into bed.

I didn't answer. Anger and hate were boiling in me – though outwardly I remained still. She could force me to kneel in this corner, but I would not give her the satisfaction of giving in.

The light was turned off, and after a while I could tell by their breathing, my mother and brother had fallen asleep. I could have crept into bed, and perhaps Mama even expected me to, but I stayed where I was. This was not about money anymore, which I wouldn't get anyway, but about so much more.

It was an endless night. My body grew stiff and started to hurt, and with the passing hours my misery increased. It got very cold, I couldn't stop shivering, and then I froze. But I would not give in, because all I had left was the belief in myself, without it, I would be nothing. My mother wouldn't break me, I promised myself. But it was a very long and horrible night.

The first streaks of gray came through the window, sparrows were chirping. It was dawn. Mama woke, turned her head and looked over to me where I was kneeling. Our eyes met, and I didn't try to disguise the hate and defiance I felt.

She sighed deeply, and I realized she was a totally different person: last night's mother was no longer here.

"Come, Gerti," she said gently, "go to bed."

I did, clothes and all, and went out like a light. A few hours later, when it was time to get up, my mother and brother acted as if nothing had happened. Everything was as usual, and after breakfast Willi and I left for school.

The money for my school bag was not mentioned again, not by my mother, and not by me. Even my brother didn't utter a word about it. I took my old bag to school, and managed somehow.

My brother never parted with money. Some years ago, he had made two decisions. The first was, not to have anything to do with our father. His second decision was of equal importance, perhaps even more so: when he grew up he would never be poor again. He was already working on it.

Willi spent nothing, he saved whatever money he got. Although far more under Mama's influence than I was, where money was concerned, he stood firm. He never gave Mama any money. If she wanted to borrow a small sum, first he made her beg for it, and then she had to sign a paper and pay interest. Strangely, she accepted these conditions.

Our mother treated Willi differently, she hardly ever shouted at him anymore. If anything, the balance of power seemed to reverse itself. Willi had power because he had money, and if Mama wanted to borrow, she had to ask nicely and say please.

At times we all worked for Tante Paula, who made shopping bags for a big firm. Mama would be paid properly I'd get ten shillings for a day's work, and Willi twenty – which I found very unjust, because I worked as well as my brother. But it didn't matter, because my money ended up with Mama, unless I needed something for school.

Willi saved his money. If Mama or Lilly didn't buy what he needed for school, he went without.

As he had savings, we no longer needed to go to the pawn shop, where they would take almost anything, even our spare clothes. How we had hated these visits, especially as we got older and Willi and I had to go on our own.

My brother had learned from the pawn shop. If Mama wanted to borrow money, she had to sign a paper, on it was the amount of the loan, when it had to be repaid, and the interest.

I felt so awful and humiliated for Mama and for me too, even for Willi – he was doing this to our own mother. But he seemed to enjoy the whole process. Mama accepted his rules, knowing otherwise he wouldn't lend her anything. The pattern established itself, and his savings grew.

Mama began treating Willi like an equal, and he became the man in our household, who made the decisions. And whatever happened, he always got the better of me. He was not only older and bigger and stronger, but good with words, able to manipulate every situation to his advantage. And I became the scapegoat.

But in spite of his increasing power, he was bored and lonely, and deeply unhappy. He had no friends, and was unable to enjoy himself, especially alone. My brother's life consisted of school, eating and sleeping, church and prayer, going for a walk, and Mama. Lilly still took him out now and again, or we helped with the sewing, but those events were rare. Nothing outside our usual routine would happen for weeks, even months.

He hated school, because he didn't get on with other children. Getting older, my brother tried to make friends, but without any success. I knew, because when we went for a walk, he confided in me. He wanted to have friends like I did, but he was too different from his peers. He'd never learned to swim or play football, and had nothing in common with boys. When he was younger, Mama had kept him away from other children. Now it seemed too late.

His problems increased as other boys got interested in girls. Willi was interested too, but he had no confidence, and could relate no more to girls than boys.

Irritated by his constant presence, Mama told him to go out. But without friends and no interests, he had nowhere to go, except for a walk – with me or alone, or with Mama. They were close, too close, I thought at times.

Perhaps he would have been different, had there been a man in our lives. But the only men we knew were priests, and we only saw them at church, or in school during religious instruction.

I'd have had no problem being a boy, and would have preferred it, because boys had fewer restrictions. They were allowed to run and to jump, turn cartwheels or stand on their heads. They could do different kinds of sport, even boxing and wrestling. But girls didn't do this. And because of my heart, I wasn't allowed anything at all.

In school, I couldn't take part in any physical exercise, not even ball games, and had to bring a doctor's certificate to be excused. But in the park with my friends I ran and played like everyone else. Coming home I had to make sure my breathing was slow and calm, and I didn't run up the stairs, because Mama would notice the slightest exertion, and tell me off, as if I wanted to damage my heart even more.

One day Christl was suddenly home during the day. Her apprenticeship had ended, and she was out of work. My sister was seventeen and a pretty girl, who hated it at home. With high unemployment, the labor exchange offered her work in the cotton mills in Lancaster, England.

"Shall I take the job and go to England?" she asked Mama.

"If you want to, then go," Mama said laconically. She had always let Christl go her own way.

Christl left within two weeks. I missed her a lot. Although she had seldom been home, to know I would see her at some time, had made a difference to my life. I felt she was on my side, though she was never there when I needed her most. But once she had given me a piece of chocolate, and a few precious times she took me with her, to the swimming bath once, another time for a day out when she didn't want to be alone with a boyfriend. We had walked alongside the Danube, and suddenly in front of us were groups of people wearing no clothes at all. We had walked into a nudist colony.

"Don't look," Christl had hissed each time we came across naked people, and obediently I looked away. It had been an adventure, and fun. I missed Christl. Everything got even worse, with just Willi at home and Mama and me.

But like a sunbeam can break through an endless gray sky, so could the sun come out for Mama and me. Suddenly my old Mama was back, the mother I knew and had loved so much when I was small. It was on such a day, when she said, quite out of the blue: "Come Gerti, let's go to the toy shop to buy you a doll."

I had two dolls already, my old Claudia, and a small black doll I had found in the park. With no one around to claim her, Mama allowed me to keep her. And now, Mama wanted to buy me another doll.

Willi was with Tante Paula – my mother was always nicer, when we were alone. But to buy me a doll? I couldn't believe it. She had never bought me a toy.

Walking through the streets holding Mama's hand, my heart was full of strange feelings. I was so happy – Mama must love me after all, or she wouldn't even think of buying me anything. But I was apprehensive too. She could turn suddenly, change her mind, and the whole thing was off.

But Mama didn't change her mind, and finally we stood in the toy shop, among the hundreds and thousands of miraculous treasures. I would have preferred a Meccano like Willi had. But it didn't really matter what Mama bought me, the miracle was that my mother was here with me, buying me something, just for me.

"Do you like this doll, Gerti?" Mama asked, pointing to a small baby doll. I nodded, too excited to speak, because next to her stood the doll of my dreams – at least, if I had ever dreamed of a doll, it would have been this one. She was slightly taller than the baby doll, and stood on straight legs, wearing red shoes.

"I think the little girl would prefer this one." The man behind the counter pointed to my dream-doll. He must have noticed I couldn't keep my eyes off her. But from the label round her neck I could see she was more expensive than the baby doll Mama liked.

"Would you rather have this one?" Mama asked me, quite normally, as if it was normal asking me a question like that. It seemed she might even buy me the doll of my dreams if I said so.

"Gerti, stop dreaming," Mama admonished me, smiling. "Would you prefer the doll with the shoes?"

In my whole life I never had to make such a hard decision. I wanted this doll so much, more than I had ever wanted anything in my life. But I knew Mama couldn't even afford the cheaper doll. How could I ask for a doll which cost more?

They were looking at me, waiting, I felt their eyes on me. I knew, if I asked, Mama would buy me the more expensive doll, because she loved me. It was such a wonderful feeling to be loved by my mother, this feeling made the decision for me.

I shook my head. "I like this one," I said, pointing to the baby doll.

"Are you sure, Gerti?" Mama asked, and when I nodded, the doll was wrapped up, Mama paid, and I took my present home. I treasured this doll, because she was the proof Mama loved me sometimes.

This was one of the few wonderful days with my mother, a day which shone like a bright and beautiful star in a dark cloudy sky. But such days were rare, and got less frequent as time went on. It seemed as if Mama was made up of several persons, the most prominent was the horrible, nasty, unreasonable mother who punished me without cause. This mother took gradually over. Several versions of her could come to the forefront, and Mama might change without any reason or cause that I could perceive.

But deeply hidden somewhere was still the mother who was loving and kind. She always appeared unexpectedly. It was this mother, in her purest form, who had bought me the doll. But even this loving mother had different shades. Usually one of them went to the market with me, to choose not only the cheapest, but the best and freshest vegetables. This Mama taught me to cook, praising me when I could prepare a whole meal by myself. It was with her I went to the communal baths every Friday, where we showered in a row with all the other women and girls. I always felt sorry for Willi, who had to shower on his own with the men and the boys.

Sometimes there was even a day we enjoyed as a family, usually once or twice a year, when we took the tram for a day out. Because of the fare, we couldn't go more often, so we enjoyed these special occasions even more. Walking along the Danube we watched the steamships going up river to Germany and down to Russia. Violets grew, and new grass started hiding the huge craters, where the bombs had ripped open the earth.

Once we took a trip to the woods. Willi liked the woods. Just like me, he needed to be close to the trees and wild flowers, and walk on soft earth. Birds were singing, a squirrel darted up a tree. This day was special, we felt close to nature. A walk in the park could not give us this feeling of being one with it all.

Willi and I asked Mama, to let us walk to the forest. From our last trip we knew, we only had to follow the rails of the 49 tram. Mama let us go, but we had to turn back, hot and thirsty, having walked for hours without reaching the wood.

I would soon return to Pupping for the summer, but Willi had no such escape. When I was not angry with him, I felt sorry for my brother. But although I often tried, I couldn't help him.

CHAPTER 13

PUPPING VIENNA, MAINLY PUPPING

As the years went by, Mama and the Pelzgasse were gradually controlling my mind, and taking over, even in Pupping. I became increasingly self-conscious, not as able to speak how I felt anymore, acting on ifs and on buts, on thoughts rather than feelings. I thought before speaking, considered what was expected, what others might think.

But although the influences of Vienna seemed to bury the real me, it was still there somewhere inside, and the longer I stayed in Pupping, the more I became my own self again. But some of Mama's conditioning sat too deep, and when Pflegevater tried to put his arm around my shoulders, I moved aside. I wanted nothing more than to throw myself into his arms, but I couldn't.

In all other ways our relationship continued as it always had been. I still led Maxl, our ox, and when I went visiting with Pflegevater, we'd sing on the way, and tell jokes. Some evenings we'd walk round the fields, observing the crops. And he was still my hero.

The village people treated me almost as if I were grown up. They greeted me in a friendly way, asked how I was, and I joined in the conversation like everyone else. But I missed the fuss they used to make of me. In Vienna I hated being the focus of attention, in Pupping I missed it.

Each year it got worse – perhaps growing up was the problem. I was not the pretty, cute little girl anymore, who sang and told jokes and made people laugh. I had to face it: I was no longer cute. Much of my sparkle had gone. After having my tonsils out, I'd put on weight, and to make matters worse, spots started to sprout on my face.

So much had changed or was changing. Loisl had left and I missed her. She was married, and lived so far away I rarely saw her. Then Nandl went to work in Linz, but at least she visited often, and on my journey home, I could see her in Linz, where I had to change trains. I travelled by myself now, and could stay overnight with Nandl, and she'd show me the sights. I enjoyed my visits, and knowing I would see her, was a comfort when I left Pupping.

With only Mirzl at home with her parents, everyone had to work harder. At harvesting time, I too worked long hours. I didn't mind, all farm children worked. As Mariandl had no set chores at home, she would join me, and help like I did. But around five our work was done.

"Get yourselves away, girls," foster-father would say. "You've worked long and hard, go and enjoy yourselves."

The family would work on, but Mariandl and I could go anywhere we wanted. If the weather was hot, we went for a swim.

Riding through the village on old borrowed bikes, we soon came to the river, and then to the weir, where the miller regulated the water-level by opening the weir. Winding a rope which pulled up a big metal plate, an opening was created at the bottom of the stream. Through this opening, the water rushed down a rock face, into a large and deep pool, reducing the water-level in the river.

If the weir stood open, which it was on that day, a strong under-current was caused in the river. This current was dangerous and could pull you down, but Mariandl and I didn't know.

We did know, however, that the pool was dangerous. We had been warned never to go near the pool, not even to paddle. People had drowned there, even horses. The water rushing down the rock face into the pool, created whirlpools, which could pull you down into the bottom of the pool which was very deep. Some who had dared never came out alive.

We heeded the warning, and only swam in the river.

After the heat of the day, it was wonderful to relax in the cool water, listening to its gurgling and splashing, the only other sound the occasional hum of a bee, or the song of a bird. I felt lazy, at peace, even swimming seemed too much effort. After practicing our strokes for a while, Mariandl and I walked upstream on the bank – it was easier than swimming against the current. Here, past the weir, we lay in the sun for a while, and when it got too hot, we didn't even have to stand up, but just turned over to roll into the stream. The current took us, carrying us gently downstream. Side by side we drifted, past the weir, until the water got shallow, and we started the whole cycle all over again.

All went well for a while. Floating on my back I looked up into the clear blue sky, feeling happy and at ease. Suddenly something was pulling me, sucking me under the water, so fast I couldn't fight it, or even know what was happening. I was under water, no above or below no air to breathe a heavy weight pressing on me. I was stuck – and hurting.

I was stuck at the opening of the weir, at the bottom of the river, but didn't know what was happening. I felt a heavy weight on my chest – and the pressure from the water behind was enormous.

I thought I would break, when suddenly the force of the current pushed me through the narrow opening. I was free and moving again, the current was taking me with it. The sound of the water was so loud, it filled my head and my body, until something hard hit my head, and a soaring pain engulfed me.

'If I don't die,' flashed through my mind, 'my brain will be damaged, I'll be an idiot for the rest of my life.' Then there was nothing at all.

When awareness returned I was surrounded by water, didn't know where up was or down, in which direction to swim. All around me was gurgling water. I felt no panic or fear, it was as if I were outside my body, observing it all. 'If I die now, I go to hell,' I thought calmly and completely detached, and passed out again.

Later, becoming aware again, I found myself swimming on the surface, and was back in my body. It was hard to breathe, it was so painful. I wanted to stay conscious, but was so tired I knew I would pass out again. Trying to feel with my foot if I could stand, I found the water too deep.

I could see Mariandl standing on the bridge above the weir, and tried calling her. But no sound came from me and everything went dark once again.

The next time awareness returned, it was like coming up from nothing – from a kind of non-existence. I was upright, only knee deep in water, walking towards the shore. Breathing was agony, especially breathing in. It was as if something was pressing on my chest, or rather, something hard and big seemed stuck inside me. Looking around, I tried to make sense of it all. Mariandl was still on the bridge looking towards me, as I walked from the pool to the shore. I had been pulled through the opening of the weir, down the rock face, and into the pool.

Tired, I felt so tired. Loud rasping breaths came from my chest, filling my body with more pain. I knew I couldn't carry on walking, I was too tired, and tried to call Mariandl again, but no sound came, except those horrible breaths. And then nothingness engulfed me once more.

"When you didn't come up again, I shut my eyes thinking, I'll never see Gerti again." I heard Mariandl's voice, it seemed to come from far away, though somehow I knew she sat next to me. But I couldn't move and every breath hurt.

I lay in the water with my head close to the shore, the water lapping in small waves around my face, but shallow enough so I could breathe. I lay there a long time, listening to Mariandl's voice, until life returned back to me. Then I dragged myself on my elbows and hands on to dry land, and stayed where I was until I recovered somewhat, and my breathing became easier. And though it still hurt, I could speak again.

On the back of my head a big lump developed. It was the size of an egg. I had to comb my hair carefully over it, and was glad of the curls, so no one would notice.

After a few days Mariandl and I went back to the river. I didn't want to, but something pulled me there. This time we checked that the weir was closed, but still I had to force myself to go into the water. The sounds, the gurgling and splashing, reminded me too much of my recent adventure, and made me uneasy. But if I avoided this challenge, I might never go in the river again. And in spite of what happened, I loved the water, and could not risk losing it. So I swam, facing my fears, but although the weir was closed, I stayed on the other side of the river. But it took several weeks, until I enjoyed swimming again.

Mariandl and I had other accidents too. Once she fell off a tree and could not get up. Luckily we were not far from her house, and as she recovered a little, she crawled there on hands and feet. No one was home, so we had a few hours to stay put, and my friend had recovered completely before her mother came home.

We often climbed trees, and jumped from the branches. Once my head hit a thick branch on the way down. I too was unable to move for a while, but was all right again later.

We got stung by bees and by wasps, once even by hornets, when we had 'borrowed' a barrel our neighbor had put out to dry in the sun. As we rolled down a slope, the insects inside the barrel got agitated and stung. This time we both ran home crying and let foster-mother look after us.

But on the whole we learned how to take care of ourselves. We knew a bee would leave its sting behind, and it had to be pulled out, and vinegar helped with some stings, even bites. Bruises and grazes could be ignored, but if a wound didn't stop bleeding, some action was required. So we plastered dry earth on the wound, for the bleeding to stop. We had discovered this method ourselves. It worked each time, and we never had any infections.

We told no one about our accidents, partly because it was so deeply ingrained in me to hide anything to do with illness, and Mariandl followed my example, but mostly because we were afraid our respective families would try to keep a closer eye on us. We might lose our freedom, which had to be avoided at all cost. That this fear was unfounded, I realized when I sprained an ankle.

On the search for new challenges, we jumped from the highest place in our neighbor's barn. A layer of straw was on the bottom, but it was thinner than we had thought. When I landed, my left ankle turned, and as my legs gave way, I sat down on the twisted ankle with a thump. It hurt like hell and my ankle increased to twice its size. Though making a valiant effort not to limp, foster-mother noticed the size of my ankle. Cold compresses were put on it, but she didn't tell me off.

I had to stay home, simply because I couldn't walk. Mariandl came every day to keep me company. We listened to the radio and discovered pop music, and learned different songs. One day Mariandl found a baby swallow which had fallen from its nest. We kept it in a box on a shelf on the wall, where the cat couldn't get it. It was a full-time job to catch insects to feed the tiny bird, and when we needed a break we gave it bread soaked in water. Our small friend always willingly opened his tiny beak to the small tweezers Nandl had given me. Finally the little swallow could fly, and we gave the small bird its freedom, releasing it, to be with its friends, and to hunt for itself.

Eventually, I too had my freedom back. First I could hobble, and then walk, but it took almost the whole summer until I was back to normal, and running again.

Apart from the occasional accident, my health was much better than in Vienna. I never had colds, rarely had any pains in my chest, and if I did, they wouldn't be as strong, and disappear quicker. All through the years in Pupping, only once was I seriously ill.

It started suddenly. I didn't know what was wrong. Every movement hurt and was a great effort. I felt terrible, burning hot one minute, then freezing cold the next, but the icy shivery cold took hold and remained. I succeeded in hiding my condition from my foster-family, making enormous efforts at meal times, and going quickly to bed in the evening. At least it wasn't harvest time, so I could get away. During the day I lay in the hot sun, shivering with cold, hardly aware what was happening.

Mariandl stayed with me, sitting quietly by my side, until the third day, when we thought I was dying. She went home for a bottle and filled it with holy water from the font in the church. Then she gave me the last rites, sprinkling me with the holy water and praying to God, first in German, then in Latin. We expected my death, and I was feeling so awful, even the thought of dying and hell didn't bother me. But to our surprise I didn't die, but got better within hours To celebrate my recovery we took a walk to the wood the next day.

Mariandl and I loved the woods for their beauty, but also because we liked foraging for berries and hazelnuts, wild herbs and plants. Through the years, the adults had taught us what was safe to eat, and which plants to avoid.

To our great joy the raspberries had ripened, and after we collected a great many, we divided the juicy red fruit equally. But we started to squabble who would have which heap of berries, which led to a fight. Whilst we were occupied in this way, maggots crawled out of the fruit. When our argument was finally settled, we didn't want the berries anymore, because fat, grayish-white grubs crawled busily all over the fruit.

I looked at my friend and she looked at me, and we burst out laughing. We had been fighting over something we didn't want anymore, yet had we eaten the raspberries without arguing, we would have enjoyed them, unaware of the maggots. How could we have been so stupid to fight over fruit?

Perhaps because we enjoyed fighting, knowing afterwards we'd still be friends. We were proud to be tough; the worst insult remained the word coward.

Yet sometimes I questioned myself, was I really as brave? Perhaps I pretended to myself. How could I be sure? I thought about this issue for days, and came to the conclusion I would have to prove myself. But how? It soon came to me: I would put myself to a test. What was I most afraid of? But I knew the answer already: dark – night – alone – in the forest.

Excluding Mariandl was difficult, but necessary. If I told her, she too might doubt my courage, and she'd want to take part in my adventure. But I had to go by myself. Facing my fears would be easy with a friend, and prove nothing.

My plan was simple: I would go to the wood when it was dark. At this late hour, I wasn't allowed to go far from the house, but my quest was important – and the chance to be found out was small. Just this one time I would break the rule. I was always outside in the evening, usually with Mariandl, sneaking past the windows of neighbor's to take bunches of grapes from their vines on the wall, or pick the best juicy plums in the orchard. Some evenings we'd sit in a tree, watching the moon and the stars and talk, while eating our spoils.

On the evening of my quest I pretended to be tired, and walked with Mariandl to the big stone, the halfway mark between our houses, where we always parted. Only I didn't go home, but took the dirt-road to the woods, to walk along the edge of the forest and come home a different way.

It was a mild summer evening and getting dark. Walking past the deserted fields, I felt edgy, butterflies stirred in my stomach. 'There is nothing to worry about,' I told myself firmly. 'Everything is as always, except that it's dark and I am alone.'

The road wound its way towards the edge of the wood. I could see a light, and knew it came from a farmhouse, ahead in the distance. When I reached the house, the path to the forest turned off to the left.

Suddenly an eerie howling filled the air, making the skin along my spine tingle, and the hair lift from my scalp as if it had a will of its own.

'A dog,' I told myself. 'There must be a dog in the farmhouse. Perhaps he is locked in, or tied up,' I reassured myself. But it didn't work, because the howling got worse, and came nearer.

Thoughts of werewolves came into my mind. 'I'm not afraid,' I told myself. But this time my old mantra didn't work, I felt like turning around and running home as fast as I could. But this would prove I was a coward – and besides, running would be stupid. If the dog was loose, he was likely to chase me.

My body had no such considerations and just wanted to be off, running as fast as it could.

I'd forgotten about my courage, and had to remind myself sternly. There was no turning back.

Walking towards the most terrifying sounds I had ever heard, I reasoned: 'If the dog is loose, running away will make him follow you. Never show a dog you are afraid.'

No other way led to the wood. So I walked on, trying not to think.

But this was impossible, as the howling sounds grew ever louder as I was nearing the house – they couldn't come from an earthly creature. Ghost stories flashed through my mind, pictures of horribly mutilated bodies ravaged by hounds with huge jaws.

I reached the house and walked past the gate. The windows were lit and I longed to be with the people inside. If I knocked on the door, they would help me. But they'd also bring me back home, and my foster-family would never trust me again. And I would definitely be a coward – and the dog wouldn't let me reach the door, anyway. Every second this terrible monster could jump out at me. Even if it was only a dog, he could bite, even kill me.

Suddenly there was silence. But this silence was worse. Was the beast waiting behind the hedge, ready to jump, to attack me? I was almost relieved when the howling sounds came back, especially when I realized I was walking away from the dog.

The howls grew fainter and stopped. It was quiet again. But I couldn't help listening, and was amazed how many sounds I could hear, alone at the edge of the wood, surrounded by bushes and trees. I reached a small clearing. The moon came out from behind a cloud, and I saw not just bushes and trees, but shadows, black shadows which moved. But I would soon reach the path leading me home.

'Just keep walking,' I told myself, 'soon you'll be home.'

Then I saw the lights of Mariandl's house in the distance, twinkling through the dark night. I had done it. Relief swept over me. I could run now. Suddenly I felt strong, exhilarated. Spreading my arms wide like wings, I ran fast like the wind, happy, and so glad it was over. I was alive and my life was wonderful, just as it was in this moment.

But bad things could happen in Pupping too, really bad things, and they always had to do with the boys, mostly with Kini. He was the leader of the village boys. There were seven, and Poldi, Mariandl's brother, was one of the gang.

The boys had always been our rivals. When we were younger, we had played together at times. Now we rarely saw them. But we knew where the boys were likely to be, just as they knew where to look for us. But we avoided them, and they only came looking if they were bored, and wanted to tease us.

Kini was about three or four years older than me, a tall, lanky youth, who had a need to prove he was the strongest, and best in everything. We had always been at loggerheads. He tried to intimidate me, calling me names, making fun of me because I was a city girl. The other boys didn't always join in his baiting. I think some boys rather liked me. But they would not go against him.

An uneasy truce remained between us, until the boys killed a hedgehog. From that day on, Kini was my enemy. I not only distrusted, but hated him.

It had happened two or three years ago, when Mariandl and I came across the boys, standing in a group on the side of the dirt road.

The hedgehog lay curled up in the grass, and the boys prodded him with sticks to make him run. When the little creature remained a spiky ball in spite of the prodding, Kini threw the first stone, and the other boys followed his lead.

I wanted to stop them. Every stone was not only hitting the hedgehog, I felt it was hitting me too.

'They'll do it all the more, if they know it upsets me,' I knew this from experience. And they would call me a soft city girl – which would not help the hedgehog either.

I couldn't fight them all – there were five – I couldn't win this fight. And I knew Kini wanted only an excuse to get his hands on me. Mariandl would be of no help. She was younger than me, and her brother belonged to the gang – and all the boys were years older. My best friend didn't share my feelings about animals. She thought I was too soft, because I came from the city.

Whilst I still searched my mind what to do, the hedgehog stretched out. It was dead. The boys lost their interest and walked off.

I couldn't stop thinking of the small prickly creature. I should have saved the hedgehog, or at least tried. Too late now, the hedgehog was dead. But I promised myself to speak up in future, and act, regardless if my chances were small. At least I would have done what was right, and would feel good inside.

The tension between Kini and me continued throughout the years. It was as if we were embittered arch enemies. Each year the situation got worse. He stalked me, trying to get me alone. I felt threatened and intimidated, and was cautious, avoiding him whenever I could. Why he followed me, I had no idea – only, that I had to be careful, it was dangerous to be alone with him.

I didn't want him to know I was afraid, it would add to his sense of power. So if Mariandl and the boys were present, I just ignored him. But he wouldn't leave me be, and at times, if his teasing got too much, I couldn't help but retaliate. With my tongue I was quicker than Kini. I won any verbal dispute, and the boys would laugh about him then. And the hate was plain to be seen in his eyes, and something else – I didn't know what it was, but it scared me. He was my enemy.

But I didn't often think about Kini. He was there, somewhere in the background, like a tiny sharp stone in my shoe, almost disappearing for a long time, but always coming back and digging in sharply. This went on for some years, until I was about ten or eleven, and Kini, fifteen, and the dreadful event happened, which had its beginning when Mariandl and I decided to write a script for a theatre performance.

Her aunt had taken her to the cinema, and in the film a man kissed his girl longingly and impressively. We had never seen a kiss such as that – how did their lips stay together for such a long time? And why would anyone kiss in this peculiar way? Was it even possible? Did something happen, unknown to us, if the lips of two people touched? And would anyone do this in real life too? And why?

Our curiosity got the better of us, so we decided to try such a kiss to see what would happen. Just in case, and to be safe, we kept the open kitchen door between our bodies, sticking our heads out from each side of the door.

The kiss was a failure, a total disappointment – it was not anything. Our lips met but did not cling, suck or linger. There was nothing, except lips pressed on lips. The whole matter was completely overrated. Perhaps we had to kiss like this when we were married and wanted babies. In the meantime no boy would come near us.

But after talking so much about kissing and acting, we decided to produce a play. But there would be no kissing, not even pretend-kissing, but instead a good fight.

It was easy enough to write the script. Once the decision was made on the outline, the words followed easily – and much could be improvised at the time of our performance.

Our script was a tale of rivalry, with two jealous men and one pretty woman. Mariandl had to play the role of the woman because she was smaller than me. In the interval she would change, to play my rival. The highlight came in the second act with the fight, where I was the winner – it was only fair, as my friend had two parts to play.

After the fight, the curtain had to come down, so Mariandl could change back to be the woman again for the happy ending – without any kissing, of course, but maybe we'd shake hands.

Our neighbor's washhouse made an ideal stage. It opened up to a covered yard, and if it rained, our viewers wouldn't get wet.

Mariandl borrowed clothes from her brother, but for me, it was more difficult. Foster-father was tall and broad shouldered, his clothes were too big. But our neighbor, Wolfgang Katzenegger, was a small man, and his wife lent me a beautiful dark suit. I just had to tuck up the sleeves and fold the trouser legs over, and use a piece of string as a belt.

Everything went according to plan. We had sold twelve tickets, and chairs stood in rows, ready for our audience.

The first act went well, with everyone applauding as the makeshift curtain went down and Mariandl changed into her brother's trousers.

The two rivals began arguing in the second act, about the beautiful woman of course. With nothing resolved, and no agreement or compromise reached, the fight became physical and we hit each other, cursing to our best ability as real men do in such a situation. The audience laughed, and although our play was not a comedy, the laughter grew louder and louder, especially when we rolled on the ground, fighting fiercely as it said in the script, and Frau Katzenegger shouted: "Get off the floor this minute, Gerti! You are wearing Wolfgang's best suit, he needs it for church in the morning."

In spite of having to shorten our fight and so ending our performance earlier, the play was such a success that we decided to stage another – although this time I had to make do with the second best and only other suit of our neighbor.

The boys had heard about the play and our plan to stage another. They came to see us, wanting to be part of the next play. Kini came too, but as he didn't speak to me, and stayed in the background, I could ignore him.

Mariandl and I wrote another script on a similar theme, and included parts for the boys. But with more actors, a bigger stage was needed. After exploring several possibilities, we decided on the beer garden in the village square. The garden had a shelter for tables and chairs in the winter. With it empty, it made an ideal stage. We only had to hang horse blankets as curtains. The guests could sit in the garden, drinking cider or beer, and we would have a big audience.

To inform everyone, we painted three posters, one each for the shop, the church, and the other pub.

Mariandl and I were confident of our success and although Kini was usually watching, I managed to ignore him, pretending not to hear his sarcastic remarks. And the boys did the same.

Finally the big day arrived. Dressed in our costumes, we checked everything one last time, just to be sure. This time, instead of painting a moustache on my face, I had brought a sweetcorn-cob, to glue its fibers on to my face.

All the he boys were here, even Kini. He kept as close to me as he could, and when I moved away, he followed. His eyes didn't leave my face, making me uneasy. But with so many children around, he couldn't hurt me, I thought. I just had to ignore him.

So I took little notice of Kini, but I could tell he was angry about it, and more so, because his group of boys were ignoring him too, as we prepared for the play.

But Kini began teasing me. I controlled myself, but when his needling remarks got too insulting, something snapped inside me. My good intentions forgotten, I retaliated, telling him what I thought of him. He grabbed me, trying to pin me against the wall. I pushed him back, all my hatred erupting, and with it my determination not to let him get the better of me. I fought with all my fury and might, but Kini was much bigger and stronger, and eventually he pinned me against the wall, holding on to my hair with one hand. His other hand tightened across my throat.

I could do nothing to him, his arms were much longer than mine and I couldn't reach him.

"Give in, Gerti," he hissed between clenched teeth, "admit I have won." His face came closer, and I was forced to look into his eyes.

"Never," I hissed back and with a last valiant effort I kicked out, hitting his shin, and broke free. But Kini held on to my hair and I felt a terrible pain as it came off my scalp.

"Didn't hurt," I shouted, though I was in agony. But I was free, and determined to stay free. Never again would I let Kini come close.

Laughing, he held up the fistful of hair as a trophy, a sign of his victory. But this time the boys were not on his side, no one else laughed, and one boy took the bunch of my hair from his hand, and gave it to me. Kini was too surprised to resist, or to admonish the boy. My enemy was in danger of losing his leadership, as the boys gathered round me, showing sympathy and concern.

"Are you OK, Gerti?" one boy asked, and "will you still be playing?" said another.

The boys formed a circle around me and Mariandl. Kini was left outside it and ignored.

"I am fine," I said, looking directly at Kini, as I held up my bunch of hair. "He has done me a favor, I don't have to use the strings from the corn cob, I can wear my own hair as a beard."

Everyone laughed, only Kini looked at me with hate in his eyes. Making fun of it, I had reversed the whole situation. He was no longer the victor.

We tied the bunch of my hair in the middle then glued it above my upper lip. It made a beautiful moustache, covering almost half of my face. But we had to get ready quickly, it was time for the play.

Kini disappeared, and I didn't see him again. He plotted his revenge, but to what length he would go, I could not have imagined.

The play was a big success, and as all the people in the beer garden had paid an entry fee, we had earned lots of money, which we shared equally between us all. We were rich, I felt happy, and hardly thought of Kini anymore.

Next morning, Loisl asked me if I had heard anything about Poldi. I shook my head.

"Is anything wrong?" I wanted to know, but Loisl just mumbled something about him going away, but didn't seem to know why.

Later, when we met, I asked Mariandl. She told me her parents found out that her brother had been with a girl, and they were doing 'it'. She had no real idea what 'it' meant, and neither did I, but we knew it was something disgusting, and had to do with parts of the body we had no names for and which had to be kept hidden. It probably was something married people did to have children, but without marriage it was sure to be a capital sin.

I was shocked about the girl, but nothing could surprise me about Poldi. After the incident with my knickers, I had never trusted him.

Later, I went looking for Loisl, ready to share the news about Poldi. Perhaps she could explain what 'it' really meant. I saw her coming from the field, and shouted: "I know what Poldi has done, Loisl."

But something was wrong, I could tell by the way she was looking at me. Never before had she looked at me in this way. Nonsense, I told myself, I had done nothing wrong. So I started telling her about Poldi.

But Loisl held up her hand, stopping me. "You don't have to tell me anything, Gerti," she said, "I already know it all."

It was the way she looked at me, so sad, disappointed, it had to be something concerning me too. But I could think of nothing I had done, so I waited.

"I know about Poldi, and I know about you," Loisl said. "No, don't say anything," she stopped me again as I tried talking. "Kini has admitted it all, he told everything. Everyone in the village knows that he did it with you."

At first, I was left speechless by the enormity of the lie.

"It's not true," was all I finally managed to say.

Loisl couldn't possibly believe this of me. Somehow I had to convince her that Kini was lying. I tried to explain, but Loisl just shook her head. She said why should Kini lie about something like that? After all, it brought trouble for him too.

I said that he wanted to hurt me; he wanted revenge. But Loisl just shook her head and walked away.

The way Mirzl looked at me, I was convinced she also knew about it, and my foster-parents would believe it too. I didn't dare to look at foster-father, afraid of what I might see in his eyes. When we sat down to eat, I tried once more to explain, but soon stopped, because it was obvious no one believed me. I was only making things worse, because they thought I was lying on top of everything else.

No one could help me, not even Mariandl. She was suddenly gone, sent to relatives for a few days. Probably, so she wouldn't be tainted by my loose morals. And this summer I couldn't even see her again, because in a few days I had to leave for Vienna.

Kini had his revenge. He was the victor, because everyone believed him, and not me. I considered seeking him out, challenging him – but I knew, this was what he was waiting for. It would give him great satisfaction to see how he had beaten and humiliated me in the end. He would never admit that his accusations were untrue and that he had lied.

There was nothing I could do.

This time I was glad to go home to Vienna. And although everyone was nice to me when I said goodbye, I knew it was just a pretense. Their eyes told me how disappointed they were in me, and how sad they felt. There was just nothing I could say or do, because no one believed me.

I had to push all my anger, fury and pain, all my hurt and desperation into this bottomless pit, where so many of my sad and painful feelings already lay waiting for more. What else could I do? How could the people I loved and trusted the most believe Kini and not me? They knew me, they should have known I would never do something so terrible.

Perhaps one day, if I was married and really determined to have a child, and there was no other way – perhaps I had to force myself to do this disgusting thing, whatever it was – but definitely not with someone like Kini.

And everyone in Pupping thought I had behaved in this way. I felt so powerless, I wanted to shout and to scream and to fight, but I knew it would only make matters worse. There was nothing I could do. Even here in Pupping I was totally without any power.

Yes, this time I was glad to go home to Vienna.

CHAPTER 14

VIENNA PLUS – 1951–52

No one in Vienna knew what had happened to me, I didn't even tell my best friends. I buried my feelings deep inside me; my feelings of anger, frustration and pain.

Here in the city, all traces of war had finally disappeared, but in our family nothing had been repaired or rebuilt. And the rubble and dust from the breakdown of our family and of the way we lived in the Pelzgasse, was settling on me; mostly gradually and slowly, but sometimes in such big heavy lumps, I didn't know how to carry it all: how to carry on living.

Because of high inflation, Papa's alimony bought less every month. We could not afford the different foods which were part of everyday life again.

Mama applied for an invalidity pension, but was turned down, and told, she was thirty-three per cent fit to work – half a per cent less would have qualified her for a pension. We were not even entitled to child benefit, because our father had his own business.

Mama applied for a council flat and went to various offices filling out forms, often waiting for hours, but without any success. She said it was because she belonged to the wrong political party, but it seemed her beliefs wouldn't allow her to join the right one.

Then she tried to get help from the state, only to be told Lilly should contribute. But my sister already helped where she could, bringing us groceries or what Willi or I needed for school. She didn't have much money, and neither did Tante Paula, who only just managed, after paying Lilly a small wage.

Somehow, our mother got through, but she became more twisted and bitter, which was reflected in our everyday life, and her endless monologues. Once more she attempted to get a council flat, but when she was turned down again, she gave up and we remained in the Pelzgasse.

Christl stayed in England. When I returned from Pupping, her bed had been replaced by a wardrobe, where Willi kept all his clothes and personal belongings. He locked his wardrobe, and kept the key on him.

My clothes remained in the small kitchen cupboard, together with Mama's things, and for my personal possessions I had a drawer. It was so unfair. Willi had a whole wardrobe to himself, and still kept his two drawers – the second drawer he 'inherited' when Christl had left. I complained bitterly. But Mama either ignored me, or threatened me with a hiding. So I gave up in the end. But my feelings of resentment, of being treated unfairly and having no power at all, these negative, hurtful emotions stayed with me, mixing with similar feelings still haunting me since Kini's lies, and my foster-family's betrayal. In Pupping I hadn't been able to do anything about the injustice I had experienced, and here in Vienna it was the same.

And did it matter what Willi had? For my few treasures was enough space in my drawer.

It contained my three dolls and their clothes, holy pictures I had been given in school and in church; water color paints, paper and pencils. From Pupping I had brought back a set of teeth from a pig. They had been boiled for hours, until nothing remained but perfect white teeth. But there were also my four books, my dearest possessions, especially my book of Hauff's fairy tales, containing stories about faraway lands, killings and ghosts, and terrifying adventures. I loved this book. Willi and I had read it so often to each other that I knew if he made a mistake.

Coming home from school one day, I opened my drawer to find it empty, except for my paints, paper, and holy pictures.

"Where are my things?" I asked Mama.

"You are too old for them, Gerti, I got rid of them all." She said it so calmly, as if she were talking about old shoes I had grown out of.

"But they are mine," I couldn't believe Mama would just 'get rid' of my treasures.

"I want my things back," I shouted, when she ignored me. I was so angry.

Mama got angry too. "There is no space in our flat," she screamed. "All the rubbish had to go – anyway, it's gone now, the binmen have taken it away with the other rubbish."

I couldn't believe everything I had treasured and thought to be mine, had suddenly gone – even the baby doll Mama had bought me. And my favorite book – this hit me the most. Now I couldn't bury myself in a book anymore to escape Mama and the Pelzgasse.

She had got rid of all my personal possessions – except my writing and painting things, but those I needed for homework. The pictures of the saints were also still here. I wouldn't have cared if they had gone – but Mama probably hadn't dared to destroy holy pictures.

Everything I valued was gone, my own mother had betrayed me completely. How could she do this to me? And why? She didn't touch Willi's belongings.

I was so angry and upset, but could do nothing, and had no one to turn to. But I wasn't able to let my pain and frustration just be, and kept on. It made Mama angrier, yet still I found it impossible to stay calm and contain myself. I wanted to scream and to shout, bang my head against the wall and hit out with my fists, but couldn't even cry and mourn my things, because there was nowhere I could be alone.

And if Mama saw tears in my eyes, she threatened to hit me and give me a reason to cry.

Willi seemed to get a weird kind of pleasure from my pain and frustration. Perhaps it relieved his boredom, I thought in more charitable moments – but those moments were rare, because he deliberately provoked me, so I'd lose my temper and go for him. He knew he'd win any fight, and enjoyed pinning me down, twisting my arms behind my back.

"Say: 'I'll never raise my hand against my brother again'." he would hiss, his face close to mine 'Or I'll really hurt you, Gerti,.'

I'd clench my teeth and stay silent, and Willi would give my arms an extra few twists to get the words out of me, before letting me go with a warning. And so it went on. He'd only give up, if I completely ignored him. But again and again I lost my temper, until something strange happened.

I was painting a horse in a meadow, and only wanted to be left in peace to get on with my work. But Willi kept baiting me, until I got so furious, something snapped in me. I picked up the square solid porcelain bowl I used for washing my brushes, and threw it. The heavy china object made straight for his temple, and I knew my brother would die if it hit him. My anger was gone, it had totally vanished, replaced by a terrible fear for his life.

Then something weird happened. Time seemed to slow down and I saw everything in very slow motion. The bowl moved so slowly through the air, I had time to think, to be aware of what was happening – aware of myself, and of my brother – though it must have been a split second. But in this split second I knew with absolute certainty, I must not kill my brother, or anyone – ever. It was like a flash of lightning – or power – or perhaps even God.

All my anger and hate were washed away by this flash of consciousness, which seemed to go on forever.

I watched as the china bowl neared Willi's temple, barely touching him, before smashing to pieces behind him against the wall. And time became its usual self again.

There was total silence – we both just sat there. But I promised myself never to lose my temper with Willi again. He was my brother, and in spite of everything, I loved him. I knew how much he suffered, and by teasing me, he relieved his boredom and pain. And perhaps he was jealous. I had some kind of life away from our mother, with my friends and in Pupping. But Willi had no one except Mama and me.

My brother didn't say one word, and I too remained silent, as I got rid of the broken pieces and wiped the water from the floor.

But having sympathy with my brother and some understanding, didn't help me, but made my life even more difficult and complex, because now I made excuses when Willi provoked me and I was angry. I was angry a lot of the time. And whatever went on, Mama agreed with my brother, or ignored us.

So much anger, frustration and fury was building up in me, and I found no way to release at least some of it. Willi had a whole wardrobe and locked it. No one would dare touch his belongings. Yet everything I had treasured was gone, and I had to pretend not to care, swallow everything down. It made me sullen, resentful and bitter. But it was not like this all the time, suddenly Mama or Willi would change, talking to me as if nothing had happened and we were on good terms. Now I was in conflict. Something in me would respond and I wanted to interact normally. But I knew I would regret it. If I opened up even a little, I would get hurt again later. Better to say nothing, and keep my emotions locked up inside me.

There was no way out. Our lives only got more complicated, and bizarre. Chaos reigned totally, and we only seemed to hurt one another.

This winter Mama got rid of Christmas, declaring we were too old for it. I missed Christmas. During the last few years we always had a small tree and some presents, usually clothes, oranges and chocolate. My sisters had always been here. But Lilly was engaged and spent Christmas with her fiancé and his parents, and Christl was in England. I missed them; everyone had a Christmas but us. In school, I pretended I too had a nice Christmas, hating to see pity in my friends' eyes.

Willi shared Mama's opinion about Christmas. He was nearly fourteen and grown up. He intended to enter an apprenticeship for business studies when he left school. Mama wanted him to become a tailor, but Willi stood firm, refusing to discuss the matter. And in spite of high unemployment, he found an apprenticeship.

He could impose his will, even against our mother. She began to lean on him, and he became the head of our household. Mama still borrowed of him, he still made her beg, and she had to sign his paper and pay interest.

Mama's illnesses also contributed to make our life so chaotic during these years. When she was taken to hospital, the church found us foster-parents. My brother and I were always split up, and didn't see each other. We both hated being with strange families, and be objects of charity. So when Willi was about thirteen, he kept nagging Mama, until she agreed to leave us by ourselves the next time. But we had to promise not to tell anyone, or attract any attention, as Social Services would put us into a children's home.

Our mother went to hospital quite soon, and we were alone. Willi wanted to look after himself, and from his half of the housekeeping money he bought a big lump of cheese and a hard sausage, bread, and some fruit, for the vitamins. But after a few days he'd had enough of cold food and asked me to cook for him. From then on I did all the housekeeping for both of us, and we had no problem at all. My brother was nice when he needed me.

Six months later, when Mama went into hospital again, Willi was already an apprentice, and we were better prepared. I shopped and cooked after school. When he came home we ate, worked out what I had spent and what to buy tomorrow. We had no quarrels, my brother knew if he upset me, he would go back to cold food.

In our free time we played Monopoly. Willi had bought the game after I'd told him about it. My brother was very different when we lived alone. He even bought a chess game with a small booklet about how to play it. With two games to play, we enjoyed ourselves.

Mama was happy to see us when we visited her in hospital. I had made her a pencil drawing of St. Stephen's Cathedral, and she was so pleased, she showed it to everyone in the ward. Afterwards Willi and I went to the pictures. I had saved enough from the housekeeping money for the tickets, and we had a really good time. I was a little apprehensive, because they showed

Blackboard Jungle, and I should have been fourteen. But Willi bought the tickets and the man let us pass. For days I sang *'Rock around the Clock,'* until Mama came home and gradually everything returned to 'normal.'

Then a letter came from Nandl. Foster-mother was in hospital with her heart, and this summer I couldn't come to Pupping.

Although I dreaded going back to Pupping after what had happened with Kini, I was desolate. Of course, I felt sorry for foster-mama, but I was so used to illnesses and hospitals, they were part of life for me, and I didn't worry too much. But to spend the whole summer in Vienna was a terrible prospect.

The school holidays came, and every day was the same. I'd go to the park, if I was lucky Helga was there, and we'd sit on a bench and talk, walk around, and watch the little ones playing. If she couldn't come, I spent a few hours walking around the streets on my own.

And then suddenly everything changed.

It was a hot day in July, it was so hot, the tar melted on the pavements. I'd been to the park and thought longingly of swimming in the river, or walking through the shady forests in Pupping.

When I came home, I found a note on our door. It was from my religious instructor, Pater Wolfschlaeger. He wanted me to come and see him.

I liked Pater Wolfschlaeger, in spite of him being a priest and teaching religion. But he also talked about Muslims and Hindus, and didn't exclude people from Heaven who were not Catholics. We didn't pray in his class and he didn't ask who went to Mass or confession.

But even with him I had not been able to speak about my problems with sinning and hell.

In theory I knew I could shed all my sins in the confessional box, but found it impossible in practice. I couldn't tell the priest all my sins, they had accumulated and grown too enormous. But at least I didn't add more sins, as I no longer went to confession or Mass. I pretended to go with my friends, but went for a walk instead. And I managed to push any thoughts about hell so deep down, they only surfaced when I had chest pains, or another reason to think I was dying.

But Pater Wolfschlaeger knew none of my problems, and I couldn't imagine why he wanted to see me. Mama had no idea either, and decided to accompany me.

Pater Wolfschlaeger was a small man, still young, and so thin I could see the bones and veins through his skin. But he was kind, and this kindness and love, and something else – something like power – or holiness perhaps – radiated from him like a light. I could always feel it when he was near.

He shook Mama's hand, and then mine, and as we sat down, he almost disappeared behind his big desk. He came straight to the point.

"I've heard the young Stary girl," Pater Wolfschlaeger paused, looked at me enquiringly, not knowing my first name. We were called by our surnames at school.

"Gerti," I informed him, as always pleased with my name. It was a nice name, not ordinary, like Hilde or Helga or Maria.

"Ah yes, Gerti, short for Gertrude." He nodded, looking thoughtfully at me, so I nodded too.

"Do you know about Saint Gertrude?" I shook my head. "Gertrude means friend of the spear," he told me. "It means a spear thrower, a warrior's name. It suits you, Gerti."

I glowed in his praise, feeling proud he recognized the warrior in me. But perhaps he knew much about being a warrior, with a name like Wolfschlaeger, a man who could beat, or would win against wolves. And quite probably he had to develop special strength and skills, because he was so small. Growing up couldn't have been easy for him.

"The reason I wanted to see you, Gerti," the priest continued, disrupting my thoughts. I was all attention now, it couldn't be something bad.

"I heard you are not going to Pupping this year, Gerti." I shook my head. He had addressed me, though Mama sat next to me. How he knew about Pupping, I couldn't imagine, because I never talked about Pupping in school.

"I thought you might be missing your holiday in the country," he said, smiling at me. "In the village I come from, I know a girl, who would very much like to share her holidays with a friend. You'd live with her and her mother, and I am sure you'd have a really good time. It's right in the country, with woods all around, and a stream, the Ranna. It's where I grew up."

Of course I wanted to go, and I think Mama was glad too. Later I learned Pater Wolfschlaeger had gone to his hometown for a weekend and asked the congregation during Mass, who would like to give a city-child a holiday. Many offered, and he picked Frau Toni, because she was the best.

Pater Wolfschlaeger took me to his village himself. We went on the train, then by bus, and we talked, as if I were grown up and he was not a priest. I managed not to be sick, but it worried me all through the journey. I was glad when the bus stopped in the village square, right in front of the post office. Frau Toni was already waiting for us. Everyone called her big Toni, and little Toni was her daughter.

Frau Toni was the postmistress. She wasn't really big, just a little bit round, and had a lovely friendly smile. "I'm glad you are here, Gerti," she greeted me. "Toni is so looking forward to showing you everything, and to have a friend her own age."

Pater Wolfschlaeger left, and I followed Frau Toni into the post office. She locked the door behind us, taking us through to the living room.

"People will knock, if they need something urgently," she said, ushering us to a table, already laid for our meal. "Otherwise they are sure to come back."

It seemed so informal and relaxed, I was sure to like it here.

Little Toni was not small, she was taller than me, but then she was three years older, nearly fourteen. But the difference in our age didn't matter, because we liked each other on sight, and soon discovered we were interested in the same things. We both liked the woods and the water, and loved reading. Toni had many books, real treasures like *Tom Sawyer* which we both loved, and Karl Mai with his fabulous adventures. She even had detective stories about *Komisar Alan Wilton*. In Vienna they had been classed as rubbish, not worth reading, and I had never managed to borrow one of the booklets. Now I could enter the world of detectives, murder and mystery, and thoroughly enjoyed it.

My new friend shared my sense of adventure, and soon we competed as to who had the most courage. Toni would creep up in the dark, to frighten me with a horrible hiss or a touch. In the beginning, I really jumped with fright, until I realized it was always Toni.

Not to be outdone, I adopted her methods and would surprise her too. She never got cross if I made her jump.

But one day my new friend proved her superiority in the art of scaremongery. Toni had given me her bedroom, and slept in her mother's room, adjacent to mine. One night, lying in bed and trying to sleep, I heard a faint scratching noise. Something strange and horrible must be under my bed, waiting to get me as soon as I slept.

Suddenly I was wide awake, listening. But all remained quiet and still.

Perhaps I had made a mistake, or a mouse had made these sounds, searching for its hole, and now it had found it.

But then this terrifying sound came again, louder this time. This was no mouse, no earthly creature could make such a sound. My hair was rising, standing on end, and shivers ran down my spine. I wanted to jump out of bed and flee, run next door to Toni and her mother.

"I am brave,' I told myself the old success-formula. But this time it didn't work, so I had to fall back on logic. 'There are no ghosts or monsters, they don't exist. Nothing can hurt me here.'

Gathering my last remnants of courage, I prepared to investigate under the bed. First I would turn on the light, so I could see what was there. I pressed the switch, but it remained dark. Refusing to give in to my fear, I bent down. But it was too dark to see anything. I was about to put my hand under the bed, when suddenly something big jumped out and came for me, giving off a loud hiss. I jumped back, ready to run for my life, when I heard a laugh which could come only from Toni.

There could be no doubt anymore, she was definitely the winner in the game of scaring people. I could stop trying, I'd never beat her.

Toni had no chores to do, and we could spend our time as we pleased. Just occasionally her mother asked us to take a letter or parcel to one of the isolated farmhouses. We loved delivering the mail, because it meant a walk through the woods, or along the river Ranna. We'd stop at the river and paddle, but the current was too strong to go in, so, if we wanted to swim, we went to the pond by the village.

Here, to my surprise and great joy, I discovered that boys could be fun. Moving in groups, we rarely came across fewer than three. They would greet Toni, asked who I was, and after trying for a few minutes to find something to say, they walked on.

Toni answered their questions, giggling in between, and afterwards she talked about the boys, and giggled some more. She liked the look of Peter, how tall he was, what did I think of him? Had I noticed the color of his eyes? So unusual – and didn't he have a nice smile?

Up to now I had never considered such matters, but to please my friend I let her talk about boys, and to my surprise found the whole thing contagious. I too started giggling and became aware of their looks, and realized the boys noticed me too. In spite of a spot or two on my face, and not being thin anymore, I looked nice, and the boys seemed to think so as well.

Toni said I was not plump at all, boys liked 'a figure', she was too thin – which I denied strongly. I thought she was pretty and just right, and told her.

We were in agreement about several boys, and really liked two. But of course, we never let on. Suddenly it was nice to be noticed by boys, they were OK. Only once a boy stepped out of line, when he said to his friend he liked my blouse with the pretty breast pocket. The boys looked at each other knowingly at the word breast, so we tossed our heads and walked off. They were not worthy of our attention.

All this talking about boys gave us the incentive to find out what happened between men and women, how babies were made. I had not given this much thought until now. In spite of the incident in Pupping with Kini, I had only vague ideas what might be involved. Even the little I knew was enough to convince me the whole matter was too disgusting, to even think about it. I didn't know what 'doing it' meant, only that it involved body parts I had no name for, and that 'it' had to be done, to have babies. At this point, my mind had always shied away – because my mother would never have done anything involving her private body parts. I was convinced of this. Yet the evidence to the contrary was apparent, I myself was the living proof she had done 'it'.

Unable to face this controversy, I had always put this subject firmly to the back of my mind, to resolve it one day in the future.

Perhaps this day had finally come, because with Toni I was able to talk about men and women, and babies. Strangely, this subject did not disgust Toni, she found it funny, bursting into spasms of laughter as we talked. And it was catching. I, too, began laughing and giggling. But the more attention we gave to it all, the more curious we became, and decided to investigate further.

Toni found a thick book on her mother's bookshelf, it was a medical book, and we studied the male and female anatomy, giggling about the drawings and all the strange Latin names written by the different body parts. And although we read the pages thoroughly, and studied the illustrations, we couldn't get the gist of it. We could not understand how this could work in practice. The man's penis had to enter the woman's vagina – by now, we knew what a penis was, we had laughed about its pictures so often and hard, it still hurt. But the vagina remained a mystery. From the drawings we could see its approximate location, and reluctantly we were prepared to admit that perhaps we each had one. But would any reasonable, self-respecting and sane woman allow a man to put the thing he used to pee, into it? Into her own body? Just thinking about it was so disgusting, we decided to drop the whole matter again, and put Frau Toni's book back on the shelf.

But we still enjoyed giggling when we met the boys, perhaps even more, now we knew about their anatomy. And the word penis kept its power to send us into fits of laughter. There was no harm in it, was there?

Better even than boys or swimming in the pond, were the forests. Endless stretches of wood, not as hilly and steep as in Pupping, but almost flat, with clearings where the sun shone through and ferns grew thickly. We picked mushrooms – we knew several varieties – and Frau Toni was glad to cook them. When the bilberries ripened, she gave us two small hand rakes. We just had to pull the rakes through the small bushes and drop the berries into the baskets. We ate what we could. Frau Toni made jam, and we sold the rest to the village grocer. I had more money than ever.

But the highlight of the holiday came when we went to a Kirtag, a village-fete – a big attraction, with games to play, and stalls with many things to buy or to do, especially as we had money. The fete was held only a few kilometers away – a walk through the wood, no longer than we walked most days. But this village was on the other side of the border, in Germany, a foreign country. Neither Toni nor I had a passport. So we could not go to the fete. But this only increased its attraction.

It was Toni's idea, but I became a willing accomplice. She said the border was just a line on the map, going right through the woods. There were no fences or walls. Toni, like all the locals, knew the woods well, and also knew where the border was, and where the guards patrolled. But how frequent the patrols were, and at what times, she had no idea.

We'd have to be very careful, not to be seen. Yes, it would be a splendid adventure.

To my surprise, Toni told her mother about our plan, and to my even bigger surprise, Frau Toni didn't object, but wished us good luck, told us to enjoy ourselves, and to be careful. Then she gave us money, and with our earnings from the berries, we had more than enough for the Kirtag. We hid the money in our socks, in case the border police caught us. It might be a crime to take money into another country, and we'd be in more trouble, if we were caught.

Our illegal crossing into Germany was really just a walk through the forest. Toni knew the way and I just went along. I could see no sign of a border, or that we had crossed it. But we must have done, because as we came out of the wood, our path widened into a dirt track, then into a road, and I could see the first houses of a village. Ahead of us, on the side of the road, stood a wooden watchtower.

And a man in uniform, obviously from the border police, was walking towards us.

I looked at Toni. "Shall we run?" I asked, but my friend shook her head. I knew she was thinking, the man was too close, he would know something was wrong if we ran, and would chase us. We had to brave it out, talk our way out, to avoid the punishment. The man stopped in front of us. "Hello girls," he said, smiling at us, but I knew our situation was serious, because he took his little black book from his pocket, and a pencil. "Where are you from and what are your names?" he asked.

We told him the truth, lying could make things only worse, and we didn't want to get into more trouble than we were in already – and apart from this, we both liked the man. He was friendly and nice, and so we admitted intending to go to the fete.

He wrote it all down, his face very stern. Then he put the book into his pocket, looked at us and smiled broadly.

"Don't look up to the watchtower, girls, "he said, "or my boss might guess what I tell you. He is watching us, so I have to send you back, or I'll be in trouble. You just turn round and walk back the way you came, until I am so far away you can't see me." He winked with one eye, as he added: "Then you can turn around and walk back to the village. Enjoy the fete and have a really nice time."

Furtively, I looked at the watchtower. The border guard followed my worried gaze, he knew my concerns.

"My boss is up there on his own," he explained. "He can't leave his post, it's not allowed, rules and regulations, you know. But he will whistle. As long as you ignore him and his whistling – don't look up and take no notice – you'll be all right. So long, girls."

He gave us another smile, and a salute, and before we had time to thank him, he had turned and was walking away.

What a kind, lovely man, Toni and I agreed, and we did exactly as he had said. The border guard up the tower whistled furiously, but we took no notice, and the people on the road didn't either.

At the fete we bought candy floss, and many raffle tickets, hoping for a big win, but it wasn't to be. We shot with rifles – the man in the booth showed us how – and won paper roses in different colors. We had a lovely time, and it was already evening when our money was spent and we went home through the woods the same way we came. Toni and I were still full of excitement, and proud about crossing the border illegally – a real adventure.

The weeks went by very quickly, and were so wonderful, I didn't want to leave when Lilly and Tante Paula came to take me back to Vienna. But I had no choice, my holiday was over.

At home, it was even harder than before to accept my life as it was. When I was away, whether in Pupping or anywhere else, people were consistent. I knew what to expect. At home it was so different. I could never be sure how Mama would react at any given moment. It was always wise to expect the worst, so I wouldn't be lulled into a false sense of security. Willi and Mama could be nice, but turn quite suddenly.

It was, as if I stood in a meadow, where many dangerous bombs and mines had been buried, waiting to explode. A wrong step, even the vibration of a word, could cause an explosion, because the mines were very sensitive. So I tried not to move and stood still. But this didn't help – it was just another trap. It was always a mistake to believe if I didn't move, I'd be safe. Some of the mines lay buried so deep, they didn't explode straight away, but after a while. And sometimes the explosion was not caused by me. It could be something Willi said, often I didn't know what had caused it, but the blast was always directed at me.

But the meadow could be so beautiful, sometimes the sun shone, and bright flowers opened their petals, inviting me to admire, enjoy being here. I'd forget the mines, begin to relax, and turn my face to the sun. It was always a mistake, a trap I fell into, again and again. The explosion would come, and if it came suddenly when I wasn't prepared, it was worse.

Not only my mother, my brother also had different faces, and could change without any reason that I could perceive. But his changes were not as extreme as my mother's.

At times, my brother could be nice to me. Highly intelligent, well read and able to talk about anything, he'd bring his point of view over well in any discussion. It could be a pleasure talking with him, even if he mostly talked about himself. He knew what he lacked, what he needed and why, and he would have liked to do something about it. He even knew what he should do, because we discussed this subject at length. But he couldn't put theory into practice, he could not change, be joyful and free and really alive.

He was so deeply unhappy, and when we went for a walk, he opened up and said he would have liked to have friends, go around with young people his own age, meet girls. He wanted to do all the things other young people did, swimming and sport and dating. But when he was small Mama had not allowed it, and in obeying her rules they became his own. Now he was older and would have been able to go against Mama's orders, but her teaching was so ingrained in him, like his own shadow, he couldn't escape it.

I felt so sorry, but couldn't help him. His only pleasure was accumulating money, but he didn't want to spend any, wouldn't even go to the pictures, if he had to pay. Once he said to me: "sister" – he often called me sister, when we talked seriously. "Sister, if you can find me something that gives me more pleasure than the money it costs, I'll spend it willingly."

All my suggestions were in vain, because my brother needed a friend for support to start something new. I felt so sorry for him, until he turned on me for no reason, and the other Willi was back, who would tease and torment me mercilessly, just to relieve his boredom, and to forget his frustration and pain.

Mama was not just two persons, but had several personalities, and I never knew what to expect. I had to be on my guard at all times. But because sometimes she could be so nice, I would forget, and we'd spend a few pleasant hours together.

As it was on this mild autumn evening soon after I came back from Toni, when Mama and I went for a walk. We strolled along the Guertel – the belt – a wide street, winding its way around the inner districts of the city, with trees and small parks dividing the traffic. It was still pleasantly warm, and we sat down on a bench, admiring the beautiful flower beds full of asters, dahlias, and tiny white flowers sprinkled between.

It was getting dark, and down the street, the Westbahnhof, which had been rebuilt since the war, shone with hundreds of neon-lights. Opposite us was the inn, where we had stood in long queues for a cup of thin soup. It all looked so different now, as if Vienna had never been in a war. Prosperous, elegant, though it was only six or seven years since we had been bombed into oblivion.

The city lights shone through the dusk, advertising in bright colours things I only knew vaguely about, like vodka or gin, and different nightclubs.

It was nice sitting with Mama in silence. I remembered when I was small, and sure of her love. I would have liked to know if she still loved me, but couldn't ask. I wanted to put my arm around her, or at least touch her hand. I knew she had suffered so much, and this was the reason she was often so mean to me. If I touched her hand, would she put an arm around me? I still tried to pluck up my courage, when Mama started to speak, and the moment was lost.

"See the lady over there, Gerti?" She looked straight ahead because pointing was rude, but I knew whom she meant. A young woman stood on the side of the street. She was wearing a dress much too short and too tight, and shoes with very high heels.

"She is not a lady, she is selling herself for money," Mama said.

I was bewildered, what did my mother mean by selling herself – who would buy her, and what for?

"She is selling her body, to men," Mama said.

I finally found my voice. "But why would men buy her?"

"To use her body, however they want, and they pay for it." Mama's voice sounded final.

I was dumbfounded, unable to utter another word. How could anyone sell themselves? It was all one had, when it really came down to it. Selling one's body without selling oneself was impossible, surely.

And what about the men?

So many questions I wanted to ask, and I looked at Mama enquiringly. She didn't look back, her face wore its closed look again, and I didn't dare to keep on. But my questions remained, and stayed in my mind, adding another dimension to what I already knew about 'it,' contributing to my negative opinion about men – though there were quite a few exceptions, I had to admit.

The whole matter disturbed me, but was also of interest. These women must be different – or something special – if they'd sell themselves. My curiosity aroused, I learned to recognize these 'ladies' by their clothes and strong makeup.

Sharing my thoughts with my friends, I found Hilde was interested too, and when we saw one of the special women on the Guertel – they usually stood at the same places – we would go past slowly to get a good look. But a few times we must have gone past too slowly or too close, because we were shouted at, with words I had never heard before.

Then, a few weeks later, just as I was beginning to adapt to being home, my whole life changed again.

Mama came home from church, and told me I could live on a farm where they wanted a girl my age. It would be good for me to live in the country. I'd have to help a bit with the work, but I did this at home, and in Pupping. If I went, it would be better for her and Willi too, because she would be able to manage better with the money.

When Mama talked so reasonable and nice to me, she always got round me, and I'd do what she wanted. She was right, I would enjoy living on a farm. Perhaps it was like being in Pupping, where I helped with the work too.

So everything was arranged, and one day in February I left for the country.

CHAPTER 15

ON THE HILL-FARM 1952

My new home was a hill-farm, high up in the mountains, surrounded by fields and thick endless woods. Only a few farms lay up here.

Herr Kahofer met me at the railway station and we walked nearly an hour up a steep narrow path to get to his farm. There was no road, or a track where mules could have gone. What couldn't be carried, grown, or made, would have to be dropped off by helicopter.

The children of the small farming community took me into their circle, and soon I belonged. We went to school together, on a Sunday to church in the morning, and in the afternoon for a walk in the woods. I had never before been part of a group, and it was wonderful, especially as the boys were so different here than in Pupping. Boys or girls, it made little difference, we all were friends, hardly ever teasing each other, except in a kind, friendly way.

I lived with the Kahofer family. Herr and Frau Kahofer, I was to address them, and it was clear from the beginning, my purpose of being here was to work. My first duty was to look after the children. Christl the oldest, was three, Anna two, and Veronika, the baby, five months old. If I wasn't in school, I had to care for the children, or do housework, and sometimes both at the same time. Except on a Sunday, but even then I was often asked to take Christl with me when I went out with my new friends on our afternoon walk.

The three cows were another one of my responsibilities. Each afternoon I had to take them out to graze for a few hours. Leading the animals out of the shed was easy enough, because they wanted to go. But getting them to where they should go was a totally different matter, especially if the grazing site was changed.

Each one of these four-legged beasts had a strong will of their own, and knew where the clover fields were. Without any reason that I could perceive, suddenly the cows would break into a gallop, ignoring me and my stick. To stop a galloping cow was impossible for me, especially if she was accompanied by her galloping sisters. There is nothing to hang on to, except the horns and the tail. I was soon to discover that either one didn't work, though for different reasons.

Herr Kahofer instructed me to get ahead of the cows, and stop them with the stick, tapping their noses. But I was never before their noses. When they started to run, I was behind, and couldn't overtake them. I had never known cows could run so fast. If they all galloped the same way, I could at least follow, and eventually persuade them to turn and come back. But if they ran in different directions, I had to make a choice which cow to follow, and where to look for her companions later without losing my cow again.

But even if I had to search in vain for a long time, eventually I always found my charges again, often in the clover field. It took all my ingenuity and persistence to convince the three determined beasts to leave a field of clover – they loved clover. But I had been instructed not to let the cows eat too much of their favorite food, because it made them very ill. But their minds were stronger than mine, as were their bodies, and I was just a child of eleven, not used to this job.

But as I liked cows and was sure they also liked me, eventually we got used to each other's ways, and my task became easier.

And once we arrived at our destination, perhaps a meadow, or a clearing in the wood, I began to enjoy myself. The cows would be munching at the new grass and the juicy spring plants, and I could relax. It was quiet and peaceful. I'd admire the violets and primroses, later the cowslips. Birds were building their nests, squirrels and rabbits came out if I sat still long enough, and a deer could emerge from the forest. I heard the first calls of the cuckoo, and as the strawberries ripened I'd feast on the juicy red berries.

Getting used to my task, I'd bring a book with me, giving the cows an occasional glance as I read. But I lost them a few times in this way. When I looked up, and realized my charges had disappeared into the wood, I panicked, frightened to death of Herr Kahofer. What would he say if I returned without his cows? Would I even dare to return without them?

But I always found my charges again, usually happily munching in one of the clover fields.

Just as I was becoming accomplished, keeping the cows in my view whilst reading my book, and my task became even enjoyable, I had to take Christl with me. A lively three-year-old can be as difficult as three cows. The whole thing combined was a stressful job, sometimes a nightmare, especially if the cows ran away, or when the child got tired and I had to carry her, and the cows smelled the clover and started to run.

If I wasn't at school or minding the cows, I had to look after all three children. I found this a heavy responsibility, especially when their parents worked in the fields and I needed help. Keeping Christl amused, whilst watching a toddler, feeding and changing a baby, was too much for me, especially as Frau Kahofer wanted me to take them outside on the lawn. Nothing was fenced in, and the toddler tended to wander off. If the baby needed attention as well, I didn't know how to cope.

I tried to discuss my problems with Frau Kahofer, but she said she was very happy with me, and to carry on as I did. But this didn't help me, because I worried, something could happen to Anna when I was busy with the baby, and couldn't watch her.

What could I do? Should I write to Mama and ask to come home? It was no better at home, my problems were just different. At least the woods surrounded me here. And as Frau Kahofer said I was doing my chores to her full satisfaction, I decided to stay and carry on as best as I could.

As I also had to help in the kitchen, I had no time at all for myself during the week. Once I had put the children to bed and the kitchen was tidy, it was late, and I was glad to go to bed. I slept in a small storeroom, sharing the space with all sorts of food, onions, garlic, apples, and a few small barrels of porkfat. A mouse came visiting me, on times even several, trying to get to the fat. But in spite of the mice and the noises they made scrabbling on the barrels, I fell into an exhausted sleep as soon as my head hit the pillow. Frau Kahofer woke me in the morning to go to school, where I could recover and relax.

For the first time in my life I liked school, it was easier than working, and I loved the long walk through the woods. Arriving in the village, I had to go shopping for Frau Kahofer. She usually needed something, sugar or flour or salt. But at least once I had been to the shop, the time was my own – apart from sitting in a classroom to do some work, but I didn't really consider this aspect of school life very much, and just let my mind drift as I relaxed.

The small village school was totally different than my school in Vienna, we only had a few class-rooms here. I was in the last class, shared by children aged between eleven to fourteen, right side the boys, the girls on the left, the youngest in front, and the oldest at the back.

Though we had a different syllabus, I managed quite well, and the walk to and from school, which I shared with my new friends, was brilliant. We talked, and we laughed, and made plans where to go next Sunday.

In the morning was church. We all went down to the village together, and no one cared that I never went to confession or Holy Communion. Afterwards came lunch, and although I had to help and wash up, the whole afternoon was mine, to do as I liked. But if Christl realized I was leaving, she wanted to come, and her mother would say: "You don't mind taking her, Gerti, you are so good with her, she likes you so much. She won't be any trouble."

What else could I do but to take her?

The woods were very beautiful, often too dense to walk through, but the children knew where even the smallest path led. We found sun-dappled clearings, covered in white with the blossoms of lily-of-the-valley, and I could smell their glorious perfume long before reaching the clearing.

Our favorite walk led to a ruined castle, where we could look way down to the village. The Turks had been stopped here and driven back, after they invaded Vienna.

Looking down to the tiny houses in the village below, and the toy cars on the narrow road, we imagined what it would have been like in the days of the siege: the fierce Turks in their turbans and outlandish clothes, brandishing their crooked sabers, their bright colored tents, and the hustle and bustle of camp life.

We were the knights, defending our homeland.

"Death to the invaders," we shouted as we prepared to pour boiling oil down the rocks, to stop the attackers. We always succeeded, the invaders were stopped, driven back, to retreat and go back to their own country, where they belonged. Victory was ours.

I enjoyed our battles, in spite of keeping an eye on Christl, so she wouldn't fall down the rock face. But the other children would help. And on the way home, when Christl got too tired to walk, one of the older boys carried her, usually Hansi. Almost sixteen, he was the oldest in our group, and already worked at his father's farm which would one day be his. He was good looking, tall, with broad shoulders and narrow hips, almost a man. Even his voice was no longer a child's. His skin was tanned from working outside in the sun, in contrast with his blond sun-bleached hair. When the wind played with it – or Christl, as she sat on his shoulders – he would fling his hair back with a move I found especially sweet. Hansi would walk by my side, and we talked. Soon our names were linked, it was always Hansi and Gerti, or the other way round, and the children acted as if he was my boyfriend.

I didn't mind, because I liked Hansi. He was everything I liked in a boy – strong and a leader, but kind, always patient with Christl – and so handsome. He was intelligent and interesting – I could talk about anything with him, he had read the same books as I, even more. Karl Mai and *Tom Sawyer*, but also serious stuff like Dostoevsky and Maxim Gorky, my favorites at the time.

He began to visit me when I minded the cows, brought me books to read, even Goethe's *Faust*, which I really enjoyed, and on his next visit we discussed living in the moment and what it meant to us, and we tried solving the witches' timetable.

Hansi always knew where to find me and just turned up. He'd offer me a cigarette and I'd smoke, rolling my tongue, to blow smoke-rings in the air as he had taught me. I felt I was growing up. Although not yet twelve, I looked older, and my figure was changing.

I was beginning to imagine a future with Hansi. Gertrude Steiner – I liked the sound: Frau Steiner. In a few years I would be sixteen, and we could marry, live on his farm and have two, no at least three children. My thoughts always came to a halt at this point, because of the way children were made, which filled me with ambivalent feelings, disgust still dominating. Could I ever bring myself to do something horrible like that? But I knew that at some time in the future I would want children. But no need to think about this just yet.

It was a warm, sunny afternoon, when I took out the cows. Christl was in the field with her father, so I got away on my own. Our destination was a clearing in the forest, a magical place. A tiny stream meandered downhill, surrounded by flowers and hazelnut bushes. Large boulders lay in the stream here and there, causing the water to ripple and make its own music. I settled close to the stream, watching a dragonfly perched on a large leaf overhanging the water.

I didn't hear his approach, suddenly Hansi stood behind me, and as I turned my head he looked down into my eyes. We smiled at each other, and he sat down beside me. It was as it always had been, yet there was a difference. I felt his presence much more – as if our bodies were touching, though there was space between us. But this space was not empty, it was filled with a tingling, a feeling of excitement – I was feeling so alive. My head turned on its own accord and our eyes met, and these feelings grew stronger – this strange wonderful magic. So I looked quickly away, down to the water.

Hansi looked away, too. I pointed out the dragonfly, swinging over the water on her long-stemmed leaf, then a squirrel darted up a tree – and everything was again as it always had been, except for a new awareness. We talked about his farm, and the work he did. Then I told him about Vienna, the first time I spoke about my personal life. I didn't tell him much, I was not in the habit of talking about Mama and home, and I didn't want Hansi to feel sorry for me.

Only too soon it was time to go. The path through the wood was so narrow, the cows had to walk one behind the other, I followed, with Hansi behind me. It was pleasantly cool, the bright sunlight diffused by the leaves of the bushes and trees, forming shadow-patterns on the path, moving and changing, as a mild breeze ruffled the leaves, and letting a sunbeam break through.

Suddenly I felt a pull, ever so slight, on the strap of my dirndl-dress, and as I turned to look back, Hansi was so close to me, our bodies almost touched. I looked into his eyes and time seemed to stand still. Then I felt his lips touch my cheek – light as a butterfly-wing.

It was just a brief kiss, but I froze. A man had kissed me. I was so shocked – so absolutely furious, that I hit him across the face, as pictures of painted women selling themselves, flashed through my mind. And I remembered whispers in school – and Pupping and Kini.

"Do you think I am one of those?" I hissed at him. I was so angry, I couldn't find the right words.

When I was married I'd let a man kiss me – perhaps even a week before – but – certainly not just like that, and without asking me.

Hansi looked bewildered, obviously I had surprised him with my attack. "I did not mean anything," he said. "I'm sorry, Gerti."

That made it worse. He had not meant anything indeed. He had kissed me and not meant anything. What did he think of me? Furiously I turned round, away from him, and stormed after the cows, leaving Hansi standing there.

Things were never the same. Hansi came to see me a few more times and tried to talk it over with me, promising it would never happen again. But I was too indignant. What was there to talk over? He had treated me as a woman of low morals. There could be no excuse. And I would make sure it could never happen again, by keeping my distance.

I tried to forget the incident, because I really liked Hansi. But it just did not work. There was something invisible between us now, which kept us apart. His visits dwindled away. We still talked when we were together in a group, but soon he didn't come to our Sunday walks, and rumors had it he was courting a sixteen-year-old girl from the village.

I put all thoughts of Hansi out of my mind, and had to do so again and again, because I missed him so much. And knowing I had done the right thing didn't help me at all.

Now when I was minding the cows, I felt sort of lonely. It was a strange feeling I never had before. In Vienna, I was always glad to be alone.

After suffering in this way for a few weeks, I decided to do something to divert my mind, but couldn't find anything suitable – until it came to me: I would ride a cow.

Riding a horse would have been better. I had loved horses as long as I could remember. My school books were full of horse-drawings – even where they shouldn't have been – but paper for drawing was scarce.

I longed to ride a horse – my Red Indian chief rode fast as the wind that rippled the long grass of the prairie – and I could only join him in my dreams. Perhaps I could bring this dream into everyday reality – it didn't have to be the prairie, a meadow was suitable too. The grass wasn't long, there were no horses, but three cows were available, hopefully, they wouldn't prove too unwilling. Perhaps with some training one of the beasts might make a suitable riding-cow.

First I had to get on the back of a cow. Holding on to the horns of my chosen one, I tried swinging myself up on her back. All my attempts failed, as the animal took fright and started to run. And though I held on to the horns, I couldn't swing myself up to a sitting position, but was hanging on the side of the poor frightened creature.

Trying to ride the other cows ended in similar ways. Hanging on to the horns of a galloping cow took all my strength, and eventually I had to let go and fall back to earth.

To make matters worse, the cows got suspicious, moving away if I approached. This task required more cunning.

Settling down to think, I observed the cows. They soon settled too, munching the juicy fresh grass, occasionally looking up, to give me a look full of suspicion. But when I sat quite still they began to relax, grazing as usual.

There must be a way to get on the back of a cow. Perhaps if I had something to use as a mount. I looked around. Several trees had been cut at the edge of the clearing, and their stumps still remained. I only had to wait until one of the four-legged creatures munched its way towards one of the tree stumps.

I had to wait quite a while, so I started singing softly to lull the suspicious beasts into a sense of security. Eventually a cow munched her way towards one of the stumps. Moving unhurriedly, I got nearer, talking softly, and when I was close enough, I stroked and scratched the cow between her horns. She looked up at me trustingly.

The right moment had come.

I stepped on the stump, grabbed her horns and jumped on her back. I never quite made it to a sitting position, because the cow started galloping and jumping straight away. But I was determined to hang on, and my hold on her horns remained firm. I was lying on my stomach on the back of a galloping cow, unable to sit up, because she jumped and bucked and twisted to shake me off.

But I would show her, this cow would soon know who was the master, and let me ride her.

This assumption proved wrong.

When the cow realized she could not throw me off by bucking and galloping, she too reverted to cunning, and began to slow down.

'She is realizing who is the boss,' I thought, 'now comes my chance.' I was ready to pull myself up, just as the animal reached the tree of her choice and started to rub her back against its trunk. I would have been ground against the tree, had I not jumped off.

I was defeated. This cow was the winner in our game, and I gave up trying to ride cows.

But at least my equestrian attempts had taken my mind off Hansi for a while, and gradually I stopped expecting to see him.

The weeks went by, and I really did not see him again.

Everything else went its usual way for a few weeks, until one morning Herr Kahofer said, because I had been so good at my jobs, and so helpful with the children, I could visit Mama for a weekend, and invite her and my brother for a holiday.

Next Saturday morning I was ready. Herr Kahofer gave me money for the train fare, and Frau Kahofer filled a basket with eggs, ham and vegetables, apples and cherries and apricots. I ran through the woods, arrived at the train-station, and three hours later I knocked at our door.

Mama was pleased I had come, and she praised me. I basked in her approval, but felt a stranger at home, although even Willi was nice to me and wanted to know all about the farm and the woods, and to my surprise he decided to come to the farm, and Mama said she'd come too.

I worried about Mama. Would she control herself when she visited me, or shout and nag, talking to herself in her usual way when she was stressed? But she was always better away from home, perhaps it would be OK. But could she manage for days, even weeks? And how could she walk uphill for so long?

But in spite of my worries, I could hardly wait for their arrival.

Finally, they stepped off the train. The long uphill walk through the wood was too much for Mama, and we had to stop frequently so she could rest, but she made it and eventually we arrived at the farmhouse. It will be all right, I reassured myself. Mama rarely made a scene in front of other people.

During the first few days all went well. It was July and the school holidays had begun. Frau Kahofer gave me less work since Mama was here, and I had time to show her and Willi around. Mama came twice for a walk in the wood, but usually settled in a chair in the garden, enjoying the sunshine. She helped with the cooking and occasionally cooked the whole meal, to give Frau Kahofer a break. In the beginning Herr Kahofer tried to interest Willi in farm work, but gave up after my brother messed up a few jobs and showed no interest. Even the children left him in peace when he ignored them completely.

But Willi liked coming when I minded the cows, and he enjoyed a walk through the forest, picking wild mushrooms and raspberries. We got on well here on the farm, it was nice having my brother around, we talked and we sang, and composed a few poems – Willi was good at making up rhymes. All went well, until we wrote a long ballad about the Kahofer family and my life here on the farm.

We described Frau Kahofer as big and mighty, the cows and the pigs and her husband as thin, and my life on the farm as much work and no play. But it was just a bit of fun, so we thought.

Frau Kahofer thought differently when she found the poem in my apron pocket. She was absolutely furious as she confronted me, and said she'd have a serious talk about me with her husband.

I was convinced I'd have to leave, but didn't really mind. I had to work like a servant – an unpaid servant, with no regular time off. At home different problems would wait for me – I didn't even want to think about those.

But no more was said about the poem – it was clear they wanted me to remain. It looked as if I would stay and grow up here, until Mama decided otherwise.

She had watched me closely since she arrived – as always, nothing much escaped my mother. She asked about my work, how my time was spent when there was school, and did I work less when she was not here, or even more? Mama was nice, she was concerned about me, and I answered more or less truthfully. Although she said no more at the time, I knew she was not happy about all the work I did. Perhaps she would still have left me here, had not something happened she could not accept.

As on most evenings, I prepared the vegetables for dinner whilst keeping an eye on the children. Christl wanted to help, and with her hands in the sink, she got wet and wiped her hands on my apron. This was too much for Mama, it was the last straw.

"No one wipes their hands on my daughter," she said to Frau Kahofer. "The child must have learned this behavior from her parents, as well as her attitude towards Gerti."

Then she told Herr and Frau Kahofer thoroughly off. In very precise words, sounding well-spoken and even reasonable, she gave her opinion. She said it was wrong, possibly criminal, and certainly against the law, giving an eleven-year-old child not only so much work to do, but also the responsibility to look after three young children, one of them still a baby. She would not allow her daughter to be used in this way.

Frau Kahofer tried to calm Mama down, and Herr Kahofer attempted to reason with her. But Mama wouldn't even listen. She told me to pack, and we left the next morning.

"You can go to Pupping for the rest of the summer, Gerti," was all she said during the train journey home. Then she was silent until we left the train in Vienna.

A week later I was in Pupping. Although on the surface everything looked the same, much had changed during the two years I had been away. Foster-mother appeared no different, but she didn't work such long hours anymore, because of her heart. Mirzl's goiter had been removed and she had a big scar on her throat. Mariandl was still my best friend and we were inseparable when she was here, but often she stayed with relatives in Aschach for days at a time, and I missed her.

Everyone treated me as they always had done. Perhaps the biggest change was in me. I felt different about my foster-family. Something was missing, and likely it was the trust I had always felt in the whole family.

Although I tried, and pretended everything was as it had been, I couldn't change how I felt. In spite of telling myself it had been Kini's fault, I felt betrayed by the people I had trusted most in this world. Knowing my foster-family thought I had 'done it' with Kini, still hurt, made me more self-conscious, uneasy and embarrassed, especially as the whole village knew about the incident too, and people might still remember.

In spite of this problem I had a few nice weeks. I helped every day in the fields, and the work was hard, but I had no serious responsibilities, as I had on the hill-farm. My working hours ended much earlier, I was free to go for a swim, or a walk in the woods. And I still went visiting with foster-father, and joined him as he was checking the progress of the various crops.

But he was no longer my hero. I still loved him, but I knew what he thought of me, and it still hurt.

CHAPTER 16

GROWING UP 13–14
VIENNA 1953–54

It was already October when I returned to Vienna, and this time it was not so easy to fit in at school. I'd been away far too long. In the small country school the content of teaching had been different, and now I had missed a whole month of the new school-year as well. But with the help of my friends I soon settled in, and a little cheating helped, to do reasonably well.

Our new German teacher, Frau Huber, assessed our grades by a test essay she gave every month. 'Describe a country,' was the first essay-title, and so we could do some research, Frau Huber gave us the title the previous day.

I had never been more than average in German, and worried how I'd manage, having been away from my class for so long. My brother was in a good mood this evening, and when I told him about the essay, he suggested writing about Egypt. He talked with so much enthusiasm about Egyptian mythology, the Pharaohs and their burial chambers, and the mystery surrounding the Pyramids even to this day, we got quite carried away. Without any prompting, he dictated a beautiful essay. I just had to copy it next day in class.

"Did you write this?" my teacher asked a few days later when she returned our papers, looking piercingly over her glasses at me.

"Yes," I said, nodding. What else could I say? But I was certain to be found out straight away, because Hilde was pushing her elbow into my ribs, and she was smirking. Frau Huber could not possibly miss it, especially as the girl on my other side was grinning and pulling faces.

But our teacher was too thrilled with my essay to notice anything amiss. She said it was brilliant, she was so pleased to have discovered a real talent for writing – and she meant me. I felt so uncomfortable, and wished Willi had just written a good essay, not a brilliant one. Now I was sure to get into trouble.

When the next essay came, I felt sick with nerves. This time I had not been able to prepare for it, and would be found out, especially as Frau Huber had already said how much she was looking forward to seeing my work. Cheating was impossible; there was no help from anywhere.

Just before we had to start writing, our teacher chalked the essay title on the blackboard in capital letters: 'If my school desk could talk'.

Somehow I had to produce a good essay. Was it even possible? Could I do it? Probably not, but at least I could try, the sensible Gerti reasoned.

'You will be found out,' another part of me answered. 'You are not brilliant like Willi.'

But I might as well go down with a bang than a whimper, the real Gerti decided. I would write what I thought, what I felt. At least I'd enjoy writing. The title was promising and open to interpretation.

So I projected my everyday feelings of boredom and frustration into my desk and gave it a voice. And because Frau Huber not only taught German but Geography too, I would write how I felt about this subject. Just hearing about other countries made me long to travel, to explore – and I was stuck in the Pelzgasse, forever it seemed. It was better, to just switch off, and think of something else – besides, the way Frau Huber was teaching, bored me.

So with all my feelings of frustration in the front of my mind, I started to write: 'And Kiel developed into a capital city,' the voice droned on, lulling me into sleep – why should I be interested in Kiel? My thoughts drifted, until suddenly I heard a rumbling and creaking – it came from my desk – and to my utter surprise it began talking. It was bored too, it said, stuck in this room with so many children, having to listen, never allowed to talk back. My desk craved change and excitement.

Entering the realms of imagination, my desk and I created a new and different world – a world of magic and adventure, where children's ideas and wishes had equal status and value to those of adults.

Now I had a beginning, I could let my fantasy go full steam ahead.

Receiving the corrected paper, I expected not only to be exposed as a liar and cheat, but also to be told off for my cheek, writing about Frau Huber's voice and finding her lessons boring. But to my surprise, our teacher just marked my paper as very good, without any remarks.

It seemed not only my brother had talent for writing, but I was talented too, and could produce a good essay if I was pushed into a corner, and was desperate. Now I knew I could do it, writing was suddenly easy, and I remained top of my class.

Once again the benefits of cheating had proven themselves. I also realized the difference expectations made. If my teacher had not expected a brilliant essay of me, I would have written an average one, as I had done for years.

Something else changed for the better in school: I began taking part in physical exercise. I had enough of sitting on the bench watching. So I didn't give the doctor's exemption-certificate to my teacher.

It was so simple – I should have tried it years ago. No one found out. I wore my under-vest, Hilde lent me her second pair of shorts, and I went in bare feet, as a few other girls did too. Initially I was bottom of my class, but as I persevered, I improved to average, except in ball games, where I became really good, especially in catching.

Mama never found out, neither did our doctor – and it made no difference to my chest pains, one way or another.

At home, I slowly turned into a difficult adolescent. My real life began with my friends: in their homes I was always welcome, and remained helpful, pleasant and polite. The parents of Hilde and Helga encouraged them to invite me, I was held up as an example, of a nice, well-brought-up girl. We giggled about it – my friends knew enough about Mama and my upbringing to see the joke – but it was nice that their parents liked me, and useful, because I could always visit my friends.

Mama was not so easily pleased – she disliked all my friends on principle. I should not have friends; they would just use me, and were unnecessary. Mama and Willi managed quite well without friends, why should I need any?

I never invited anyone home, because I was so ashamed of my background. Our flat was dingy and small and there was no privacy to talk.

But unable to prevent me from having friends, Mama insisted on meeting them. Whenever possible, they had to come and collect me. Mama made it as embarrassing as she could, asking lots of questions to delay our departure, giving me chores like the like washing up to do, before we could leave – but at least my friends helped me.

My relationship with my brother did not change for the better, if anything, it got worse. Whatever he knew, he would unexpectedly use against me, so I didn't say much at home. But the less I told Willi, the more he tried to find out, in any way possible. Nothing was safe from him. He went through my belongings if I wasn't here to prevent him. And he still tried to provoke me, just to relieve his boredom.

One day, a fresh wind blew into our lives: Christl came home. It was lovely to see her. She talked about her life in England – she had lived in a town with small one-storey houses lining the street. My sister had lodged with a family, and had a large bedroom just for herself. There was a garden in the back she could sit in –and a bathroom. I could not imagine such luxury.

She had worked in a cotton mill, a dusty job, she said. Dust had been everywhere. It was very damp, but not cold in the winter, and people ate spaghetti, which came out of a tin.

A new, strange way of life opened up as I listened. My sister considered returning to England, this time permanently, because she had fallen in love with a young Ukrainian man, Stephan Kelner, and he wanted to marry her.

"Shall I get married, Mama?" she asked.

"If you want to marry him, Christl," our mother just said, "then marry him."

She didn't even ask much about Stefan.

For me all this happened too quickly. I had so many questions. What was Stefan like? How old was he? But Mama and Willi didn't seem to care. And instead of answering my questions, my sister just said I was too young to understand about love.

Within a few days Christl decided she would get married and go back to England – but I thought our life in the Pelzgasse was also a reason. Two days prior to leaving, she asked me: "would you like to come with me, when I visit our father?"

Her question hit me like a flash of lightning out of a blue cloudless sky. I had no idea Christl had contact with Papa – that it was even possible to see him.

My father had always seemed this huge, nebulous monster, an impression derived from Mama's 'talks.'

And it was true that he didn't care about us, as Mama had said. He had never increased our alimony in spite of high inflation, and never been to see how we lived.

But what if all my assumptions were not quite right?

Of course I wanted to see him – to see for myself what he was like. But first I had to promise my sister to keep this visit a secret from everyone, whatever happened, especially from Mama.

For the last two or three years, I had thought more and more about my father. I only really knew about him from Mama, and as the years went by, I had begun questioning her words. There must be another side to Papa, he could not be the unfeeling monster, or she wouldn't have married him.

I wanted a father so badly – I needed my own father. When I was small, I had pushed every thought about him away. But that had changed. I thought about him when things were bad – and they were so often very bad.

"Just like your father," Mama would say disapprovingly if I showed an interest in something, just ordinary things like mountains, or sport, art, or psychology. To her, anything more than the daily routine which included church and prayer, was not only unnecessary, but wrong, and possibly dangerous or even sinful.

"Just like your father," expressed total condemnation.

'Why shouldn't I be like my father?' I'd ask in my mind. I couldn't say these words aloud, or I'd make things worse with my cheek, and Mama might slap me. Only in my mind could I talk back.

'It's only natural that I am like my father. It's your fault Mama, your own, you chose him. How can you blame me if I am like him?'

It was so unjust, so hurtful to blame me, when she had chosen him in the first place. I would never say these words to my children, except when I praised them.

If Papa was really this bad, why had she married him?

When I was deeply unhappy and had no one to talk to, I thought perhaps my father would understand. I wanted to know what he looked like, what he thought. I wanted to know him.

And now Christl had asked, did I want to meet him?

Of course I did.

We took the tram to the second district, walked down the street, and on the next corner was Papa's workshop. Christl opened the door and went in without knocking, as if she had the right to walk in and out as she pleased. I followed more slowly, apprehensive, not knowing what to expect.

We stood in a huge workroom. Several men were busy working on pieces of furniture, and a strong smell of wood-glue was in the air, coming from a black stove, where a strange brown mass bubbled in a pan. Suddenly an enormous black cat jumped on to the work bench where I stood, its yellow eyes staring unblinkingly at me.

One of the men looked up from his work. "Meister," he called.

It was strange to hear my father addressed as master. But I couldn't think about it for long, I was too worried. Would Papa be glad to see me? Would he talk to me? And if he did want to see me, why had I never met him before? Surely he could have found a way. Probably he didn't care one way or the other – I must not expect anything, so I wouldn't be hurt.

But at least I was meeting him, find out what he was like.

The door next to the stove opened, and my father walked through. He looked like an ordinary man, quite normal, not outstanding in any way. Not tall, just average, and slim. Not old and not young. Thick brown hair, streaked with gray at the temple; a high forehead, unusual gray-blue eyes, strangely in contrast with his tanned skin. The nose was straight, slightly big.

He is nice, I thought with surprise, and then I wondered why it surprised me so much. Had I really expected a monster?

"Hallo, Gerti," he said. I shook hands with my father and he spoke to me as if he always had known me. I found this peculiar, because to me he was a stranger. I was tongue-tied, didn't know what to say, so I just answered his questions about school. Then we talked about the cat who was making friends with me now, and as a second cat came and also wanted my attention, I began to relax, having something I could do with my hands. The cats were unusually large, and as I stroked them, they started to purr like two chainsaws.

"They catch the rats," Papa said, smiling faintly, the corners of his lips just lifting, as he added: "At least they chase them away."

He began to cut pieces of meat for the impatient animals, then gave me the task of cutting more meat, and feeding both cats.

As I was occupied in this way, Papa and Christl wandered away, and I couldn't hear what they said. Later, when Christl and I said goodbye, my father gave me his telephone number and a few coins, and asked me to ring him. Perhaps we could meet some time, he suggested.

A few days later I phoned him. I had never before used a phone, and was nervous. But following the instructions written in the booth, I finally heard Papa's voice. He seemed pleased that I called him, and suggested meeting him in the park the next day.

It was strange, being with my father. At first I was apprehensive and shy, but gradually I relaxed as Papa asked what I liked doing, what I thought about this or that, what I read, and about Pupping. No adult had ever wanted to know what I thought, and gradually as I talked and my father listened, my nervousness eased. He really seemed to be interested in my opinions, and as he told me a little about his interests too, we slowly began to know each other.

We met about once a month. I didn't tell Mama, and my father also thought it was better so. We both knew Mama would be furious, and try to prevent our meetings. And I didn't want to cause her more pain, she was hurting so much already. Yet I felt I had the right to see my father, I had a right to both my parents. In theory at least. In reality – my reality – it was impossible. Mama would never allow it, if she knew.

Papa never talked bad about Mama, or asked about her – he never talked about her at all. We both avoided this subject as best we could. And as we always went somewhere – a museum perhaps, or a walk through the inner city – we had plenty to talk about. He told me fascinating stories about the old churches we visited and the magnificent buildings from the Austrian Empire. My father knew who had built them and when, the long process each piece of stained-glass window went through, how it was done and by whom.

Every sculpture, each stone, told a story, and Papa knew so much about it all; he was breathing life into history and art as he talked.

He also told me about the sewers running underneath the city, and how he and his friends had run from one part of Vienna to another; right underneath all the houses and people, just as the rats did.

All the entrances were closed off now, and Papa refused to show me where they were – in case I would find my way into the sewers too, I suspected. He quickly changed to a different topic as he realized my interest, and told me about his travels.

I listened spellbound to my father's adventures in foreign countries – expeditions to Egypt – and to India, with its yogis and fire-walkers and fakirs. I too wanted to visit these places; geography and history were suddenly interesting.

The winter passed, and it was spring when one day, out of the blue, Mama told me she had arranged for me to go to Pupping. I could stay for six months, and go to school there. I was surprised, especially as she gave me no reason at all, and I hadn't noticed any correspondence. Perhaps Mama had found out I had contact with Papa, and wanted to keep us apart. But would she be able to contain her anger if she knew? Yet Mama was unpredictable. It was wise not to ask questions, and as I preferred Pupping to Vienna, I was happy to go.

As always, I enjoyed staying in Pupping. The small school in Eferding was like the country school I had gone to when I lived at the hill-farm. I cycled the four kilometers to school on foster-father's old bike – a feat in itself, because my bike-riding skills were limited, and lorries drove close by. But in spite of the odd wobble, I enjoyed the ride. Mariandl and other children from the area cycled too, but Kini had left school and worked on his father's farm. I never saw him again. But the emotional distance between me and my foster-family remained, although no one ever mentioned anything about Kini.

I never even talked with Mariandl about it. What was the point?

Being older, I worked much harder, almost like the adults, often until seven in the evening. At times, it was backbreaking work in the fields, but afterwards Mariandl and I went for a walk in the woods, or we swam in the river. We were still best friends, and Sundays were still magic. After church, the whole day was ours to spend as we pleased.

It seemed as if I was staying in Pupping for good, until Mama's letter arrived. In September I had to return home, for my last year at school. To have good grades in my last school report was important; it could affect my future.

So once more I settled in Vienna and re-established my friendships. I would have a full year in the same class, as well as the same school, for the first time in my life.

At the beginning of the new school year all went well, I did very little work and managed OK. The pattern seemed set for the remainder of my last year, when suddenly everything changed, because our headmaster decided to test all the children who were leaving that year.

We were given test papers with many questions, and I wrote down the answers as best as could, unaware it was an intelligence test. I was unaware of the problems to come. I had the highest score in our class, only one boy in the whole school had one extra point.

I often wished I'd given wrong answers, because from that day my peace in school vanished. My teachers suddenly took an interest in me, wanted to develop my talents, and were trying to bring out the best in me.

They asked what I wanted to do when I grew up? Would I like to go to college and study? I was in the top stream, and could transfer to a gymnasium. If I took Latin, I could go on to university.

It seemed I could be anything, get any job or profession, if I just put my mind to it.

At first I almost believed what my teachers said. Perhaps there was a way I could study, and develop my talents, as Frau Huber said. I even enjoyed the unaccustomed positive attention for a while. My drawings were looked at with different eyes now. If they were not as tidy as my teacher had always wanted, now it was because I had special talents. I was encouraged to talk about books I had read, and my thoughts and ideas. Suddenly I seemed to have a brilliant future, and nothing could stop me.

My future ended as quickly as it had begun, with Mama's visit to school.

A letter had come from my headmaster, an invitation to discuss my future. My mother was most annoyed, but decided to go, and I went along, because I was invited too.

All the way to school Mama's anger increased. I tried to reassure her, I wasn't in trouble, I just had done well in a test. It made little difference. She was less angry with me now, but more with my teachers, for putting impossible ideas in my head.

And I should know better too, she said.

The meeting was short. Mama didn't even listen to the director. She interrupted his friendly words, and told him I was going to be a tailoress and the matter was closed. She wouldn't even allow Frau Huber to speak, and told her not to put impossible dreams into my mind.

I felt their pitying looks, and knew what they thought. I was so embarrassed. Mama turned to go, taking my hand and pulling me with her. Not another word was spoken. All the way home we walked in silence. And not one word was lost on the subject again.

At school, nothing was spoken about my future either anymore. My teachers said no longer, I could be what I wanted, if I was prepared to work for it. I was aware they felt sorry for me and would have liked to help, but we all knew, even if I did get a grant, without support from home, higher education was impossible.

Mama had made up her mind: I would become a tailoress. There was little point in resisting. I could have tried to get a different apprenticeship, like my brother, but I felt totally defeated. Did it matter? What was the point of it? I couldn't study for a profession I really wanted. Did it matter if I became a tailoress or a hairdresser? I didn't want to be either.

I was only thirteen, and wasn't able to pit myself against my mother. She was persuasive, her reasons made sense. We had high unemployment – but I needn't look far, I could go to Tante Paula, who would be happy to take me, as Lilly was leaving.

The last hope was my father. I phoned him and we met in the park. I told him about the test, that my teachers thought I should go to college – and that I hated sewing and didn't want to be a tailoress.

Papa listened, asked a few questions, and was silent for a while.

"Would you like to live with us?" he suddenly asked.

I couldn't believe it. Papa had never even hinted I could live with him.

"Can I study?" I wanted to know, when I got over my surprise sufficiently to have my voice back.

"Possibly," Papa didn't commit himself, but at least gave me hope.

"I would rent a room for you with a family," he continued, dispelling any idea of me actually sharing his home.

"Our flat is much too small, you need your own room, Gerti," he said, when he saw the disappointment in my eyes.

My own room! I would give anything for my own room. No more interference from Willi, I could have quiet around me, real silence. I would be able to read all by myself, without being disturbed.

The matter was settled.

"Yes, Papa," I smiled at him happily. "I would like to come very much." Everything would be wonderful – I would have a future.

Papa explained I couldn't come straight away, the matter would have to be taken to court. Mama had custody, and would never let me go voluntarily, we both knew that. But he'd speak with his lawyer straight away, as we needed to know where we stood legally. And it could all take a long time. We had to be patient, and wait.

"It will be hard on you, once your mother hears from the court," my father said, concern in his voice. "Will you be able to cope with it, Gerti?"

I nodded. It would be hard for us all, but especially for Mama – she would be so upset. I hated to cause her additional pain. Already I felt guilty. But I wanted to get away from the Pelzgasse so badly – I needed to get away. I felt stifled at home, could never be me, never let my guard down and just relax.

"I want to come," I said again. "No matter what."

Papa insisted I say nothing to Mama for the time being. First, he would talk with a solicitor and find out how to proceed, and what our chances were. The court might refuse my father's request for custody. If this happened, there was nothing he could do. I would have to remain with my mother until I was eighteen. It was better I acted as if I knew nothing until Mama was informed, which could take several months. In the meantime I had to carry on as 'normal'.

So I carried on, but at least I had hope.

In the meantime Mama arranged my life to her satisfaction. When I finished school I could have a holiday in Pupping, then start my apprenticeship with Tante Paula. My aunt needed help in her shop, as Lilly would no longer be with her when she got married.

My big sister would soon be Frau Heller. Her fiancé Karl was nice, a quiet young man, who seemed to take everything in his stride, even Mama and the Pelzgasse. He and Lilly rented a small flat, an hour's tram ride away.

The wedding would be held in Maria Zell, and Willi was invited as a witness. I pushed any thoughts about this injustice away. After all, it was Lilly's big day, she could arrange it as she pleased – and perhaps they had not enough money to pay for Mama and me too. And we'd be at the reception – I looked forward to it very much.

Finally, the big day had come, my sister was married and we celebrated her wedding. I had a really good time at the reception, eating delicious food and drinking wine for the first time. I enjoyed myself, until I looked at Mama. She had drunk a few glasses of wine and was talking and laughing. And as she raised her glass, the man sitting next to her kissed her on the cheek.

I expected my mother to slap his face, but she just laughed.

I was so shocked. My mother had allowed a man to kiss her. Had I not seen it with my own eyes, I would not have believed it.

It brought all my thoughts about men and women and sex to the forefront of my mind once again. What shocked and confused me the most was the thought that my mother must have done 'it'.

But perhaps it was normal – after all, everybody seemed to have done it. Perhaps I was wrong the way I thought about 'it'. And perhaps I had done Hansi an injustice when I hit him, just for a kiss on the cheek – when even my mother had allowed her cheek to be kissed.

I couldn't keep my eyes off Mama. I had never seen her like this before. She was 'normal'– she was like other people. I couldn't get over it. She seemed happy and laughed a lot. Not that it lasted, the next day everything was as it always had been. But it made me think. The subject of men, women and sex was getting more and more complex.

One morning I noticed blood on my clothes, and didn't know what to do. I washed everything as best I could before going to school. What was wrong with me? Was I ill? I hoped whatever it was, would go away as quickly as it had come.

When I came home, Mama said: "Why didn't you say you are having a period, Gerti?"

I had no idea what a period was. I couldn't ask Mama, who clearly thought I should know all about it. She gave me the necessary things, and explained how to use them. She obviously knew what this terrible period was, and didn't seem worried about it. But I had to wait until the next day to get answers in school from my friends. Hilde had no idea either, but Helga was relieved to talk about this curse, which had happened to her some months ago.

She gave me a lot of information, and reluctantly I had to accept, we were women, if I liked it or not. But everything got more complicated, nothing was black and white anymore. Perhaps I had overreacted, hitting Hansi, perhaps kissing was OK after all.

One girl in our class bragged openly and without any shame about some quite peculiar things she was doing with boys – but perhaps she was lying. Why would she do things like that? When I asked her, she said it was fun. I was puzzled, because none of it sounded like fun to me. But perhaps for some girls it was fun, otherwise why would women allow men to touch them, and allow – whatever it was, if it was not pleasant at least some of the time? And now at least I knew, 'it' was really called sex.

Perhaps it was OK to have sex, if you were married and deeply in love.

In novels, I had read about romance and being in love. I read more now. It was always about true love, and the wonders of being in love. But how it was in real life, I still didn't know, and decided to wait and keep an open mind, and collect more evidence, until the matter of sex became clear, one way or another.

A few weeks passed, then Mama came home from the doctor one evening and said Dr Melka wanted to see me. This had never happened before, and with trepidation I set off to visit the doctor on the next afternoon after school.

Dr Melka was an attractive woman, still young looking, although I had known her most of my life. When my turn came, I went into the consulting room, and the doctor got up and came to meet me. We shook hands.

"Sit down, Gerti," she said. "Nothing to worry about, I just wanted to talk with you."

I sat down and waited. What did she want to talk to me about? Now I was seriously worried.

"I thought you are old enough – you are turning into a young lady – I thought in future you could come alone, without your mother."

I nodded and smiled, as our eyes met. Dr Melka knew Mama well, and thought as I did. It would be much better to leave Mama out of my life in every possible way.

"Thank you, Dr Melka," I stood up, ready to go.

"Not so fast," she indicated I should sit back down again. "I really want to talk with you, Gerti. I think you are old enough now, to know and to understand what it means to live with a heart defect."

It was the last thing I wanted to know. The greater part of my life I had attempted to ignore my heart, and live a normal life – at least as far as that was possible in our flat in the Pelzgasse – and with my family.

But Dr Melka would not be deterred from talking to me on this subject.

"Do you still get chest pains?" she asked.

Reluctantly I nodded. "Sometimes."

"I'm afraid you have to accept that your condition is incurable. You have to live with it. But you can still have a good life, Gerti. You can do most things –in moderation. You must not exert yourself."

She put her hand on my arm which was resting on the edge of her desk. Did she realize the word moderation was like a death-blow to me? I didn't want a moderate life – I wanted to live my life fully, go to extremes. I wanted to swim across fast flowing rivers, run and climb mountains. I wanted to make up for everything I had to endure in the Pelzgasse. I wanted a full, an interesting and adventurous life.

"You can walk, but don't run," Dr Melka continued, seemingly unaware of the turmoil within me.

"Swim, but just a width in the pool, perhaps even two, and then rest." She smiled as if everything was all right now, adding kindly: "You really can live a full, happy life, right to a ripe old age Gerti, as long as you take care."

The doctor stood up, to signal the visit was over. "Any further questions Gerti?" she asked.

I shook my head, unable to speak, struggling to hold back my tears. But no one must know how I felt. I contained my pain, held it tightly inside me, as I shook hands with the doctor and walked through the door and through the waiting room, where people looked at me as if they knew.

Then I stood in the corridor, finally alone. I felt as if I had received a blow – I felt stunned, lightheaded, sick to the core. My thoughts went round and round in my head.

I should walk but not run? So I could live to a ripe old age? As if I cared, if I couldn't live my life fully – the life I had planned. So many things I wanted to do, and they all involved physical effort: rock climbing, crossing glaciers, riding horses, exploring jungles in faraway countries.

In my life there could be no moderation. If I really wanted my life to be real, I had to go past myself, past my boundaries – higher and ever higher – further and further. I wanted to learn judo, win championships. I wanted to excel in whatever I did.

Already I had made a small start by taking part in all physical activities at school. I had made huge efforts, and was getting better. And now I should be sensible, do things in moderation. Stay within my limits.

Moderation was not for me – and I would find my own limits. What was the point in living to a ripe old age, if I couldn't be me?

I stood in the corridor for a long, long time, leaning against the window and looking at the peeling wall in front of me, the beige and maroon floor tiles. Each time I heard footsteps, I turned round, to look at the sycamore tree outside in the yard, to hide my tears.

When I finally left the building, I knew what to do.

I would climb mountains, swim rivers, live as I wanted to. Perhaps the time would come soon, when I had to pay for it, and I would die. But I would have to die at some time anyway. And at least for a while I would really have lived. To walk and not run was no life for me.

I pushed everything to do with my heart and other illnesses and obstacles, away from me. I would think no more about it. If I had chest pains, I would either ignore or endure them, as I always had done. My life, my real life, was just beginning.

My school-life was ending, and after my holiday in Pupping, my apprenticeship with Tante Paula would start. It was not what I wanted, but at least I would have more freedom, and a little money, to begin bringing some of my dreams into reality. Perhaps I would be able to live with my father. Then my life would really change, I would be in heaven. But I couldn't rely on it, Papa was still making inquiries, and I had heard nothing.

Our relationship wasn't straight forward. I admired him greatly, was so proud to be his daughter. But we weren't close. I had never been able to open fully up to him. Telling my father about the intelligence test, that I would like to study, and how much I wanted to learn judo, was the nearest I had come to confide in him. But I couldn't open my heart to him and tell him how I really felt.

Perhaps it was because I didn't know his feelings for me. He had never put his arm around my shoulder, or kissed me goodbye. He never showed that I mattered to him. In that respect, he was just like my mother. We were as distant physically, as we were emotionally.

But he must want me, I told myself, otherwise he would not have asked me to live with him. Perhaps our relationship would change once I was away from Mama. Perhaps we could really talk then, perhaps I could even tell him about my heart condition. Although on second thoughts this was a bad idea, because he might stop me from sport. For the time being I would tell no one.

Finally, the day came when I left school. I had good grades in my school-leaving-certificate, but it didn't matter. I would begin my apprenticeship with Tante Paula after my holiday in Pupping.

No one in Pupping had ever asked about my heart, and I didn't tell them now. I doubted if Mama had let them know, because I worked hard and long in the fields. My heart was no worse for it. I always felt better in Pupping.

CHAPTER 17

WORKING
VIENNA 1954

Coming home to Vienna I found our lives changed and to my surprise for the better this time. Mama was working full time. And though her health was still poor, and she had to stay in hospital on occasion, she kept working for Firma Horzizka, who produced first-class ladies' coats. As Mama was only able to do light work, she was allowed to sit in an armchair, and do the necessary hand sewing. But she worked forty-eight hours per week.

Now she was so busy, Mama had less time to focus on me, and our relationship improved. But nothing improved between my brother and me.

Willi was in the last year of his apprenticeship and doing well; he had decided to become a book keeper. A handsome young man, he was always well dressed, wearing the right tie to his shirt. Going to work he wore one of his suits, a hat, and a smart woollen coat in the winter.

He could talk with eloquence about any subject, but still had no friends, and was lonely. And he still took delight in teasing me, perhaps in a more grown up way, but just as hurtful, perhaps even more so. I always had to be on my guard.

At least our financial problems had eased. Mama earned money, Willi contributed, as I did, now I was an apprentice. We were no longer so desperately poor, could afford to eat meat during the week too on occasion, or sausages with our vegetables. And on a Saturday afternoon, Mama would take me to the pictures. Willi never came, he didn't like the romantic love stories Mama and I enjoyed.

Going to the cinema with my mother was wonderful – we were close again. I was careful not to spoil these special occasions through saying the wrong thing, but we didn't need to talk much, except about the film. But when Mama was nice to me I felt very guilty about Papa, though I rarely saw him, and he had said no more about coming to live with him.

But if he was busy, so was I, since I was working.

I worked forty-four hours weekly, but shouldn't have worked at all yet, because I was only thirteen. But in November, at fourteen, my apprenticeship would start officially, and I'd attend college one day every week.

I didn't learn much about making clothes, because Tante Paula still produced the same bags she had done for years. As she got paid for each bag, we had to be fast. But now and again a customer came through the door and ordered a dress, and we put the bags to the side. After long discussions and looking at styles and patterns the customer made a decision and Tante Paula took the measurements. Later she cut the material, pinned and tucked it all together, and proceeded with the machine sewing. The rest was my job, and when the garment was finished, I had to iron it, and deliver it on my way home.

I still hated sewing, and now I had to sew all day long. But at least I got paid. Not much, just thirty-six shillings. I had to give Mama twenty for my keep, but if I didn't take the tram and walked the three kilometers to work, I had sixteen shillings to spend. My most urgent need was for clothes. Tante Paula bought the material and under her supervision I made my first dress, then a skirt and blouse, and later a coat – all in working time. Every week my aunt deducted five shillings for the material from my pay, until I'd paid her back – which never happened, because I always needed something else.

My aunt was kind on the whole, and we talked as we sewed. Never before had I talked so much with an adult, but then I was an adult too now. I heard about Onkel Bert who was stationed in Romania during the war, driving a lorry. Tante Paula had travelled to Bucharest, and lived in an isolated mill, just to see her husband now and again. When Onkel Bert was killed, Tante Paula came back to Vienna again, but she was glad she spent what time they had left, with her husband.

Though she bore a strong resemblance to Mama physically, my aunt was very different in every other way. She talked a lot, was adventurous, and best of all, she was superstitious. But though I could have, I didn't want to talk about the small happy beings of my childhood anymore. They belonged to the past. I had become very rational, I even had stopped dreaming consciously, probably when I was working such long hours on the hill-farm, where I slept deeply as soon as my head hit the pillow.

My black panther was still around, and I still went to his island. I had a second place too where I went when I needed a refuge: a mountain lake, where deer and other forest creatures visited me at the shore.

But perhaps it was all imagination, or superstition. Tante Paula's various superstitions were fun, though we both took them with a pinch of salt. Chimney sweeps were lucky, and walking under ladders had definite rules, as did black cats. And if Tante Paula had a dream, her little book would come out to help her to translate the dream into numbers for the lottery. And though I had my doubts, I had to admit that my aunt often won quite a bit of money through her dreams.

As I learned how to make dresses and blouses and skirts, I also learned not only about dreams, but about astrology as well. To my surprise, my problems were connected with the planets – Venus for the year I was born in – and Mars because I was a Scorpio.

If we didn't have much work, we'd visit Frau Jellinek, who read the cards and looked into our future. But If Tante Paula did not agree with her future, she took certain cards out of the pack.

"Now you can tell me," she'd say to her friend, a faint smile on her lips. "I don't want to know anything bad."

And although Frau Jellinek was put out and grumbled, murmuring words in a language I didn't understand, and telling my aunt, it couldn't work that way, in the end she did what my aunt wanted, reading the cards that were left, until Tante Paula found her future agreeable.

Had Mama not said so many bad things against my aunt, I probably would have settled quite happily with Tante Paula, in spite of my hate for sewing. But I couldn't altogether wipe away the conditioning I had grown up with. Even now, Mama maintained, Tante Paula took advantage of me, using me to sew bags and paying me only a few shillings, because I was an apprentice.

But what could I do? Hopefully I soon would be able to live with my father and give up sewing forever.

I still met him sometimes. His application had been made to the court – but the matter would take more time, he said, and we could do nothing but wait.

Then one day, a letter from Social Services arrived, asking me to visit. Mama must have had a letter as well, because she already knew that my father had applied for custody. She was furious.

I felt so sorry for Mama, it was my fault. I was causing all this pain and anger.

I tried to explain that I needed my father in my life, and wanted to live with him, because our flat was too small. But Mama wouldn't listen. She just shouted, I should go to live with him. I would regret it, and crawl back to her, on my knees would I beg her to have me back. But once I shut the door behind me, she wanted nothing more to do with me.

"Don't think you can come back, Gerti," Mama screamed again and again. "Go to your father, and see where it gets you." She took both my arms and shook me, glaring into my eyes.

"Where has he been all those years? He didn't care if you were dead or alive. Now he wants you, now, because you are growing up."

She pushed me away from her, and I could feel her disgust. "Just go to your father," she said, turning from me.

I felt terrible. How could I have done something so awful? How could I have hurt Mama like that? After all she had been through, sacrificing herself for us children – for me!

And what she said about Papa was true.

But there was no way back now.

But I couldn't go to my father, the lady from Social Services said. She would prepare a report. Then it was up to the court. I was questioned at length about my life, and she asked did I want to live with my father? She'd talk with Mama as well, then write her report. But until a decision was made, everything had to stay as it was.

So everything did. I was afraid to return home, but I had no other choice. Eventually, Mama calmed down, and after a few weeks not even Willi said much anymore. And with Mama busy working and running the household, she had little time or energy left. And so everything somehow continued.

Perhaps to divert my mind, Tante Paula suggested, I should visit a dancing class. Every young girl or boy between fourteen and seventeen went to dancing school. It was the place a first romance blossomed, as boys would ask to take a girl home after class.

I met my friend Hilde after work. "Why don't you come with me?" I asked. "It will be fun."

My old school friend agreed. She was two years older than I, and quite plain, but she met the boy of her dreams, Herbert Moll. He was really good looking though not my type, but then, lately, no one seemed to be my type. Now and again a boy asked to walk me home, but I only enjoyed it if we walked together with Hilde and Herbert. We talked and we laughed, even danced in the street once – a quiet side street where only few people walked by, smiling indulgently, perhaps remembering when they were young.

Though romance didn't blossom for me, dancing school was fun. I was enjoying myself like all the other teenagers – a name just invented, and catching on fast.

Mama didn't agree with my new pastime, because it was already nine when I came home, and she and my brother were already in bed and asleep. I undressed in the kitchen and tried to slip into my bed without waking her – if she woke, she'd tell me off, sometimes far into the night. Willi would join in, until gradually, one by one, we would drift into sleep.

Hilde and Herbert became engaged, and my friend learned about the physical side of love. She enjoyed sex in its various forms, and was happy to tell me all about it. I didn't doubt her words – but could sex really be fun? Perhaps, if you were in love, as Hilde was, and you knew you were going to marry your lover.

In spite of all the new information, I couldn't see myself ever getting married, or do the weird things Hilde described, but decided to keep an open mind. I was only fourteen – Hilde was sixteen, perhaps I too would think differently in two years' time.

My first year with Tante Paula came to its end. It was July, and because we had not much work to do, she suggested I should have an unpaid, extra-long holiday in Pupping. But in September I had to return for my second year in college.

As always, I enjoyed being in Pupping, though much was different. The biggest change lay in Mariandl. She was no longer a tomboy, and refused point blank to go to the wood, or even near it.

"Young ladies don't go to the wood on their own," she said. It seemed young ladies could do very little alone, without boys. I found this strange. I loved the woods more than anything and felt safer alone, than with a boy around.

Mariandl was away for days at times, with an aunt in Aschach, so I saw little of her. We were still friends and when she was here we talked, and occasionally went swimming. But the closeness had gone. I missed the old Mariandl, and the way we had been in the past. I felt kind of lonely and consoled myself by walking in the woods whenever I could. I was more aware, saw much more – foxes with their young, and deer coming out to graze, it was nice being alone in nature. But I missed sharing everything with my best friend, as I had always done.

But occasionally, quite suddenly and unexpectedly, Mariandl was her old self again, and it would be like old times. We'd sit in a tree and look at the moon and the stars, and talk about old times – when we had become blood brothers – or rather blood sisters – cutting our arms, mixing our blood to join us forever.

We were both sad when September came, and I had to return home.

CHAPTER 18

THE STEAMER TO TULLN

I had decided to travel home by steamship this year, from Aschach down the Danube to Vienna. I'd heard how beautiful this journey was. Looking forward to my adventure, I took the bus to Aschach and boarded the steamer.

It was early, with the morning mist still hanging thickly over the countryside. Once the sun came out it would be a warm, sunny day.

The Danube winds its way gracefully through farmland and open meadows, past villages and towns, with castles and beautiful palaces perched on top of wooded hills, overlooking the mighty river. I had imagined sitting on deck with the sun shining warm on my face, drinking in the beauty around me, occasionally glancing at the silvery waves below. A new and wonderful view would be waiting around every bend of the river. A spray of water might occasionally reach me – but with the late summer sun shining hot on my face, I would soon be dry again.

But it didn't turn out this way.

The spray of water was the only part of my imagery which became real. The castles and the rest did exist, but without the warm sun it was not as wonderful as I had thought, because it was cold. The misty morning had not turned into the warm, golden day I had anticipated. Quite suddenly it was autumn, with a cold drizzle in the air.

For a while I stood on deck, looking at the marvellous, ever changing view, but eventually the wet and the cold drove me inside, and for a while I sat in a room crowded with people. It would be a long journey, I thought, disappointed my dream had turned sour, and a long boring journey lay ahead of me.

Becoming restless, I got up, wandered around the passages, until I came to a window overlooking the engine room. It was warm here, the engines were moving, hissing and making strange noises as if being alive and working hard to power the ship. I liked it here, feeling comfortable, as I stood unobserved with no one around. After watching the engines for a while, I took out my paperback and began to read.

Suddenly I felt someone's presence and looked up. A few feet away stood a man, looking down at the engine room too – a very good-looking man, tall, and well dressed.

I ignored him and concentrated on my book. After a while he stepped closer, as if he too wanted to study the workings of the engines in more detail, but then he looked at me, asked about the book, and we began to talk. He was surprisingly easy to talk with, although he was the kind of man I normally had little opportunity to meet: a businessman, travelling from Passau to Vienna.

We talked about everything under the sun, and I felt as if I had known him all my life – as if everything until now had been a prelude, a preparation just for this moment. He was the most interesting and exciting person I had ever met. His name was Rolf Merker; he lived in Passau, and was going to Vienna on business. For the same reasons as I, he had decided to travel by steamer, and he too was disappointed the weather had changed.

Rolf was thirty-eight, had soft velvety-brown eyes and dark hair with a streak of silver at the left temple. Tall and slim, he looked elegant in his dark business suit. And he was married.

He mentioned it so casually as part of our conversation, yet it gave me a jolt. Then I wondered why it should do that, Rolf was just a pleasant man I shared a long journey with.

We kept talking, and his marriage didn't seem to matter any longer. I enjoyed his company, and he clearly enjoyed mine. Never before had I talked so freely with an adult – but then, I was an adult too now. Already I had worked for a year, I was almost fifteen, and told him so when he asked my age. I could tell him everything, it was a wonderful feeling, a feeling I had never experienced. But I didn't really think about any of this, I was only aware I felt happy, different somehow. Although there was space between us, it was as if we stood close, the air between us was filled with a charge of excitement. I felt so alive. The rain was forgotten as we wandered about the ship, and although the weather had not changed and it was still cold and damp, for me, a warm golden sun shone from a dazzling blue sky.

I said whatever came into my mind – even about Mama and Willi I talked – I felt so totally accepted. Rolf didn't judge me; he liked me just as I was. It was an exhilarating feeling, a feeling of freedom from my life of restriction, a feeling of love? But I didn't question anything, just lived in the moment.

Eventually, hours later, the rain ceased as we stood by the glass door leading to the deck. Here was a notice board. Absently I looked at the various notices, advertising events along the path of the Danube. "Flower festival in Tulln." I read, my thoughts somewhere else. Soon I would be back in Vienna, back in my old life.

"It's today," said Rolf. "Would you like to see the flower festival, Gerti?"

As I looked up into his soft brown eyes, our souls seemed to meet, just for an instant. I wanted to say yes, wanted to prolong being with him for as long as possible. Never in my whole life had I wanted anything more. I loved him. Then, like a downpour from a grey sky, reasoning returned. If I agreed, would he think I was agreeing to much more? And to what? I couldn't formulate my thoughts beyond that point, and tried again. Would he think I was agreeing to a kiss? But kissing might be wonderful – at least with Rolf. I got lost in my imagination.

For a while we stood in silence, looking out through the door, where the grey skies were breaking up, and a sliver of pale watery-blue sky broke through, highlighted by a ray of sunshine. Was it a sign?

If I agreed to go to the festival, would Rolf take it as licence for a kiss – or more? I shied away from the thought. Anyway, I couldn't leave the ship, how would I get home?

"We could take the train to Vienna later," Rolf suggested. "In the evening – or next morning."

I shook my head, although I wanted so much to say yes. It would be wonderful to spend a few long hours with Rolf. But Mama's warnings were suddenly right in the front of my mind: never trust a stranger.

But he was no stranger, I felt closer to him, than to anyone. I trusted Rolf, so I decided to be open.

"I would love to come to the festival with you," my words came easier, now I had started. "But –" I didn't how to continue, without sounding like a silly child.

I tried again. "I could only come as a friend," I said. It wasn't easy to put my objections into words, but I had to make myself clear. "If you expect more," I hesitated. How could I explain? How could I make him understand?

"If you expect more," I repeated, finding it increasingly difficult to talk, because Rolf looked at me with a smile on his lips
and so much tenderness in his eyes, I could easily drown in my
feelings, and wanted to.

"If you expect more," I repeated quickly, "you would be disappointed, and we'd better stay on board."

There, I had said it, and perhaps it was the end of my romance.
But Rolf was still smiling, tenderly, perhaps a little amused.

"I shall do nothing you don´t want me to do, Gerti," he promised, looking serious now.

His words left all possibilities open, it was cop-out, and I knew
it, and knew that he would try. But I also knew he'd only go as
far as I allowed him to, and I was quite certain what I did not
want. It would be OK, because it was up to me; the rules were
established: I would be safe. I could trust him to keep his promise – and I knew I could trust myself. We would spend a beautiful afternoon and evening together, take a train later, or even –
but that decision could wait, until sometime later.

So we left the ship and walked into Tulln, but because of the
rain the festival had ended early. Not that it mattered. We meandered around the town, had a snack in a cafe, and walked on.

The weather improved and the sun came out. And because I
didn't want to lose Rolf so soon, I agreed to stay in Tulln overnight – in separate rooms of course.

Walking into the small hotel, Rolf seemed edgy. "If anyone asks,"
he said so quietly, he almost whispered, "tell them I am your uncle, Gerti. You are only fourteen after all."

"I am nearly fifteen," I pointed out indignantly, but according to Rolf that made little difference in the eyes of the law. If anything went wrong, he would be in serious trouble.

"What can go wrong?" I asked, but Rolf didn't answer, he was busy booking our rooms. We left our luggage there, and went to eat.

I had never eaten in a hotel – I had never eaten out before, and worried, in case my table manners would let me down. But this didn't seem the case, and I relaxed and began to enjoy the evening. I was dining with a handsome man, an attentive man of the world who liked my company; a man – not a boy. The waiter brought the menu and I ordered liver fried in egg and breadcrumbs, and potato salad. My meal would be easier to eat, than the chicken Rolf had ordered. I took care to use my knife and fork correctly, but no one took any notice. Everything was like in a film, or in one of the novels I had read. It was a great adventure, a beautiful evening to remember, and I was in love.

Later we walked out of the village, and stopped under a tree. Rolf took me in his arms and kissed me: long kisses, completely new kisses – kisses I had not known could exist, and were wonderful. It was magic, a new, intense magic. Rolf was close to me, touching me, moving his hands from my shoulders and arms towards my breasts. Alarm bells began ringing and I took his hands and placed them firmly back on my shoulders. He laughed, gently, tenderly, and said in time I would learn not to mind a loving touch. I would even like it.

But he realised I did mind, and left his hands where I had put them.

Later, as he brought me to my room, he kissed me again. And somehow it happened I was in his arms, and we sat on my bed. It was wonderful being so close to Rolf. Our kisses grew deeper and longer, I wanted time to stand still. But time went on, and it was getting increasingly difficult to keep control of his hands, their touch was too close, too intimate. Danger signals flashed through my mind, because Rolf was no longer amused when I pushed him away.

"Send me away," he said finally. "Send me away, Gerti, if you really still mean no."

It had to stop, I knew. I felt so sad when I told him to go.

Rolf kissed me tenderly, and left, and I heard the door closing gently behind him. I felt awful.

It had been so wonderful being held close, and now it was over. For so many years, I had missed the physical contact with another human being. Mama had not touched me with affection since I was small, and my foster-parents had accepted not to hug or to kiss me.

Not only was I in love, and completely new feelings flooded my body, but out of nowhere, long forgotten old feelings appeared suddenly – feelings of being held, safely, with love.

It took a long time until I fell asleep, and knowing I had done the right thing, did not make me feel any better.

Next morning after breakfast, we went for a last walk, before boarding the train. Coming across a small wood we sat down under a tree, on fallen leaves still damp from yesterday's rain. Rolf kissed me, but today his kisses were different, Rolf was different, there was an urgency about his kisses. Suddenly I felt threatened, I had a strange feeling of danger, something warned me to be cautious.

I pushed Rolf away, jumped up, and without any further words I walked out of the wood and back to the village, with Rolf keeping pace. I kept a distance between us, acting on instinct, on my gut-feeling, which told me to get among people as quick as I could.

Walking fast, I started talking, and kept talking, about what I don't know. Even at the time I probably didn't know, or what Rolf said, or even if he said anything.

In the street amongst people, I relaxed. Everything seemed to be fine again. We ate a quick lunch, and caught the train to Vienna. Rolf had a business meeting, I wanted to go and see my father. We arranged to meet at the railway station at six, to spend an hour or two together, before Rolf took the train back to Passau, and I went home. In case anything went wrong, I gave him Tante Paula's address.

Everything did go wrong. I got away a little late from Papa, and had to wait for my tram. I was twenty minutes late when I arrived at the Westbahnhof, and Rolf wasn't here. I couldn't believe he had not waited; I wanted to see him so much, at least this one last time. I walked all-round the station looking for Rolf, but could not find him. Unhappy and sad, I walked home.

A few days later, a letter arrived at Tante Paula's address. Rolf wrote he had been delayed and arrived twenty-five minutes late, and couldn't find me. He was sorry to have missed me, and hoped we could meet, next time he came to Vienna. Much love from Rolf, the short letter ended.

Perhaps this should have been the end, but I knew it was not. I dreamed of Rolf and lived for my memories. It wasn't even so important, that I couldn't see him. He existed, was in my life, a big part of my life, and I knew he thought of me too. We'd never make love, but I would see him again.

In the meantime, to take my mind off Rolf, I went out with a different boy every week. After working a long day in Tante Paula's shop, the evenings and weekends were mine.

CHAPTER 19

1956

Since Rolf had come into my life, young men seemed to be everywhere, and not only was I aware of their presence, they noticed me too. As a well brought up Viennese girl, I ignored any attempts to chat me up, but now and again there was an exception. If he was very persistent as well as attractive, and clever enough to make me laugh, the ice was broken, and I might agree to a date. But nothing serious developed, and I hardly met anyone more than three times. Somehow it always ended – usually when a good night kiss wasn't enough for him anymore.

But other boys were waiting already, and the game was fun. A kiss was nothing serious any more. But everything else would have to wait for the man I wanted to share my life with.

By now, in theory I knew a lot about making love, because my friend Helga, who would soon marry her fiancé Herbert, enlightened me about some of the enjoyable aspects of sex. In spite of this theoretical knowledge, I couldn't imagine what it would really be like, but I could wait to find out a little longer. I didn't want to get involved yet. Dating was enough for now, it was fun; I liked the excitement and the attention.

I still loved Rolf and thought of him often. But we could never belong to each other, though I would see him again, I was quite certain of it. To distract myself, I went out with a different boy almost each week. The evenings and weekends were mine, and like Christl before me, I was rarely at home. Mama couldn't stop me going out, although she tried.

When I wanted to be alone, I took the tram to the outskirts of the city, to walk in the Viennese woods. Or I went out with friends, and sometimes to the swimming pool, where I met Heinz one day. We both held on to the rail having a rest, and after we talked for a while, he asked me for a date.

He was very good-looking. Tall, blond, with green eyes which could change colour until they were blue, and as deep as the sea. Heinz was a student, a few years older than me, and we'd meet almost every day.

We would go to the pictures, or to a café, and sit over a coke and talk. After walking me home, we'd walk round the block again, to be together just a little longer. It seemed something wonderful had found its beginning – unfortunately it should find its end as quickly as it had begun.

It was a mild evening, and we sat on a bench in the park. A full moon stood in the sky, the air was warm, though it was already October. No one was around and we kissed, and in between kissing we talked – nice talk, and nice endless kisses. But I could not lose myself completely in my wonderful feelings, because now and again Heinz seemed to lose control of his hands, and I had to remind him firmly of the boundaries.

But more recently, I had begun to have doubts about my self-erected boundaries, asking myself – purely theoretically of course – what it would be like to make love with a perfect young man like Heinz. If what Helga had told me was true, it would be the most wonderful and amazing experience.

I liked everything about him, I really liked Heinz, perhaps I loved him. What would 'it' be like? What would it be like to make love with a beautiful young man like Heinz? Surely it must be the most wonderful thing in the world, and for tonight, Rolf was forgotten.

What would it be like? Did everyone feel the same way? What was it like for a man? What would it mean to Heinz?

I knew, before me, he had an affair, with an older woman – a woman of twenty-five. So Heinz would know. I hesitated to question him about such a delicate subject, but I really did want to know.

So when the subject filtered into our conversation, I took the opportunity to ask: "What is it like to make love, Heinz, what does it feel like? And what is it like afterwards?"

He pondered about this question for a while, until he said: "Well, one really can't compare it with anything, Gerti, but in a way, sex is like a good meal. Afterwards, you feel so fulfilled and contented."

My romantic thoughts disappeared. I was so angry. How could he compare something which joined two people in love, with a meal?

I was not only angry; I was hurt, and got up to leave. I was walking so fast, Heinz almost had to run to keep up with me, as he tried to find out what was wrong. He said he wanted to talk things over, talk about it – whatever it was.

But what was there to talk about? He had said too much already.

I refused to see him again, but couldn't tell him why. I didn't want him to know how hurt I was. And so our romance found its end.

And although I missed him so much, I knew I'd made the right decision. Although this was no help at all.

But a few days later, Rolf reappeared in my life, completely out of the blue. I was at work as the door opened and he stood there, smiling at me. I introduced him to my aunt, and we made polite conversation for a while, until Tante Paula said I could leave.

We went to a café, to finally talk on our own. But something had changed. Though I still liked Rolf and was happy to see him, this special magic we had shared, seemed to be gone. The excitement – the glow – was no longer there. Rolf was just a man I liked very much, that was all.

But it was good to be with him, he was still my close friend. "I have to meet some people on business, Gerti," Rolf said later. "Would you like to come?"

He called a taxi, and we met a few men in a restaurant. Over a meal the conversation was general, and later, the men talked business. Rolf had another appointment, and offered to take me home.

But one of the men, Charles Bonner from London, had finished for the day, and wanted to see something of Vienna. He said he would appreciate a conducted tour, and assured Rolf, he would take good care of me if I showed him around.

I looked at Rolf, a question in my eyes. When he said it was up to me, I agreed to show Charles the city. Perhaps it was better to say goodbye to Rolf here, I didn't want to acknowledge or discuss this strange change which had happened between us. And I didn't want to kiss him goodbye.

Still, it was strange to let go of feelings which I'd held on for so long. It seemed as if a big part of myself was leaving too. As I said goodbye to Rolf, we were both sad. He also knew something between us was different. I was missing this something already; it had sustained me when things had been tough. But it was gone, we both knew it. Saying goodbye was easy this time, as I left the restaurant with Charles.

I had never really appreciated Vienna. Perhaps because I longed for quiet places, and to be surrounded by nature and not buildings, even if these buildings were palaces. So my heart wasn't really in, as we sat in a taxi, driving through the Ringstrasse, where I pointed out the parliament and the famous opera house. Finally I decided to show Charles the Prater. In the cabin of the Riesenrad, the giant wheel, high above Vienna, we both admired the city sprawling beneath us, a magnificent sight, even for me, who knew it all so well.

The first street lights illuminated the beauty of the city – soon it would be getting dark. Leaving the shelter of the Riesenrad I noticed it was starting to rain, and Charles waved down a taxi.

"Where shall we go?" he asked, once we were settled inside, out of the rain. Where could I take a sophisticated business man in Vienna at night? I didn't know. So Charles asked the taxi driver.

"Go to the Moulin Rouge," the man said.

I protested, because the Moulin Rouge was one of Vienna's top night clubs. I could not go there. I was only fifteen, dressed in a blue skirt and yellow cardigan, and wearing socks with my flat walking shoes. Unless wearing nylons and high heels, a girl wasn't suitably dressed for the evening. And an evening dress was essential, going to a night club.

"I am not dressed for a night club," I said. "I came straight from work."

With a wave of his manicured hand, the perfectly dressed Mr Bonner pushed my concerns away. "If you have sufficient money," he said with conviction, "you can go anywhere, dressed in anything."

Easy for him to say, dressed as he was in his expensive, beautifully-made suit.

But before I could convince him otherwise, our taxi had arrived in front of the Moulin Rouge. A man in uniform with an enormous red umbrella stood at the entrance. He came up to our taxi, holding the umbrella over me as I got out, as if my yellow cotton cardigan deserved his protection more, than the elegant evening gowns of the women exiting the next car.

I looked around. The city was so alive. In spite of the bad weather, the streets were teeming with people – laughing, happy people. The rain added to Vienna's charm, because the streetlights and brightly coloured neon lights reflected themselves in the wet asphalt of the pavements and streets. It was so exciting – a real adventure.

I had never been to a night-club, but tried to act as if it were an everyday event for me. We went along a corridor, past an open door, where, in the dim light, I could see an empty stage and people moving to soft music on the dance floor. Charles walked upstairs, as if he knew where to go. The waiter led us to a small table, with curtains around. One side was open for the waiter to serve, and we could watch the stage and the dance floor on the opposite side, as the curtain was open. And I would make quite certain it would stay this way.

The waiter came for our order, and I thought this was a good opportunity to try the drinks I had read so much about in my novels. And as I couldn't make up my mind between whisky or gin, Charles ordered me both. To my disappointment I liked neither, but to be polite I took an occasional sip from one of the glasses.

The show began. Charles was watching with interest, I watched in total disbelief and disgust. Naked women were posing on discs which turned round and round. How could these women show themselves like that?

But I didn't say one word about it to Charles, who was still a stranger to me. It was too embarrassing. But although I hadn't asked, and really didn't want to know – at least not from Charles – my companion casually informed me, the women were not allowed to move if they were completely naked. This was the reason they stood on turning discs, so they could show everything and still stay within the law.

I ignored this information, it was really quite inappropriate to discuss such a subject.

An interval followed, and Charles asked me to dance. I refused, feeling too conspicuous in my clothes. Every woman here wore an evening gown and high heels. But apart from this, I didn't want to dance with Charles. The way he had looked at the naked women had put me right off. I wanted to be away from him, as far as possible, and as soon as I could.

The show started again, and a singer came on. Then three women danced – but they didn't really dance, just moved their bodies in odd ways, wriggling like snakes. These women were naked too, just wearing a small patch of some sort of material, which didn't hide anything. As I watched the way Charles stared at these women, I was glad he was sat at the opposite side of the small table, rather than next to me.

Finally the show was over, and we took a taxi home. I sat in the corner of the car, as far away from Charles as possible. Please God, I prayed, make him stay in his corner. After the way he had looked at these women, I could not bear the thought of even shaking his hand. But God listened to me that time. Charles just said goodbye, and thanked me for a pleasant evening. I got out of the taxi, and it drove off.

It was strange, but with Charles, Rolf also went out of my life. I still thought about him now and again, but our love was in the past, a beautiful memory I'd always treasure. I would always like Rolf and wish him well, but I knew I would not see him again, and didn't want to.

CHAPTER 20

In November I was fifteen, and my small world was changing fast. But bigger and even more serious changes took place around me. History was in the making, affecting us all because the Hungarian revolution happened right here on our doorstep. Daily, we heard horror stories about people trying to escape the Communist regime, and getting killed in the process.

We all tried to help. I could do little more than direct someone to an address written on a crumpled piece of paper, or take him there, if he couldn't understand my directions.

In my life, the jump to freedom was yet to come. I still waited for my escape from restriction and poverty, into a wonderful life with Papa, where I could finally give up sewing, and study for a bright future. I just had to wait.

In the meantime, I continued working at Tante Paula's, hating every aspect of making clothes. In spite of this hurdle, I had successfully completed my first year at college. A third of my apprenticeship was over.

My life at home was still hell, and I spent as much time with my friends as I could.

Mama continued working, though she was often so ill, she had to spend time in hospital. She must have been good at her job, not only was she kept on, but allowed to sit in a comfortable chair, doing the hand sewing. In a first class saloon in these days, much was sewn by hand.

I looked after our household when Mama was ill, but we were used to it and had been for years.

As Mama was more preoccupied with her own life and had less time for mine, we got on better. But nothing improved between my brother and me.

Willi had finished his apprenticeship and was earning well, but he was no happier. He was tall and slim, and in a skinny kind of way, my brother was handsome. But not all girls liked muscles, and my friends liked his looks. But although I still took him with me now and again, hoping he might find a girlfriend, or at least go on a date, it never worked out. In a conversation, my brother lectured, showing off with his knowledge, but if someone else took the lead, he became silent as if he were sulking. Even if he liked a girl, he never managed to ask for a date.

In his job, he must have been different, he seemed to have no problems at all, and got promoted quickly. But he never met any of his colleagues away from work, and in his private life he hardly communicated with anyone except Mama and me, and Lilly occasionally. But he couldn't cope with her husband, and only wanted to see her alone. He wouldn't visit her, because our two beautiful and well-brought-up nephews might have sticky fingers and touch his trousers – touch him. My brother didn't like being touched, he needed to stay separate.

Yet I knew how he hated his isolation, because sometimes he still talked about his problems to me.

With Mama he had never been able to talk about his concerns, and this didn't change, although now he definitely was the man of the house. When it came to a difference of opinion between him and Mama, my brother would have his way. She seemed almost afraid, although he never abused her physically.

Mama had not hit him since he was a small child. With me, her hand would 'slip' even now, if I provoked her. But with Willi she controlled herself, as if she too sensed the danger, the anger and violence behind his rigid control. Ridicule and sarcasm were his only safety valves to let off some steam. He still provoked me, so I'd lose my temper and lash out at him. Then he would fight me. He never threw the first punch; at worst he would grab me to pin me down. But I had learned to control myself, and so we no longer fought physically.

In spite of my anger and resentment, I felt sorry for my brother, and tried to help him. We'd go for a walk some evenings through the city streets, or take a tram to the woods to walk among the trees and talk – or rather Willi talked and I would listen. When he had finished talking I'd make some suggestions, trying to find a way, so he'd mix with girls his age. Dancing school would get him used to being with young people in a social environment – or he could take swimming lessons – girls liked to go to the lido in the summer.

Willi liked my ideas, but could never bring himself to act on them. "It's too late, sister," he would say. He still called me sister when we talked seriously.

"I'd be the oldest in dancing school, and stick out like a sore thumb. And children learn how to swim; it is too late for me."

Willi stuck to his isolation. I couldn't help him, only listen when he wanted to talk, and play chess when I was home and he was in a good mood.

Then to my amazement, my brother became interested in self-defence and judo. As he explained the principles of judo, I got interested too, and bought the booklet Willi had seen advertised. When Mama went shopping, we started to practice. But as I threw Willi over my shoulder as it said in the book, he fell against the kitchen cupboard. After this accident he wouldn't continue, ignoring my suggestion to move next to his bed. Willi had had enough – he wouldn't even take his turn and throw me.

So I practiced with my friend Barbara, who had such a big spacious bedroom we could put her mattress on the floor. In spite of this precaution, she landed next to it on the hard floor, and refused to continue. Hilde had nowhere to practice and showed no interest, she was far too involved with her boyfriend. I had no choice but to postpone judo, but promised myself I would continue one day, if possible with a teacher, to learn this sport properly.

Willi found a more suitable hobby, discovering an interest in photography. But it was a lonely hobby, except when we travelled to the woods together, and he took photos of the sunset, the beauty and abundance of nature, and of me.

But the good times we had together were rare. More often Willi teased me, or nagged, and always tried to find out as much about my life as he could, only to twist my words, to make Mama angry with me. She would join in to berate me with words – ugly words – that still had the power to hurt, even after hearing them for so many years.

I had to keep silent and pretend indifference. If I showed any sign of anger or upset, Willi would prod even more, getting pleasure from my pain. This happened when he 'found' my diary.

Tante Paula had bought me this beautiful little book for my birthday. It was bound in red leather and had a key to lock it. It was my most treasured possession. When I was on my own, I could write down my thoughts, and how I felt. I took my diary with me when I went to the woods, where I settled down under a big tree – sometimes I'd even climb up to sit in its branches. I liked sitting quietly, surrounded by nature. Here I could think and write in peace. I had already written my life story, confiding in my diary how I felt about Mama and Willi, and everything about Papa – even about Rolf and staying in Tulln I had written about.

I kept the diary hidden in my drawer between my books and other stuff for college, and I always locked it securely, looking forward to the next time I could open it and write without restrictions. But the joy in my diary should change into the opposite, and in a terrible way.

One day, as I came home, Mama was preparing our meal on the kitchen table, Willi sat next to her by the window. In front of him, next to the onions Mama was peeling, lay my little red diary. It was open. The leather strap with the lock had been cut. As I entered the kitchen, Willi looked up, and then continued with what he had been doing: reading from my diary in a loud voice.

"Thief!" I hissed, trying to grab my book. But Willi stood up, holding it high over his head, out of my reach.

"I really love him," he quoted, raising his voice to imitate me. "Rolf."

I wanted to hit him, really hurt him. But this was what my brother wanted to achieve. If I instigated a fight, he could beat me, as he had done when we were children. He was waiting for me to lash out, sneering at me, holding on to my diary.

I had to stay calm. It took all my efforts, but I succeeded, and sat down.

Willi knew he could provoke me no further, and put my book on the table. I took it, picked up my handbag and ran out of the flat.

Aimlessly, I walked through the streets. I felt violated, raped somehow, my innermost feelings laid open to the ridicule of my brother and mother. She had been part of it too, at the very least Mama had known, and hadn't stopped Willi. She had not said a word when he read from it. Probably they'd read it together, making fun of me. I felt physically sick. As far back as I could remember I had kept my thoughts and feelings to myself, to protect myself from their ridicule, and from my brother's sarcastic remarks. Now they knew my innermost secrets. They knew about Rolf, about Papa – they even knew what I thought about Willi and Mama themselves. How could I ever go back and face them? My only hope was my father.

I phoned and asked could I come, but Papa said no, he could get into trouble. He had not heard from court, and I had to go back to my mother.

But I couldn't go home, and though it was already very late, I went to my friend Barbara. Her mother opened the door and beckoned me in. She was friendly and welcoming, so different from my mother. Barbara was lucky, she had a happy, a normal home. We went to her bedroom, and I told her everything. My friend listened as it all poured out of me, but she couldn't help me, nobody could. It was nearly midnight; I had to leave and had nowhere I could go but home. There was no other choice if I didn't want to walk the streets all night.

Our flat was in darkness, my mother and brother had gone to bed, and were probably sleeping. Through the kitchen window came enough light, to see Mama had left a plate with my meal on the table, as if nothing was wrong. Although I was very hungry, I could not touch even a mouthful.

I quickly undressed, and crept quietly into my bed next to Mama's, holding my breath. This was the moment when she was most likely to wake and shout at me. But although I could tell from her breathing she was awake, Mama stayed silent.

Next morning, we all went to work as if nothing had happened. And nothing more was said, but my brother had a new weapon. He would quote whole sentences, even paragraphs, out of my diary, just as I had written them. Willi had a good memory.

I had to stay silent, swallow my tears, my anger and pain. What else could I do? If I retaliated, if I said anything, I would make it all worse, giving more fuel to my brother.

Somehow we carried on. Mama ignored what had happened, and what was still going on between us, and so it went on for a few weeks, until our lives suddenly changed, because Willi had to join the army for nine months. It was compulsory.

Life was much easier with my brother away, and became even better, when Christl came home for a holiday, with her husband and Larysa, my lovely niece, who was two by now. They stayed with Christl's friend, and when they went out, I looked after Larysa.

I was very sad when they left.

A few more months went by, and then Willi returned home from the army. He was very glad to be back, he hated army life. On his brief visits home, he'd only told us they had to sleep in bunk beds, and wear night shirts. But now we learned a little bit more.

The rigorous exercise had been his biggest problem, and marching came close behind. My brother was always out of step. His biggest problem was that he could not get on with the other recruits, or with the officers. Eventually Willi was transferred to an office and excused from all training. But in his new position, he did so well, he was promoted and came home with a star.

My brother said, he only had promotion because he searched through all the drawers and papers, and found out a few things which he used to his advantage. He was probably lying, but you could never be sure with him.

With Willi home, life was settling back into its old routine, when on a mild February day I came home from work. Opening the door, I stopped in surprise. My mattress stood on the floor. Mama had a saw in her hand and was sawing my bed in half. Her face was an unhealthy red and her breathing labored.

I just stood there, struck dumb with astonishment. I didn't know what to do. Mama just carried on with the sawing, without saying a word. Finally, with the job done, she straightened up and looked into my eyes, breathing heavily. She was furious.

"Don't look so stupid, Gerti," she shouted. "You don't need your bed anymore. Go, get out of my sight – go to your father."

I didn't know what to do. I had heard nothing from court, or from Papa. Yet Mama was shouting again that I should go. But how could I? I couldn't leave her this way.

"Just go," Mama was still shouting, waving the saw in front of my face. "He is waiting for you. And believe me; it is better for you, if you go now – immediately."

She started hacking with the saw on the parts of the bed.

What was I to do? I couldn't leave my mother this way. I wanted to tell her how much I loved her, that I would come visiting and wanted her to visit me as well. I needed to explain I was not rejecting her, just because I wanted my father as well. It was not fair, to make me choose between my parents.

And I needed her to know; my spirit was dying in this small hole we lived in, where flowers and plants died because there was no light or fresh air. Where there was no privacy at all, not even to wash on my own – where I could never be me.

I would have my own room. She should be pleased for me. I'd be able to study, have a profession I liked. My father had agreed that I could learn judo, and travel with him to interesting and exotic places like India and Japan. I would have new opportunities, make something of my life. My mother should be happy for me.

Most of all I wanted to say how much I loved her, and appreciated all the sacrifices she had made for me, and that I understood how difficult it had all been for her. I wanted her to know, that I would always love her.

I opened my mouth to put some of my feelings into words, and moved towards my mother. If I could touch her, put my arms around her, just once. Mama paused in her sawing and looked up. There was so much fury and pain in her eyes – I closed my mouth and swallowed my words – and my emotions. It was no use. So I went, quietly closing the door behind me, her words echoing in my head: "If you go through this door now, Gerti, you can never come back."

I carried on walking, there was no going back.

Papa was waiting for me in the street. I couldn't speak, and he stayed silent, too. He just took my school bag which I still held in my hand; put it in front of him on the motor scooter. I climbed on the back seat, and we drove off, towards my new life. I should have been happy, instead I was terribly sad.

And I really could have done with an arm around my shoulder, and someone holding me to feel safe, to feel safe enough to cry. But this wasn't happening. Although my father had taken charge of me, I was still so terribly alone.

CHAPTER 21

PAPA

Papa's flat was light and sunny, with oil paintings on the walls, and many art-objects everywhere, my first impression was of a museum. But I was only ever a visitor here.

I would live with Frau Hammer, just round the corner, which was OK. My dreams of having my own room were finally reality. No one rifling through my belongings, I'd have the privacy I longed for. I could read without interruption, perhaps I'd even start a new diary, having burnt my old diary in our small stove in the Pelzgasse.

Everything would be different; I was on my way to a normal, wonderful life. At least this was what I assumed.

My new home was a nice and comfortable flat, belonging to the Hammers. After Frau Hammer showed me my room, the children claimed my attention. But I didn't mind – I liked children. And any time I wanted to, I could go to my room – it was small, but had everything I needed.

I still felt awful, because of Mama, and the way I'd left. But it had been the right thing to do, I told myself. A new life was waiting, a life I'd enjoy, and a life with a future. I could stop my apprenticeship, return to college and go on to university. I would learn judo, and travel with my father. He had promised. It was the beginning of a marvelous life.

Reality turned out quite differently. I did have my own room, but was hardly ever allowed to be there until it was bedtime. A waste of electricity, Frau Hammer said if I tried to read there by myself.

"You can read in the living room, Gerti," I was told, "where we all are."

But I longed to be alone. And the only waste of electricity would have been a light-bulb; nothing else was in my room using electricity, not even a heater. I had no heating in my room at all, but although it was still bitterly cold now in February, I would still have liked to read for an hour, before going to bed. During the week I had no more time, anyway.

At six I had to leave to get to work on time, and should have finished by quarter to five, but lately my aunt gave me extra chores, always at the last minute, and when I finally got home, it was after six and the family had already eaten. My meal would be waiting on the table, usually it was cold.

When I first came, I offered to help with the dishes, now it was expected of me – a day's washing up waited for me every evening. Once I added my plate to all the other dishes. But before I could escape, Frau Hammer called: "Don't forget the dishes, Gerti."

Washing up was my job already.

Soon I had a second duty to perform each day: I had to put the children to bed. At first Frau Hammer asked me very nicely. "Would you mind, Gerti? They are asking for you."

At the time I didn't mind, and would not have minded at other times, had it not become another daily chore which I had to perform however tired I was.

I liked the children, which made it more difficult to have time to myself because they liked me too, surrounding me whenever they could. I didn't have the heart to reject them, and so my day ended bathing three children under five, putting them to bed and telling stories. Then I had to get their clothes ready for the following morning. What had begun as a favor became a duty, another daily chore.

By now it was eight or even later, and I would have liked to get ready for bed, and read for a while before going to sleep. But Frau Hammer had other ideas.

"No sense in wasting electricity," were her usual words. "You can read in the living room, where we are."

But I couldn't relax, feeling alien and strange in their presence. The couple moved around, or sat talking. I couldn't concentrate on my book. So I said good night, went to my room, to read in bed for a while. But after a few minutes Frau Hammer opened my door, said good night, and turned the light off.

I tried to talk about it with Papa, but he was on her side.

"It's only right you share the household chores, Gerti," he said. "After all, you live there."

He didn't seem to understand why I wanted to be in my room. My sweet golden dream was turning rapidly sour. My father only listened to what he wanted to hear, which was Frau Hammer's voice.

But not all was lost; we still had our Saturdays, which we always spent together.

Around eleven I would go to Papa's workshop, where I waited for him as he finished and locked up. Then we went to his flat for lunch, which Mina prepared. I didn't mind Papa's wife, the divorce was long in the past. But Mina and I never got close, she always stayed in the background, polite but impersonal, taking little notice or interest in me, and she never came with us.

I still enjoyed going out with Papa. Now he was again the father I had come to know and admired so much. Perhaps deep down I loved him. I forgot my disappointments, and enjoyed the hours we spent together. Each time we went out, he found something new I could learn from: small side streets, hidden in the inner city, ancient houses with dark heavy doors. To me, they had always been just old houses, but now I learned about their past. Papa was a master craftsman, having restored the carpentry work in many of Vienna's buildings. I learned how to tell when a house was built, about the craftsmen at the time and their tools, the way they worked.

Many a Saturday was spent in a museum, or in one of the spectacular palaces, built when Austria was a large empire. Even cemeteries were interesting; so many famous people like Mozart, Schubert and Beethoven lay buried here. Papa knew not only their life stories, but also snippets about their personal lives.

His enthusiasm about stained-glass windows was catching, as we explored old churches, and he explained the staining process, at a time when everything was very different.

I began to visualize how the city must have been a long time ago – teeming with people in old-fashioned clothes, living their lives and creating their world – an ever changing world, leading through our ancestors and grandparents to the present and to us. And from us to our children, towards a future we could only imagine. One day we would be their past, we would be history.

We'd discuss our thoughts over a drink in a cafe, and if I was lucky Papa would tell me about his travels to Africa, India, South

America or Egypt. Magic existed, strange things went on, which our advanced modern science had no explanation for.

I was spellbound. Sometimes I wondered if my father realized how much I appreciated these hours we spent together. How much I admired him, wanted to get to know him, not just as my father, but the brilliant man he was.

Probably he didn't know, because I couldn't show my feelings, my admiration for him. The conditioning of my childhood sat too deep – it had never been safe to show how I felt. Perhaps this would change, if I felt more secure.

But as time went on I became even less secure. I felt let down, betrayed, because Papa did not keep his promises. My life was turning out completely differently, than we had planned.

I had my own room; that was true. It was quite adequate, and would have been heaven, had I been able to spend more time there. As it was, I hardly had time anyway. I didn't mind helping with the children or the household, I had always helped, wherever I lived. But all the chores I was expected to do when I came home from work were too much. Even on the week-ends I was kept busy.

I wasn't allowed to go anywhere on my own, couldn't visit my friends or invite them, and had to ask Frau Hammer's permission for whatever I wanted to do.

Trying to talk with Papa about it was pointless, he wouldn't listen. Frau Hammer had got to him before me; he believed I just had to help a little. So I stopped trying to discuss my situation with him, especially as his other promises also crumbled to dust. Our plans for my future had disappeared, as if they never existed. When I talked about studying, Papa insisted I continue my apprenticeship with Tante Paula – too much time had passed, he said, I was fifteen now.

"Another eighteen months and your apprenticeship is finished. Work a few years, and then qualify as a master tailor. I'll buy you a shop, Gerti, and you are set for life."

What I wanted for my future was of no interest to Papa anymore. And when I reminded him what he had promised, he became angry, and shouted that everything was different now, and the subject was closed.

My future was no longer full of promise, but broke into pieces in front of my eyes and I could do nothing about it.

But my dream to learn judo was left, and this dream I would realize, whatever it took. My father's friend Hubert was a judo expert, he would advise us, perhaps even teach me himself. When Papa went to visit this friend, I was so happy. Finally I would learn judo. I was so excited, when I visited Papa, to find out when I could start. But his words changed everything.

"Judo is too masculine for a girl," I was told now. "Your muscles would develop too much Gerti. You wouldn't find a husband. Men don't like muscular women."

I didn't want a husband, I wanted to learn judo. And I didn't mind – or care – about my muscles, one way or the other. They could develop any way they liked. But Papa's mind was made up and he refused to discuss the matter further. Another dream vanished, and not much was left.

Doubts began to rise up in my mind. Had I made a mistake? Should I have stayed with my mother? I didn't even live with my father, but he kept a much tighter control over my life, than my mother had ever done. I began to revolt, silently at first, somewhere deep inside of me. But it showed, and my new attitude didn't help our relationship, and the communication between us got even worse. I still wanted to know my father better, get behind the facade. And I was aware he tried to get to know me too, find out how I really was. But instead of listening to me, discussing how I felt, he went about it in a roundabout way, which I resented bitterly.

"The youth of today," my father murmured one day, putting his paper down on the table. "Teenage pregnancies – it seems most teenagers these days have sex."

Over his spectacles, he looked enquiringly into my eyes, as if he was waiting.

Waiting for what? To see how disgusted I was at the thought? That I said: 'Oh no Papa, I would never do that. I am a virgin, Papa, and I will stay a virgin, until the day I marry.'

He would not hear these words from me, treating me this way. How could he? The whole subject was disgusting. And my father suspected me of sleeping around! If he really wanted to know about me, he should ask. In this roundabout way he would discover nothing, at least not something that was true. I would show him, and treat him the way he treated me.

I looked him in the eyes, smiled faintly, shrugging one shoulder. "Why not?" I agreed, as if my friends and I went to bed with all sorts. Let him think I would hop into bed with every agreeable man, one part of me reasoned. Let him think what he wanted. Serve him right, if he's hurt.

But I was hurting too.

That he should think so little of me deeply upset me. And that he read statistics from the paper, talking about today's youth, to find out what I thought, to get my reaction, was even worse. I would not play his game.

He should know me better, and if he wanted to know something about me, he should ask straight out. I was not just another teenager, another statistic, but his daughter. He should have trusted me. Clearly he did not, so it would serve him right to think the worst of me.

Let him think what he wants to, I told myself again. But at the same time I was desolate, that my own father thought such terrible things of me. I was his daughter, and he should trust me.

As it was obvious, he did not, it served him right if now he thought the worst of me. But all of it upset me deeply, though I had practiced all my life not to show how I felt.

Next time we met, Papa told me about his friend Robert, who accompanied him on his expeditions. How handsome and how brilliant he was, excelling in his profession although he was only twenty-five. Now, every time I saw Papa, he mentioned this man, and I began to suspect he had a reason. Perhaps he thought it should be Robert, with whom I slept around.

Or was he trying to find out how I really acted around men? He could trust Robert to report back to him.

But I would not play his games, whatever they were.

Meandering through the city on our Saturday walk, as if by accident, we met Robert. He was indeed handsome. Tall, with a good figure, brown wavy hair surrounded a beautifully chiseled face. He was almost too good-looking to be true, he really looked like one of the Greek statues that Papa had likened him to. If I had met this man in a different way, I might have been interested. But I resented Papa pushing him at me – I could do my own choosing – thank you very much.

Robert would be taboo for me.

Now, we often met Robert on a Saturday as if by accident, and he would join us. And sometimes, when Papa had to meet a customer, Robert would wait with me in a cafe. This maneuver repeated itself a few times in different ways and then my father invited us both to his flat. Robert was really charming and attentive, but I didn't know if he was interested in me, or pretended to, as a favour to Papa. And after considering everything carefully, I decided to avoid any risk, and get rid of my would-be suitor once and for all.

As Robert was a well-educated and experienced man, I thought he might be put off if I acted the silly adolescent. Starting slowly at first so he wouldn't suspect anything, I fell into the worst Viennese dialect on occasion, and started giggling quite inappropriately, covering my mouth with my hand, as if I were embarrassed. I pretended my previous good behavior had been for my father's benefit, and now Robert saw the real me.

Soon I spoke in my worst Viennese slang if I was alone with Robert, and talked about subjects he was not interested in. This was difficult at first, because he seemed to have almost as much knowledge as Papa. But he knew nothing about judo, so I had one subject, and another I found in water sports, as Robert admitted to being a poor swimmer. In case all this talking about swimming and judo, delivered in my worst dialect, was not enough to drive Robert away, I acted very juvenile, made silly jokes, laughed overly loud, or giggled.

My ploy was successful. Within a few weeks Robert disappeared from my life as suddenly as he had come, and Papa talked no longer about him.

But my father didn't give up his psychological games so easily and Pepi came into my life. Perhaps he thought Robert had been too mature and sophisticated, and I might be more interested in a boy my age.

Pepi was one of my father's apprentices; I had often seen him when I came to the workshop. He was a nice boy, tall and slim, with curly dark hair and a cheeky grin. I had nothing against him, until Papa decided to bring Pepi with us on a Saturday.

My father had got an old bike for me, and I looked forward to ride with him to the Prater, a fairground, surrounded by a nature park, with leafy trees, lawns and fields. There was little traffic, it would be a pleasure riding our bikes, and we could even go on dirt tracks, where there was no traffic at all.

Though I looked forward to this new venture, I didn't trust my father. Why did he bring Pepi along? He had not even said anything about it before. When I came to the workshop, Papa was ready to go, and so was Pepi.

Perhaps this was another of my father's psychological games. Did he really think I was so stupid, not to be aware of his plans, his actions, and of the games he played? But two could play this game; I would turn things around, and watch how Papa would react. For this I needed Pepi's co-operation.

During the next outing I talked with Pepi. Until now, I had just thrown the odd word at the lad, in between ignoring him altogether, because Papa had upset me. I really shouldn't have taken it out on Pepi, it wasn't his fault, and he had to go if the 'Meister' invited him to come along. It was an honor.

Pepi rode by my side with Papa behind – an ideal opportunity to talk, and to my surprise I found we had much in common. He also liked swimming and playing chess, and had an axe to grind with my father.

Pepi had grown up in a children's home, and the Meister helped him to a good start in life, by teaching him carpentry – even restoring antiques – and Pepi's future was secure. But my father took advantage of Pepi, by making him work extra hours without pay. He had not asked Pepi if he wanted to come with us, he had just told him. Saturday afternoon was Pepi's free time. He should have been asked.

I agreed wholeheartedly. I didn't want to tell Pepi too much about me, and it wasn't necessary, because he was glad to talk about himself, to let off steam. His life wasn't easy, living in a hostel, without support or help from anyone. And he wanted his Saturdays free again – which suited me fine, because I wanted Papa to myself.

I designed the plan, but Pepi was a willing accomplice. We would test Papa, and see how the master reacted. We would pretend to be interested in each other, but in a way Papa would not like.

When my father caught up with us, I was ready to play my part.

"Can I go to the Alte Donau with Pepi tomorrow? We'll take out a boat, and go rowing?" I asked, ever so casually. The Alte Donau is a side arm of the Danube, with lots of leisure facilities, and boats for rent.

Papa was taken aback, and seemed to consider this new, unexpected situation. But I didn't want him to have time to think, so I continued: "I like Pepi." I pushed my point home. "It will be fun. We just found we share other interests too, like chess. We can practice together."

"Where will you play?" Papa seemed to have problems with this new development, this was happening too quickly for him.

"Oh," I hesitated, pretending to think.

"Well, Pepi lives in a hostel, we can't go there." I paused, looked at my accomplice, then at my father and smiled, as if an idea had come to me. "He can come to my place," I said, beaming at Papa, "we'll play in my room."

The atmosphere changed. The warm spring day turned chilly suddenly, an icy wind blasted from Papa's direction, as he glared at me. He didn't say a word. But I knew I had achieved my objective.

Pepi didn't come with us anymore on a Saturday. I didn't know if Papa realized what I was up to, or if he thought my promiscuity was breaking through. It didn't matter. I had achieved what I had wanted to.

He finally dropped the subject of men. He didn't talk any longer about the youth of today, and stopped his psychological tests. Obviously he had found out enough about me.

So our lives and our relationship continued in their roundabout ways. Nothing materialized as I had expected and as Papa had promised. My wishes and plans for my future were ignored, and I had to continue with my training as a tailoress. And my life with Frau Hammer was only getting worse. If Papa was not around, she was in charge of me – she even said so.

My apprenticeship with Tante Paula continued, and I still attended college once a week. Every Friday I went to the Maerzstrasse, just round the corner from the Pelzgasse, where Mama was.

When I thought of her, I was hurting as much as on the day I'd left her, perhaps even more so, because I might never see her again. I loved my mother so much and I missed her – but she had told me, never to come back. Her door was closed to me forever.

What if I did knock at her door? She would throw me out, I was certain. "Don't come back," Mama had said. But even if she would have nothing to do with me, if I knocked on her door, at least I would have tried. If she threw me out, it would be no worse than it was already.

So next Friday after school I went to visit Mama.

As I entered the building, it took all my determination not to turn back, as the old, well-remembered smell of damp and decay enveloped me, as well as the feeling of despair.

I knocked and Mama opened the door. Somehow, I don't know how it happened, but I was suddenly in her arms – the first time since I had been a small child. We both cried. It was the first time ever I saw Mama cry, and the first and only time we cried together. Everything was all right again, all the barriers washed away by our tears. I was so happy. Mama was talking, but I hardly heard what she said. That my mother was holding me in her arms, was the only thing that mattered. I loved her so much, and now I knew that deep in her heart she loved me too.

We talked, in short, disjointed sentences – how I was, what I was doing, where I lived, how Mama and Willi were. We both were sad when I had to leave, but I'd back. I'd visit every Friday now, and if I managed to get away from Frau Hammer, I came on Sunday too. Willi was home then. He too seemed glad to see me, although he didn't say so, and acted as if it was normal I was there.

Now, I no longer lived at home, we got on better, especially with Mama my relationship changed. She really surprised me. No recriminations, no: 'I told you so.' Not that I said much about Papa or my life with the Hammers. But Mama knew I wasn't happy, she could always tell.

I couldn't keep my visits secret, at least not those on Sundays, as I had to account for my time. Now, my father talked badly of Mama, just as she had done about him – though he didn't carry on as long, but simply left. Why couldn't they leave me out of whatever was between them? It had nothing to do with me. Why couldn't I see both my parents, wherever I lived?

My relationship with my mother had so much improved, but with my father and the Hammers everything got only worse. My mother had trusted me; I appreciated this only now, when I realized my father had no trust in me at all. With Mama, in my free time, I had more or less come and gone as I pleased. This was over; the freedom I was used to had gone completely. Papa had taken firm control of my life through Frau Hammer. If I was late from work, he always knew, Frau Hammer told him on the telephone. And she would shout and nag, claiming she and her husband were responsible for me. I must always come home immediately from work or college, or ask beforehand, if I wanted to go somewhere.

But if I did ask, could I visit Mama or my friends, I was refused. There was always a reason why I couldn't visit Mama, or Helga and Hilde. To go alone for a walk was not allowed either, about a cinema visit or going swimming ... I didn't even dare to ask.

It was impossible to get things right. Even if I tried to get home from work on time, I rarely succeeded as Tante Paula always kept me late, and gave me extra chores, just when it was time to go. Or I had to run errands, deliver a dress or buy something on the way home; as she was my boss, I couldn't refuse and got into trouble when I arrived home.

But I still enjoyed my walks with Papa at the weekend, and our bike rides through the Prater. But we came no closer. The barriers were firmly in place, emotionally, and physically.

Tante Paula made matters worse, uttering strange, obscure warnings about men, emphasizing they were not to be trusted. "One can't trust any man, no matter who it is – not a relative, not even one's own father," she would say. "Don't let anyone get too close, Gerti."

I didn't understand what she was trying to tell me. Was she warning me about Papa? I didn't trust him now anyway. But I became even more suspicious about things I had never thought of before. Riding on the back of his scooter one day, Papa said to put my hands in his pockets, as it was such a cold day. Tante Paula's warnings flashed through my mind. I wouldn't have put my hands in his pockets, had they fallen off with frostbite.

Absolutely everything went from bad to worse. I was upset, because my father had broken his promises, and refused to talk about my future and what I wanted to be and do. And as the weeks went by, he started lecturing me about the value of money, stressing how much he paid Frau Hammer for my keep. He added it up – or rather made me do it. He even talked about the alimony he had sent Mama for my keep, during all the years.

I remained silent, what could I say? In my heart I told him, I had not asked to be born, he had created me. He had responsibilities. But had I spoken these words, I would have been told off for my cheek and ingratitude.

There was only one bright spot left on the horizon: our holiday together. I would travel to India with Papa and his friends. He had told me so much about India, and I was looking forward to it so very much. For me, this journey was not just about seeing India. I was hoping that without the influence of Frau Hammer, Papa would see me in a different light.

But one day, as I began to talk about the journey to India, Papa said I couldn't come.

"Only men are coming on this expedition," he said. "We sleep in tents. To take a girl is unthinkable."

This was the end of my dream. My father would not even talk about it; he just said the discussion had ended. My last dream had ended, and with it the last opportunity to improve our relationship.

CHAPTER 22

PAPA

With Easter approaching, Frau Hammer asked if I had to go to work on Good Friday. Suspecting she wanted my help with spring cleaning, I said quickly: "I have promised my mother to visit her." No more was said on the subject, which surprised me, because Frau Hammer usually never gave in, if she wanted my help.

But it was strange. Although both she and Papa tried to prevent me from seeing Mama, they always gave me chores, rather than forbade it, as they did with everything else. I suspected the court had stipulated Mama should be allowed access, but I never found out. I didn't think about it much, all I could do, was to visit her, when I could.

I still hoped to visit Mama on Good Friday, because for now, nothing more was said on the subject.

Next day was Sunday; I was in bed still asleep, when my father stormed into my room. He looked furious, but just said: "Come into the kitchen, at once," and left again.

What was the matter? What was wrong? I wasn't aware of any problem; I had done nothing out of the usual.

I threw some clothes on and followed him. As I opened the kitchen door, I saw Frau Hammer, arms folded across her ample chest; she looked at me with a gleam of triumph in her eyes. I knew something was wrong, but as I saw the satisfied smirk on her husband's face I became very uneasy.

My father must have stood next to the kitchen door, I hadn't seen him, and his blow took me by surprise. He struck me across the face, and the force of it sent me reeling across the large kitchen, where I landed in a heap.

"That's what you get, Gerti, for refusing to help with the housework," he said calmly. His voice quiet, almost relaxed, made the situation even more unreal and bizarre.

I could not believe what had happened. How could my father do this to me? And in front of these people? Even the children were present and looked down on me, as I lay on the floor, trying to get myself together again. I wanted to hide my innermost feelings, the pain and humiliation I felt. How could he treat me like this – his own daughter?

I tried to make my face look blank, void of expression, as I slowly got to my feet. I would not allow him to see how hurt I was, or show the astonishment I felt over this attack. I had done nothing – nothing wrong – I had done nothing wrong at all. How could he hit me – and in front of the whole family. I looked up into his face. When he saw defiance in my eyes, he got so furious, he started punching me, hitting me with strong, heavy blows, and then kicking me, as I collapsed on the kitchen floor, unable to move. I lay at their feet like a dog, totally humiliated and in pain.

I didn't know what he said – or if he said anything even. It took all my strength and willpower, not to show what I felt. My face should be without expression, like a mask, so one could see what was inside of me.

Eventually, slowly, I got to my feet.

I knew my face was blank, but my eyes spoke of my defiance and fury, as I stood in front of him, blood coming from my mouth, dripping down to the brown linoleum floor.

He was talking, I now realized, but it took a while until I could understand his words.

I should be grateful to him, he said, and to Herr and Frau Hammer too. They provided me with a nice home, with good wholesome food – I even had my own room. I had everything I needed, and more, and I dared, I dared, refuse to give a little help. I did not appreciate what they all did for me.

Frau Hammer chimed in, supporting my father, saying what a good man he was to take such good care of me, and show so much concern.

Basking in her praise, he confirmed how well they looked after me. All three were united in their opinion; I had to change, pull my weight, and be grateful for what they did for me.

I stood on the same spot, unable to move or to speak. Everything was so unreal, so bizarre, as if I were in a nightmare, and would wake any minute. I could not understand what had happened – what was still happening – and why it should be my fault. Even now, as I stood, hurting all over, with blood running down my face, they were still telling me off.

It couldn't be that I was responsible for my father's action. It was he, after all, who had beaten me with his fists, until I collapsed on the floor. My blood was still dripping all over me.

Ignoring the blood and the pain, I said nothing. I looked at my father one last time, turned, and went to my room. I just wanted to be away from these people, who didn't know me at all, pulling me to pieces, in between praising each other.

No one stopped me from leaving the kitchen, they just continued talking.

I sat down in my chair, where I stayed, how long I didn't know. My mouth stopped bleeding, but I stayed where I was, without moving, feeling nothing. Around me was emptiness, a vacuum, nothing was real. Inside of me was this same feeling of emptiness, until suddenly I was gripped by an immense anger. It was so unjust! All I had done was trying to visit my mother. Was this a crime? I hadn't even refused to help – though I had tried to escape Frau Hammer for a day, I admitted now to myself. But was this so terrible? Even if I had refused to help with the cleaning, it didn't warrant his attack – nothing could justify such treatment. He had no right to strike me – especially so brutally.

My father had not even given me an opportunity to tell him my side of the story.

Sometime later, Papa knocked on my door. I didn't answer, but he came in anyway. Pulling a chair up, he sat down opposite me and began speaking. But although I heard him, I didn't understand what he said. His voice seemed to come from somewhere far in the distance. Around me was still this bubble of nothingness, this complete vacuum. I was unable to speak or to move. When I didn't react, he got up and went to the door. Before he left, he turned his head, and looked at me. Suddenly I could understand his last words. "From now on," he said, "you will do exactly as Frau Hammer tells you."

I was alone again. Perhaps now I could think about what had happened, and what I should do.

I was nothing but a servant here – an unpaid servant with no regular time off – with hardly any time to myself at all, without any say over my life. My father had all the power over me, he was my legal guardian, and now he had custody as well.

Only a few months ago I told the authorities, that I wanted to live with him. What a fool I had been. I had never lived with him; I lived with the Hammers as their servant. And my father believed everything they said. He trusted them, not me, his daughter. He had not even asked to hear my side of it all, given me no opportunity to explain.

I could do nothing, he had control, had all the power. I would be here for three more years until I was eighteen. Only then I could live where I chose. Three years were an eternity – I was here only three months – but three years? I couldn't endure it. There had to be a way to escape, a way out.

But if I ran away, the police would bring me back. If I told them he hit me? They would say it was his right as a parent to chastise me, especially after Papa told them, how difficult and disobedient I was. Frau Hammer would only be too glad to give evidence, as would her husband.

But in my heart I knew, no father has the right to act in this way. Papa often said that a branch had to bend, to avoid breaking. But this branch would not break, nor would it bend – not to him, not to the Hammers. I must find a way out.

What if there is no way out? What then?

There was silence in me, until a small voice from deep within me whispered: 'There is always death.'

But I was afraid of dying, of going to hell. If I killed myself, I would go to hell, of this I was sure. Suicide was a capital sin, one of the worst kinds; warranting hell; where I would stay for eternity.

But I was already in hell, now, and three years in this hell would be an eternity.

Did I have the courage to kill myself? And how would I do it? I thought for a while, quite detached, considering various options, and decided it would be easiest to cut my wrist with a razor blade. The blood would flow out of my vein, out of my body – I would die. Visualizing my death, a strange feeling of peace overcame me.

I had found a way out, my last way out – but not yet. This option was a kind of insurance to be kept in reserve, if I could find no other way.

Suddenly new doubts arose. Would I be able to, did I have what it takes to cut my wrist? To cut into my own body?

I wasn't certain, but needed to know, and must find out. So I decided to cut my wrist, but on the outside of the arm, where there was no danger. But if I could cut myself on one side of the wrist, I could do it on the other side, too.

I looked for a razor blade, and gingerly began cutting through my skin. Tiny blood-droplets appeared, staying there. But to be effective, the cut must be deeper. Slicing the skin had been easy, but to put enough pressure on the blade to cut deep was different. I felt strangely reluctant to press harder, to cut deeper into my flesh, into my own body. It was not the pain I was afraid of, but something else. Something deep within me was revolting. I had to overcome whatever it was.

'You have to do it, Gerti, if you really want to be certain you can kill yourself,' I told myself firmly. 'So get on with it, just press down hard on the blade.'

I did. At first more pale flesh opened up as I cut deeper, and more tiny droplets of blood appeared, until suddenly my blood flowed freely – lots of blood. Now I could stop.

The cut was about four centimeters long, and one centimeter deep – which would be deep enough. To stop the blood from staining everything, I grabbed my cardigan and put it under my arm, absently watching the yellow fabric turning red.

I felt different suddenly, amazingly strong – free and strong, as if mine was the power over life and death. Out of this new feeling, I decided to make a promise, a blood oath, like the Red Indians, my friends from long ago, when I was a child.

Until now, I had avoided every thought to do with my father. Now I was strong enough to think about him. What did I really feel towards him? Did I hate him? Should I hate him, after what he had done?

At least my thoughts were clear again. But I still felt strange, as if I was looking down at me. As if a part of me was just observing, as if it was not me who sat here, thinking about hate, whilst watching drops of my blood falling on to the beige linoleum floor.

And as one part of me still thought about hate, another whispered I should do something about the blood, because it was staining my clothes and the floor.

Why should I care, said another Gerti.

At least I felt better. In me was peace, the flowing blood had taken my anger and desperation away, so far, the real Gerti could come back. Suddenly it became clear to me, that hate could never achieve something good, something useful. I would only damage myself.

I would not waste my feelings, my energies, on hate.

But my relationship with my father was finished. I would never feel for him as a daughter, never again accept him as my father. He would not be a father to me anymore.

Now I was ready for my oath, for my blood-oath.

It seemed only right to stand up. "From now on," I said quietly but firmly, "I will never again acknowledge you as my father. As long as this scar can be seen, you will get no acknowledgement from me, as my father."

To add weight to my oath and perhaps because the flowing blood strengthened me – gave me a sort of a high – I cut three times across the heavily bleeding wound. Now it would take longer to heal, and the scar would be visible for a long time, adding power to my oath.

From that day on I controlled myself tightly. If a way out existed, I would find it. And the less my father knew what was going on inside me, the better. For now, I would do everything Herr and Frau Hammer demanded, I would do as I was told. If Papa thought, I had accepted my lot, his suspicion would decrease and he'd watch me less, as Frau Hammer would too, making it easier to get away.

But where I could flee to, I had no idea.

Next day Papa came to my room, wanting to talk with me. He pushed a chair opposite to where I sat, and waited to hear what I would say. But I remained silent. It was too late for talking; I had nothing to say anymore. Noticing the bandage under my sleeve, he asked what had happened. I said I had cut myself accidentally, it was just a scratch. When he realized I would not open up, he left.

Frau Hammer didn't try talking with me, she just kept me busy. When I was not at Tante Paula's, I had to help spring clean the flat, whilst listening to her lectures, which had two themes: be grateful to your father, and you don't know how good and easy you have it here, Gerti.

As I worked by her side, trying not to listen, I constantly had to remind myself to keep calm, not to talk back and to pretend to have accepted my fate.

Finally, after days of hard work, all the cleaning was done. It was Easter Sunday. Just as we finished that morning's chores, the doorbell rang. I stood next to Frau Hammer as she opened the door. My mother stood in front of us – I couldn't believe my eyes. In my wildest dreams I would not have thought it possible, that Mama would brave the hour-long tram journey to come and see me.

But she had come – after all that had happened, after what I had done.

Mama stood face to face with Frau Hammer, who clearly didn't know how to deal with this situation, though she seemed to know who stood before her. And Mama made it clear, in case Frau Hammer had any doubt.

"I've come to see my daughter," she said in a firm voice, a challenge in her eyes. I could feel her determination; she was not going to be put off. Frau Hammer must have realized it too; she stood back from the door. "Just for once," she said to me, "you can take your mother to your room."

Mama sat with me in my room. "Since you did not come," she said, smiling at me, "I came to see you, Gerti."

I was so happy. My mother had come to see me, she cared, and she loved me. Mama opened her bag and took out Easter eggs – real eggs, hard boiled, colored red, blue and yellow. Then she gave me three oranges.

"I am sure you don't get enough vitamin C here." She smiled again, and I smiled too, remembering how she had always made sure we ate enough fruit to get plenty of vitamin C. And she was right, I didn't get much vitamin C, an apple or an orange was a rare treat. But I didn't want to think about fruit, it was so good to be with my mother, after believing I had no one who cared.

But I couldn't tell Mama what had happened. This was my own doing; it was entirely my fault I was here. I had wanted to go to my father. It would only upset Mama if I told her the way Papa had hit me, and she couldn't help. I was in my father's care, which was legally binding.

So we sat together and talked, just about small things, and the big heavy lumps stayed in my heart. But it was good to be with Mama, and when she left I felt much better, as I went back to the kitchen to help with the cooking.

Not much happened during the next few weeks. My escape plans remained nebulous, nothing turned up to give me new ideas. Then another problem emerged – but this time it was a problem for my father. He didn't know what to do with me when he travelled to India. Tante Paula was closing the shop in July and August, and intended to give me an unpaid holiday. I wanted to go to Pupping, but my father wouldn't agree.

"You are too young to go anywhere without supervision," he said, refusing to 'waste another word on this subject.' I couldn't believe it. I had stayed in Pupping since I was four – always on my own. Now I was fifteen, he thought me too young. What about all the other times I had been in Pupping? I was younger then, and he hadn't cared. My father had always been my legal guardian.

Papa said he knew nothing about Pupping. I asked him to come for a visit with me, and see for himself. It only took three hours by train. But he just shook his head, turned around and left.

Frau Hammer found the solution to Papa's dilemma. Her father had a saw mill in the country; the family spent the school holidays there. I could go with them for six weeks, and for the first two weeks of my holiday, Papa would send me to a holiday camp, arranged by my college. I would be well supervised, he assured me. My holidays had been arranged – end of discussion.

I could accept going to a holiday camp, perhaps I might even enjoy it. But six weeks with Frau Hammer and her family, was a terrible prospect. Perhaps I should run away from the holiday camp, but I still had no idea where to go. Anywhere in Austria, the police would find me, and bring me back to Papa and Frau Hammer.

Vague ideas formed in my mind about girls being abducted, and sold to the orient. The papers were full of stories, how they ended up in brothels somewhere abroad.

A few times I had been approached by men who pretended to be film producers, who said they were looking for girls with talent and looks. Anyone in their right mind knew what was behind it. But perhaps I could make use of such an offer, allow myself to be abducted, and flee when I was abroad. I was old enough to work for my living. But how could I avoid being kissed – or something worse?

Apart from it all, I didn't need to go to a holiday camp to be abducted, the prospects were much better here in Vienna.

I decided to wait a little longer, to see what opportunities would present themselves, and in the meantime think again about what I could do. But as time went by, and no one wanted to abduct me and nothing unusual happened, I suffered increasingly under the monotony of my daily life. I had nothing to look forward to, all I did was work. I was so tired in the evening after finishing my chores; I just fell into bed and slept.

At five thirty I had to get up for work, getting home in the evening around six. Then I ate and washed up, carrying on working for Frau Hammer until eight or nine, when I was glad to go to bed. On the weekends I looked after the children and worked in the house. I still spent time with my father, but now I didn't enjoy it anymore, and neither did Papa. We were just pretending, playing happy families. It was a lie and we both knew it. Our conversations were superficial; we were just making noises, because to be silent was even worse.

I couldn't visit my friends or invite them. If I wanted to go anywhere, I had to ask permission. And when I did, there was always a reason – an excuse – why I couldn't go.

But I still visited Mama in my lunch break from college on a Friday. She finished early at work, to be home for me. But I couldn't tell her what was going on, it would upset her too much and affect her health – and she couldn't help me anyway. And I still was afraid she might say, she had warned me about Papa.

I tried to talk with Tante Paula – although I could not even tell her the truth about Papa, and how desperate I really was.

"I told you not to trust him," my aunt said, as we sat eating our lunch. "Be careful, Gerti." Then she thrust a small book across the table at me. "You are old enough to know these things now – read it, Gerti."

I looked at the book; it was about sexually transmitted diseases. What on earth did my aunt think of me? Or was she implying something about my father? I was too embarrassed to ask, so I said no more to Tante Paula about my problems.

Totally cut off from anyone to confide in, my life became unbearable. I did everything Frau Hammer told me, but after completing one job, the next one was already lined up for me. And whilst I worked I had to listen to her constant nagging. She kept me occupied until I went to bed, totally exhausted. I didn't even have time or enough energy to read a few pages in a book.

One morning, as I was getting ready to leave for work, I'd had enough. Frau Hammer kept on and on, nagging, and rubbing it in. Had I really thought I could get away so easily, go to Pupping on my own? I was only a child, needing discipline and supervision, which I would get when we went on holiday. There would be plenty for me to do. Her sister had two children; I could look after them, as well as her three. Oh yes, there would be plenty for me to do, she repeated, plenty of housework, in such a big household.

She was baiting me, waiting for me to talk back, to lose my control. If I retaliated, she could complain to my father. Refusing to give her this pleasure, I stayed silent, and when she paused for breath I asked: "Can I go now, Frau Hammer, or I'll be late for work?"

"Don't forget to come home early," was her parting shot. "It's laundry day, I need you to do the washing with me."

I found it increasingly difficult to stay calm. She wanted me to lose my temper, to complain to my father. Well – I'd had enough – I would give her a reason to complain. Tonight I would not go home, but stay away. It was hard work to do all the washing by hand for the whole family. I had always helped willingly. But today she could do it without me. I would not be her willing slave.

I reached this decision as I walked towards the tram-stop, ignoring the boy who tried chatting me up. I wasn't interested, I was too traumatized, and too much was on my mind – until I realized, if I didn't go home this evening, I had time on my hands. Perhaps a date would be good for me, take my mind off my problems – and he looked very nice. He was also very persistent, and finally I had to smile, and agreed to meet him this evening.

As I got off the tram, Paul was waiting for me. He was an attractive young man, with fair, curly hair, and a ready smile, slightly crooked, conjuring up a cute dimple in his left cheek. We walked for a while, taking the street towards the Prater, with its fairground surrounded by lawns, flower-beds and bushes, and benches strategically placed under flowering trees. It was almost summer, a beautiful, warm evening, with a few hours of daylight ahead of us yet.

Once it got dark, the Prater would change its appearance. The families went home, and gangs of leather-clad youths rode around on their motor bikes, looking for trouble. Prostitutes of the cheapest kind would appear, with their pimps somewhere around to protect them. I didn't know all the details, but I knew it wasn't safe in the Prater, once it got dark.

But now in June it would be light for hours – and I wasn't alone.

We sat down in one of the beer gardens, in the shade of a flowering tree, and had a snack. Paul was a nice, interesting young man, about nineteen, and I would have enjoyed myself, could I have stopped worrying. But my mind was going round in circles; I couldn't stop thinking about my dilemma, and what would happen once I got home.

Later, as we walked for a time, we talked, but I was so tired. I was totally exhausted, and needed to sit down. So we settled under a tree, children were playing, running after a ball, and under the next tree a family had spread out their blankets, having a picnic. I told Paul a little about myself. I wanted him to know he was wasting his time with me. I might have allowed him to chat me up, but there was no more I would allow.

Paul smiled, his eyes crinkling, he knew what I meant. "It's OK, Gerti," he said. "I understand."

He was a really nice boy, I thought, sighing contentedly, as he assured me he would act like a gentleman. And as he put his arm around me, I leaned my head on his shoulder. A yawn escaped me – I was so tired. Sleep overtook me, suddenly, unexpectedly, and I knew nothing until I woke with a start, feeling something strange on my throat.

It was already dark; I must have slept for a long time. At first I didn't know where I was. But when I became aware of my situation, I pushed Paul away and jumped to my feet. What was the matter with me? How could I have fallen asleep – just like that – with a strange man sitting next to me? I looked at Paul. He was not strange anymore, but still, he was not someone I could trust completely.

I was furious with myself. I walked so fast, I was almost running; I needed to get away from the dark bushes and trees towards the brightly lit fairground. Paul was keeping up beside me, trying to apologize. I was apologizing too; I should not have fallen asleep. The way I had behaved, I couldn't blame him if he had thought – my mind refused to go further. But although I felt uncomfortable in Paul's presence now, I was glad he was here, because groups of youths in black leather-gear circled around on their motor bikes. Now and again they stopped to talk to one of the women standing around, wearing short, skintight dresses and glaringly loud makeup – the Prater prostitutes, I had heard about.

Finally we reached the streets, and I felt safe. Paul said he wanted to see me again, in spite of everything, because he really liked me. I had to smile; I liked him too, in spite of everything. But I knew I would not get the opportunity to see him.

I tried once more to tell him what my home life was like, but he insisted; if we couldn't make another date, at least we could stay in contact. He wrote his address on a piece of paper, and wanted me to take it.

"You might change your mind," he said. "Or you might need a friend. You can always come to this address if you need help. You can count on me, Gerti."

I was touched. He was really sweet. In other circumstances, perhaps. But I had more serious considerations now, so I pushed the piece of paper into my handbag, as I hurried towards home. I had no home, but I had to go somewhere to sleep. I had to go back to the Hammers.

Rounding the last corner, I quickly said goodbye to Paul, in case my father was looking for me. I was right. Paul had only just turned around, when I saw my father coming towards me.

"Where have you been?" he asked. "It's almost midnight."

He spoke quietly here on the street with people passing by, but I could tell from his eyes how angry he was.

I had prepared myself for his question. "I went for a walk," I said equally calmly. "I sat down, and because I was so tired, I fell asleep."

"Alone?"

I nodded. Why did he stare at my throat? Later, looking into the mirror I saw the red mark. I knew from my friends what it meant, and Papa obviously had known it too.

My father had reported me missing, and in the morning I had to go to the police station. I was questioned first by a man, then a woman. I told the same story each time I had told to my father – and my polo-neck jumper hid the mark on my throat.

Both officers assured me I could confide in them, and I was tempted to tell the one, who was a woman, what my life was like with Frau Hammer. But how could I trust the police? They would be on Frau Hammer's side, if even my own father was.

No point in telling anything to anyone, my words would only be used against me. So I stuck to my story – it was true after all, I just left out some details. When the officers saw I would not say more, they let me go.

From now on, the hostilities were barely veiled on either side. I became the sullen, uncooperative and ungrateful girl, my father had seen in me for a long time. If there had been any doubt in his mind, it was gone now. I had proven what kind of a girl I was: promiscuous, in need of a firm hand. My father was glad; Herr and Frau Hammer were willing to provide this firm hand, when he wasn't around. He talked like this in front of me, wanting me to hear what he thought of me, and that I didn't stand the slightest chance against him or the Hammers.

Because he was going to India, Papa intended to transfer his rights as my legal guardian to Herr Hammer, giving him full authority over me. I was present when they discussed all the details, and designed a document, which was legally binding, and would be witnessed by my father's solicitor. Papa repeated again and again, I had no choice, but to do what either of the couple told me. My father signed the paper in my presence, and handed it over to Herr Hammer to keep.

He was handing me over too. I felt like a dog, given to a new owner, an owner not to be trusted, who would abuse and mistreat, instead of giving care.

It was the last time I saw my father. After handing over the certificate, he shook hands with the couple and left. No goodbye, Gerti, or see you in a few months when I am back from India.' My father just left without saying a word to me.

Two days later, my holiday started. I would spend the first two weeks in a youth hostel, and then join the Hammer family for six whole weeks – if I didn't find a way to avoid this fate. I could but try.

CHAPTER 23

BOAT TROUBLE

My holiday turned out quite differently than I had expected. My father must have made a mistake; he'd never have sent me here, had he known we were not supervised at all.

As long as we made our beds and were in by midnight, we could do as we pleased. A teacher was always on duty, but just for emergencies, and if we didn't seek her out, we were left to our own devices. I could hardly believe it. Papa must have been misinformed, or I would not be here. But whatever the reason, I would enjoy myself, my problems could wait. From this beautiful place I would not run away.

The youth hostel was built at the foot of a hill, with trees all around, and a small waterfall at the back. Almost daily I went to the waterfall, to stand under the streaming water, feeling its magic power washing away my pain and disappointment. Somehow my life would go on.

We were a mixed group, boys as well as girls, although the girls outweighed the boys by far. Not that I was interested in boys. I was too traumatised by what had happened in the space of just five months. The dream I had cherished for years, the dream of a father who loved me and cared, had turned into a nightmare. I needed time to think, be by myself, alone with the healing power of nature, which was so freely and abundantly provided for me.

Yet I felt lonely, and longed for the easy camaraderie the other young people enjoyed. I wanted to be part of the group. But I couldn't join in, and if one of the girls invited me, or just came along, I felt uncomfortable. I seemed to have nothing in common with anyone. They talked about boys, clothes, makeup and dancing, all subjects which held little interest for me now, and I couldn't talk about what was on my mind. So I said little, and avoided company. Soon I was left to my own devices.

I was so glad to be here. Being surrounded by woods and mountains gave me new sustenance, and to swim in the lake at any time I wanted, was unbelievably wonderful. The Wolfgangsee is an enormous lake, surrounded by mountains and hills. Just a ten minute walk from the lake, at the foot of a mountain, was our hostel. Looking up at the steep wooded slopes, I felt the need to stand right at the top, free like the wind. It was freedom I had missed most. With Mama I'd had a certain amount of freedom – I had her trust. I realised it only now, when it was too late. I had jumped from the frying pan into the fire, in my desire to escape the confines of the Pelzgasse, and to be with my father.

But here I had found a refuge, just for a while, and I would take full advantage to find myself again. Nature provided all I needed to recover and heal. I loved the mountains and hills, and climbed one after the other. It was wonderful to feel the wind in my face as I stood on the summit, free as the falcons and hawks above me. Never before had I been so high up in the mountains.

I saw deer stepping out of the trees, and as I climbed higher, mountain goats were jumping down rock faces; marmots scurried around or stood still, watching for danger, disappearing quickly at my approach.

It was a hot summer, thirty degrees in the shade. In spite of the heat I spent every day in the hills. I came across meadows with Almenraush, and found Enzian, dark velvety blue, rare in its beauty. As I climbed higher, the trees disappeared, and Latschen, the small crippled fir trees, took their place.

One day, close to the top of a mountain, I discovered a beautiful lake: the Schwarzensee. The black lake was true to its name. I stripped off, and slipped into the water. It was icy cold, despite the sizzling heat. I swam, dived and revelled in the feeling of freedom in the icy wetness. It was like a dream I didn't want to end. The cold finally drove me out, and my chest pains, which I had managed to ignore so far. I sat on the water's edge, waiting for the pains to ease off, before starting the long way back down the mountain.

"You swam in the Schwarzensee?" A local youth said when I came in for my meal and told him where I had been.

"Well, you are lucky to be alive. This lake is fed by underground streams; it's not safe to swim, because of the strong underwater currents."

Strange, I thought, I had felt only peace and enjoyment. The lake had been kind to me.

All of nature was kind and nurtured me, helping me to heal. I began to feel better, until something terrible happened.

This particular day started like all the others. As it was already exceptionally hot in the morning, I decided to spend the day by the lake. I would settle in the shade of a tree and read my book, swim in between, and perhaps take a rowing boat out into the lake, where I could be totally alone, with just water in every direction. Although all kinds of boats, even ships, crossed the lake, it was so big; you hardly ever saw a boat, except far in the distance.

It was still early morning as I settled close to the water under a tree, and after reading for a while, I got up for a swim. A man nearby seemed to have the same intention. One of his legs was amputated above the knee, and he used crutches to get along. By the edge of the water he manoeuvred himself into a sitting position, put his crutches down, and awkwardly pushed with his arms until he was deep enough in the water to swim.

'How brave,' I thought, admiring his courage. 'He is not hiding from people. In spite of being disabled, he carries on living.'

He was a big, strong man, with bulging muscles, about forty years old. Perhaps he had lost his leg in the war, I thought, feeling sorry for him.

As I swam out into the lake I forgot the man until he surfaced by my side, and started talking to me. I'd have ignored him, thinking he was trying to pick me up, but because of his disability I reconsidered. Perhaps it had taken all his courage to speak to me. So I responded to his words about the hot weather and the beauty of the lake, then turned around and swam towards shore. But the man followed me. On land, as he needed time to get on his crutches, I lost him as I walked on. I settled down on my towel, expecting him to walk past, but he sat down next to me.

Reluctant to hurt his feelings, I waited a few minutes, then got up and said goodbye. He looked up reproachfully. "Surely you are not leaving yet, on such a beautiful day?" he asked.

"I am taking a boat out," I answered reluctantly, anxious to be away from him.

"I'd love to come out on the lake," he said. "Could we share a boat?"

It was the last thing I wanted, but how could I refuse such a simple request to a man with only one leg? He'd think I didn't want to be seen with him, because he was a cripple. I had to agree.

So we hired a boat and I rowed out into the open waters. I liked rowing, but my companion was not content just to sit on the bench, he also wanted to row, and insisted on sitting by my side, and to row together with me. I tried it, but we couldn't find the right rhythm. I suggested he do the rowing, and I would sit on the bench, and relax. But he stopped me.

"Let's row alternatively," he suggested. "When my oar comes up, you dip yours in."

I tried. "Now you are getting it," he approved. "The Red Indians row like that."

He laughed, a weird laugh, but though I wondered what he found so funny, my mind was still on the Red Indians, as suddenly, without any warning, he threw himself at me.

He was on top of me with his leg between mine, his hands trying to rip my bathing suit from my body as I fell back, hitting my head. I fought back, and tried to get out from under him. But he was too strong – too heavy for me, and his weight kept me fixed where I was. The sides of the boat restricted my movements, kept me his prisoner. I couldn't push him from me, he was too strong, and his weight was squashing me.

Grabbing my hands, forcing them over my head, he held both my wrists with one hand. With his other hand, he was pulling, ripping my bathing suit from my shoulder, my breast, his fingers hurting me. At the same time he tried kissing me, and all I could do was move my head from one side to the other to avoid his mouth.

My bathing suit was a tight fit, made of strong elastic material, which wouldn't rip. It fitted tight on my legs, so tight, his fingers couldn't get very far, especially as I kept fighting, and now and again I got one of my hands free, though not for long. He was too strong, I knew I could not win this battle, I was already exhausted, and I was terrified.

My head was underneath the top bench – I couldn't push him off. Escape seemed impossible. With one hand he held my wrists over my head, his other hand tearing and pulling on my suit, hurting me.

Although I was terrified, some inner part of me remained quite still and detached, noticing every detail – absently almost, as if this had nothing to do with me. It was this inner Gerti, who said, you are in the middle of a huge lake, no one can help you. You must help yourself, Gerti.

But he was too strong for me, and had all the advantages in the confines of the boat. I was in pain and exhausted, how much longer would I be able to fight him off?

But the inner Gerti refused to give up, she would not surrender. It was she who made me aware that my hair was getting wet, and it was her voice telling me, it was wet, because so much water was in the boat. Through her, I realised how strongly the boat was heaving from side to side, as if it would capsize. I hoped it would, but these boats were built for inexperienced tourists and broad and stable. Perhaps I could make it capsize – use the rocking motion of the boat? I felt a glimmer of hope, and realized how close I was to giving up. Fear and exhaustion, and the hopelessness of my situation threatened to overwhelm me. But I must not give up.

Knowing I was fighting for my life, I struggled harder, which made the boat heave even more. But though it almost stood on its side, it wouldn't capsize. Suddenly out of nowhere, an idea was in my mind, and I adjusted my movements to become completely one with the rhythm of the boat.

In the meantime my attacker succeeded in ripping the bathing suit from my breasts, but I had to ignore his hands, and concentrate, and when boat almost stood on its side, in this split second, I arched my body up high, pushing him with my last strength. As his weight eased, I slid from underneath him into the water, just as the boat stood on its side.

Swimming away as fast as I could, I didn't dare to look back. When eventually I did glance back, I saw the boat had not capsized; the man was still in the boat, shouting something at me.

I was too far away to understand his words. Perhaps he was angry – or he was afraid I would drown – they would look for him if I did. We had hired the boat together, the police were sure to question him if I drowned.

It would be easy to drown in this lake, miles from land, with no boat in sight. I was only a moderate swimmer, I would never make it to shore.

On the other hand, my chances were better here in the water, than they had been in the boat.

What should I do now? Start swimming towards shore? Or follow the boat, knowing I could hold on, if I became too exhausted?

The man was sitting in the bottom of the boat. In the water, he would probably be no danger to me. I could outswim him, I was sure to be quicker, having two legs.

And, surely he would not be able to rape me in the water?

All the while he kept shouting, and as I swam closer I understood his words: "You'll drown, come back into the boat, I won't touch you."

I didn't believe him, but what else could I do?

I was already exhausted, not just from swimming, but the fight and my terror and pain had taken their toll. I would never make it to shore. But I couldn't trust his words, and must be on guard.

"Will you sit at the front and row?" I finally called back.

He pulled himself up, sat down on the bench, and took the oars. If he made one move towards me, I'd simply jump back into the water. I wouldn't be any worse off, better perhaps. I'd get some rest, and we would be closer to shore. Or a boat might come along in the meantime.

Keeping my eyes on him, I pulled myself up on the side of the boat, climbed in, and sat down on the back bench. He stayed where he was, rowing steadily, his strong hands on the oars. I kept watching these hands, in case he should attack me again. It gave me a horrible feeling, but it was easier than looking at his face. And I had to watch him, be alert to any danger, ready to jump into the water.

But nothing further happened, he just kept talking. This stranger, whose name I didn't know although he nearly raped me, kept talking as if he couldn't stop. He tried to excuse his behaviour, said he lost control, and that I had no idea what his life was like. No woman wanted anything to do with him.

I stayed silent, holding on tightly to myself, just wanting to reach the shore safely. I had been so scared, was still afraid now, the danger was not yet past.

But he was scared too, I felt it, and could tell by the way he talked. He was scared in case I went to the police. He didn't say so, but kept asking me what I would do now.

What could I do? I should report him. But he'd deny everything, and what proof did I have? Absolutely none; it would be my word against his. We had taken the boat out together; I had rowed out on the lake of my own free will. He might even claim I had tried to seduce him, and this was my revenge because he refused. Whatever happened, I would get the blame, I had gone off with a stranger, and nice girls didn't do that.

What could I say in my defence? That I'd felt sorry for him, because he had only one leg? It sounded lame to me now, though it was the truth.

I imagined my father, receiving the news, and what he would say. Frau Hammer would swear to my bad character, telling everyone how promiscuous I was.

Finally the boat reached the shore; I stepped out and walked away as fast as I could. Let him return the boat, he could do with it as he pleased. I didn't look back, picked up my clothes and walked on. My knees wobbled, my whole body started to shake. I felt terrible. Now that I was safe, my whole being seemed to shake, and I was close to collapse. I lay down on the ground – near a group of people for safety – and stayed there, semi-conscious. Sometime later I dressed, and walked back to the hostel. I told no one what happened, and I tried not to think of what might have been.

That evening, I stood under the waterfall for a long, long time, numb at first, and then beginning to feel the power of the water washing away what had happened: the man, his touch on my skin, and my fear.

The next few days I tried finding my balance again. I walked in the wood, but was too weak to go far. When I finally went to the lake, I had to force myself to go into the water. But I would not allow this man to spoil my enjoyment. It was over, he couldn't hurt me anymore. It was unlikely I would see him again.

I wanted to enjoy what was left of my holiday. Only too soon I would have to return to Vienna to my old problems and the new ones to come.

I didn't believe any more that something might turn up, to stop my return to the Hammers. After what had happened, I would take no chances, and definitely not with a man.

Slowly I recovered, and returned to the mountains and hills. On my last day I went up the highest peak all around which I had saved as a kind of a going-away present. This was the only mountain around I had not yet climbed. It was hotter than ever, and proved a long and difficult climb, but the view from the summit was worth it. Above and around me was only sky, and birds of prey, circling, completely free. My whole world, which suddenly seemed small and of no significance at all, was way down below.

Looking down, I saw a whole valley covered with beautiful deep pink flowers, a carpet of Almenrausch. I knew these flowers were protected, but with so many, I could surely pick some for Mama. She loved flowers, and these were special, as they only grew high on the hills, where she couldn't climb to anymore. Tomorrow I was going back, and would take the flowers to Mama, before facing the Hammers.

Mama loved her flowers, I had wrapped them in wet paper and a thick towel, and the blooms had stayed fresh. We sat in the kitchen and talked – about the hills I had climbed, the beautiful lake, and the waterfall. I kept to myself what had happened, what went on inside me, my fears of the future and of the next day.

Willi came home from work. Mama and I cooked our meal and we ate. Even Willi was nice all evening.

"Why don't you stay the night?" Mama asked, because it was late. I was surprised by this invitation which I hadn't expected. I wanted to stay, though I would get into trouble with the Hammers, my jailers. What the hell, I thought. I was in enough trouble already, it couldn't get much worse and at least I would have this one night with my mother.

Early next morning, just as I had dressed, a knock came on the door and Herr Hammer stood there. He said I must come with him, I was his responsibility. And although he said nothing more in front of Mama, I knew this would come later. But I had to go with this man; my father had signed me over to him. What else could I do?

"We'll pick up some cases from the flat, and take the train for the country. My wife and children are already there, waiting," Herr Hammer said after we'd left. He said nothing else, until we entered his flat.

His calm and politeness had suddenly gone. He closed the door, grabbed my hands, his fingers between mine, squeezing them, whilst pressing my hands back, to hurt me.

"Kneel!" he hissed. "Kneel down on the floor, Gerti; say you are sorry, and that you won't give me any more trouble."

In spite of the pain, I could only look at him in amazement. Did he really think I would kneel to him, a young man, barely ten years older than me? Or that I would kneel to anyone? But I soon realised he meant it, as he increased the pressure on my fingers, and bent them back further.

"Kneel down in front of me," he shouted, losing his cool, hurting me even more.

'Nothing will make me kneel to you,' I silently promised myself as the pressure increased, and the pain was so severe, I thought my fingers would break. Suddenly something clicked in my finger joints, and in me something clicked too. It was no longer I who stood there, determined not to kneel. I, my real self, was up here above, watching.

But when Herr Hammer let go of my hands, I was my old self again.

Without another word, he handed me two bags to carry, and took the rest of the luggage. We took the tram to the station, and boarded the train. Not a word was spoken until we arrived in a small village in lower Austria. We got on the bus, and soon arrived at our destination.

The house stood on its own within acres of ground. A big, solid building, with cows and horses around, and a large saw mill and outbuildings close by. Around it all a brick wall, six foot high, solidly built, the only opening a gate, which was in full view of the house. Everything seemed well built and solid – to me it looked like a prison, and it felt as such, as Herr Hammer took me through the gate, and closed it behind us.

My father had told me of the beautiful woods all around, in a last attempt to make me accept this 'holiday'. He had said I'd be able to go for walks in the forest and by the stream. I had doubted his words, and was proven right. My working day started early in the morning, and I was lucky if I could finish in the evening by eight.

I had to look after five children, help with the cooking and cleaning, and do all the dishes. It was a big household, and I soon gave up working fast to finish my chores, because it was pointless. As soon as I finished, I was given another job, until it was time for bed in the evening. Thankfully, I had a bedroom to myself.

I knew my reputation had gone before me, because Frau Hammers' relatives treated me as if I could not be trusted. When I asked to go for a walk after finishing my chores in the evening, I was told no one had time, and I couldn't go by myself.

I was a prisoner. With a high brick wall surrounding the property, I'd have to run through the gate, which was overlooked by the kitchen windows. I would risk someone following me, bringing me back. But even if I managed to run away, where could I go? The police would return me back here, because my father had put me into the care of the Hammers.

But my life here was unbearable. I was not only treated as a servant, but like a prisoner. No one talked with me, except to give me another job to do. My only friends were the children I was in charge of. I couldn't help being friendly, play with them when I had enough time. I wouldn't take it out on the children, it wasn't their fault. But with the adults I turned into the sullen, difficult adolescent I was treated as. I didn't rebel openly, but was surly, overly polite, on the edge of insulting.

But I didn't care anymore, I had nothing to lose.

A few days passed in this way, until Maria, the oldest child, brought me a letter from a man who worked in the saw mill. His name was Andreas, and he wrote that he had found no opportunity to meet me, but hoped to remedy this soon.

I asked Maria who gave her the note, but the six-year-old wasn't very good, describing this man.

I ignored the letter, but the next day Maria brought me another note, asking me to meet him in the evening, next to the gate by the walnut tree.

Again I ignored the letter. I was in too much trouble already, and to get away was impossible anyway.

Out in the yard with the children the next morning, Maria produced a beaker and asked me to get her some water from the pump in front of the house. I was just about to give her the full cup, when I saw him. He had walked right up to us, and stood in front of me, the child, waiting for her water, between us.

I forgot Maria and her water, because as I looked up, something strange happened. This man was so familiar, as if I had known him my whole life. But I had never seen him before, because him I would have remembered. He was about twenty, tall with wavy blond hair, his skin bronzed by the sun. In his deep hazel eyes I could have got lost in. He looked at me, and whispered so quietly only I could hear: "I will be waiting for you. Tonight at eight."

I knew I was being watched through the kitchen window.

So what, I thought, let them watch. There is no crime I am not already guilty of in their eyes.

Not that I considered anything clearly, my half formulated thoughts disappeared as I looked into his eyes. It was as if our souls met. Slowly, just with one finger, he tilted my chin up, bent down – over Maria who stood between us – and kissed me. It was a gentle kiss, our lips barely touched, but it took me to another world, another time. I was almost in trance. Everything glowed in a mysterious light. Time seemed to slow down. I watched myself from somewhere outside of me, watched both of us – watched as the water from the cup dripped slowly down, to the child's upturned face between us. After an eternity – or perhaps just a second or two – the kiss ended, I turned, and walked slowly away. I knew I would never see him again – they would see to it. But I did not regret the kiss; it had been so beautiful.

Now I had shown my loose morals in front of witnesses, my life became even worse. Not only Herr and Frau Hammer, but her relatives also took every opportunity to tell me, that I couldn't be trusted. Now I was only allowed to take the children in the garden if an adult was close by.

At every opportunity someone reminded me that my father had entrusted me to their care, and they would not disappoint him, even if they had to watch me day and night. Now I was really a prisoner. I almost gave up, until something in me started to rebel. Enough was enough; I could cope no longer with this. I had to escape, whatever the consequences. But my escape must be planned and executed carefully, if it failed, my life would be worse and my next escape even more difficult, if not impossible.

So I tried to keep calm, pushed my feelings to one side, to consider my situation logically. Could it be that my father and Frau Hammer had overlooked something? Was there a weak point in their calculations, which I could use to my advantage? Even if Papa had left me in the care of these people, had they the right to make me work from seven in the morning to eight at night, sometimes longer? The law didn't allow young people to work more than forty-four hours per week – this I knew from Tante Paula and my contract as an apprentice. Perhaps if I told the authorities, they'd help me. But would they believe me? Should I take the chance?

I knew which authorities to go to, after my session with the police in Vienna. But the whole matter had to be considered thoroughly before I made an escape plan.

The next day was Sunday, and to my surprise, after finishing the dishes after lunch, Frau Hammer gave me the afternoon free. "But don't leave the grounds, Gerti," she called after me.

I took a book to the garden, and sat down in the shade of a horse-chestnut tree, pretending to read. Instead, I tried to think of a plan. But I couldn't get my thoughts straight. I needed someone to confide in, someone to talk with. But there was no one; I had only myself to talk to, and to rely on.

"You always complain you are treated as a child," I said to myself. I looked around, but no one was there to hear me. Just to be safe, I continued the conversation silently in my head.

'This is your opportunity to be an adult, to make your own decisions, alone.'

But I didn't know how. My burdens were too heavy; they were threatening to overwhelm me.

Should I give in, abandon every thought of escape and stick the six weeks out – I had survived one week, only five were left. But even if I did manage somehow and returned to Vienna – it would be no better there. Something had to change. I had to escape; I had already made this decision and only needed to work out how to do it.

I would plan my escape like an adult and succeed, so I wouldn't be brought back like a disobedient child.

My thoughts flew this way and that, but I couldn't think of a plan – how could I make such a big decision without talking to anyone? If I only Hilde was here, or better still, my friend Mariandl from Pupping. I felt so alone. No one was here for me. Perhaps Papa was right. Perhaps it really was me, who was the problem – the difficult, stubborn and ungrateful child, the promiscuous adolescent I was treated as.

I pushed these thoughts away. I must not think like this. It wasn't the truth, and I would prove it.

'Show you are an adult, Gerti,' I challenged myself. 'Stop moaning and feeling sorry for yourself, and think constructively.'

So I began to formulate my plan.

The first problem was where to run to. There was only one possible answer: I had to go to my mother. Although we had never spoken of it, deep down I knew Mama would take me back, in spite of what she had said when I went to my father. But I needed to ask her.

I didn't want to return to my mother. I loved her; we got on well now, but probably only because I no longer lived at home. If our flat had been bigger and I had a room to escape to, it could have been all right in spite of Willi – although he too had been much nicer to me since I'd left. But this could change, once I was back.

But where else could I go? Pupping came to my mind, but the authorities were unlikely to agree. The children's services might let me go back to my mother, but not to somewhere they knew nothing about. Besides, I had never been invited to stay in Pupping for good.

I would have to go back to Mama. But first I needed to ask her.

I would travel back to Vienna, go to Mama, then to the police – to the juvenile section – and explain why I had run away. I could give several reasons, but would stress the amount of hours I had to work.

I would present myself as a nice, trustworthy girl, so the police officers believed me.

Now, I only had to find a way to get away with a few hours start. Luckily I had enough money for the fare.

How could I get away? Should I creep away quietly during the night? But with dogs in the house and in the grounds, I might be discovered. And the doors would be locked, the windows downstairs had iron bars, and the gate might be locked too. During the night there wouldn't be a bus to get me to the railway station. No, I would have to think of a way Frau Hammer would allow me to leave, or better still, that she sent me to go on the bus.

I needed to be on my way to Vienna before she suspected anything, so I wouldn't be reported missing, perhaps even found, and brought back. After considering various options, I decided to pretend I needed a doctor. About medical matters, Frau Hammer took her responsibility seriously. If she believed I was ill, she would make sure I saw a doctor.

What could be wrong with me? Nothing too serious or a doctor would be sent for. My heart had to be kept out of it altogether. Papa knew nothing about it, and so it should stay. The less the grown-ups knew about me, the better, I had discovered long ago.

I took a close look at my body, but found nothing, apart from a few spots on my legs, probably from insect bites. They were lumpy and red, and some had turned into blisters. If I scratched them they would bleed.

Perhaps I should modify my behaviour. If Frau Hammer thought her methods were successful, that I had given in and was trying to mend my ways, she might not watch me as closely, making it easier to get away.

But I needed to start gradually not to arouse any suspicion. And to lose no time I would begin now. And so, as the children came into the garden, I played with them. Later, I told them stories, making sure we settled under a tree close to the open window. Now, Frau Hammer could not only see how well I got on with the children, she also could hear us.

During the next two days I became more polite, but I was careful not to overact, in case of arousing suspicion. But everyone just seemed pleased to break me of my bad habits. Frau Hammer even pointed out how much better it was for all of us, since I had finally seen my mistakes, and tried to do better. Soon I volunteered for jobs, and was polite and helpful.

On the third day I started limping. When Frau Hammer asked what was wrong, I pointed to the patches on my legs. They were red and infected from my constant rubbing and scratching.

"You have got to go to the doctor, Gerti," she said straight away. I pulled a face, pretending this was the last thing I wanted. But Frau Hammer insisted I should go the next morning.

I was lucky with the weather, it rained, and I could wear my anorak, which was wide and had an elasticated bottom. I'd hide a change of clothes underneath. Squeezing a pair of shoes under my armpits, I had to be careful not to relax my arms, or the shoes might drop through the elastic, and my other clothes would fall out as well. My handbag was overfull with my personal things and my book. But no one noticed, and all went well. Pushing the kitchen door open, I stuck my head through and called: "I'm off for the bus, see you later, Frau Hammer."

As I walked through the gate, everything was suddenly different – I felt different. My body felt light, as if a heavy weight had gone from my shoulders. The sun broke through the clouds, the trees and the bushes seemed to come alive and were vibrant with colour, with beauty and magic, giving off a beautiful glow. With a little regret I thought of the boy who had kissed me. In his kiss there had been beauty and innocence, our lips barely touching, our bodies so far apart a child could stand between us. Yet there had been magic – for an instance our souls had met.

I pushed these thoughts away. I must stay in the present. With a long way ahead of me, I had to take care, each step of the way.

It turned out to be easier, than I had dared to hope; everything went exactly to plan. I took the bus, bought my ticket, but instead of getting off for the doctor, I stayed until the last stop, which was the station. The morning train came, and I was already reaching Vienna, when I might still have sat in the doctor's waiting room.

Entering our building, the old, well remembered smell of damp and decay hit me, bringing with it the usual feelings of despair. I ignored them. I would just have to put up with the Pelzgasse for a few more years. There was worse. At least I had some kind of freedom here with my mother, and I had her trust.

I would never have thought it possible, but I was glad to come home again.

Mama wasn't even surprised to see me. I told her why I had run away, but didn't go into details. I only said I had to work all the time, and was allowed no freedom. I could not bring myself to ask Mama if I could come back, but she did it for me. "Why don't you stay here with me, Gerti?" she said simply, and in her eyes I saw understanding and love.

"Yes, Mama," was all I had to say, and we smiled at each other. But it was not quite as easy, I told her, some things had yet to be sorted.

"I can't stay yet," I explained, "because Herr Hammer will call the police. I have to go to the authorities first and tell them my side of the story."

It felt strange, entering the police building. Not so long ago I had been forced to come here, now I came voluntarily. Last time I had been a difficult adolescent, now I played the role of a well brought up girl, who had got into difficulties through no fault of her own. I told the officer who stood at the entrance, that I had run away, and could I please speak with someone who dealt with cases like mine. I felt elated, as if something gave me a push in the right direction – I had to hold myself back not to giggle. I was playing a role, and I knew I was succeeding; only one more hurdle had to be overcome. But I must remain serious.

'Remember Gerti,' I told myself, 'good impressions count. And first impressions are especially important.'

The officers were nice to me, but I was questioned for hours. First by a woman, conferring in whispers with a man, who, although present most of the time, didn't speak with me. Sometimes he left the room – perhaps to check on the facts, or to find proof for the things I said. I told only the truth, as I answered the same questions again and again: Why did I live with the Hammers? How had I come to be with my father, if I previously lived with my mother? And where was he? Why was I not living with him, but Frau Hammer? Where was he now? And why did I run away?

I explained that my father had gone to India for the summer, and left me in the care of the Hammers. And that I had run away, because I had to work from morning until late in the evening each day, had no free time and was not allowed to leave the house.

I kept quiet about Herr Hammer bending my fingers to make me kneel. It sounded too unlikely. They might not believe me, and doubt other things too. And I said nothing of my father's assault. But I did explain how he had signed me over to the Hammers and my life since then.

The hours went by, and I was questioned about the same things again and again, though they tried to formulate their questions differently, to trip me up. But as I stuck to the truth, I just had to repeat everything, each time I was asked. I didn't exaggerate, rather played things down, because I was embarrassed about it all, and would have preferred not to talk about it. This only supported the role I played, the role of the nice, well-brought-up Viennese girl.

But I didn't really have to play this role, because I was this nice girl, but only in part, because I was also the sullen, troublesome adolescent. But she was not allowed to come to this interview. I spoke nicely, with just a touch of Viennese dialect.

Again and again I was asked: where was my father? But I could only say somewhere in India. They must have tried finding him, or to get a forwarding address. The Hammers had also been questioned; I could hear the officers whisper about it when they went to the far end of the room. It always seemed to end with: "if he is so concerned about his daughter, why does no one know where he is?"

All afternoon they tried finding my father, but failed. I had to wait, was given a sandwich and a Coke. Then the woman officer asked me: "Is there anywhere you can stay, Gerti?"

"I can stay with my mother," I said. "Or I could go to Pupping, where I used to go every summer." As I told her about Pupping, I got so carried away, the officer smiled, though she stopped me by raising her hand.

"I can't give you permission to go to Pupping," she said, "but for the time being you can stay with your mother. The court will make the final decision about your future, but," she looked into my eyes and smiled reassuringly, "don't worry, Gerti. You won't go back to Frau Hammer ever again."

I only went back to pick up my clothes, weeks later, after the court had decided I should stay with my mother permanently; she now had custody of me again. The decision had been made in my father's absence: the police had failed to trace him, not even a forwarding address had been found.

I didn't see my father again until three years had passed. I was visiting Lilly, and as I walked up the garden path towards her door, my nephew Peter came to meet me. He took my hand. "Tante Gerti, come," he said. "I'll show you my Opa."

And there he was, standing in front of me – his grandfather – my father. Papa said nothing, he seemed to be waiting. But I had nothing to say. So we just looked at each other in silence.

"We do know each other already," I finally said to Peter, as I turned to walk towards the house, away from my father. I did not turn round as I heard the garden gate close softly behind him, as he left.

CHAPTER 24

VIENNA 1956

I was so glad to be back home; I did everything I could to get along better with Mama and Willi. I appreciated my mother much more; she had come to my rescue when I was close to despair, in spite of having caused her so much pain and anguish. My father, I pushed out of my mind, in the same way I had done as a small child. I would not think about him anymore.

Mama seemed to be glad to have me back, and to my surprise, even my brother was nice to me, never mentioning the past, and that I had wanted to go to Papa. Before I had left, he would not have missed such an opportunity to torment me. Perhaps he too was glad I was back, even his sarcastic remarks were not as frequent, and not so harsh any more.

But I also was different. We both had grown up; Willi was no longer a boy.

With his apprenticeship finished, he was a book keeper and earned well. His firm had kept him on, and recently he had been appointed head of a small office, dealing with debt – an advanced position for someone so young. Now he was able to make good use of this talent to get people to pay up what they owed.

For the first time in my life I was glad to be in the Pelzgasse. I could go out to meet my friends without having to account for every hour, though Mama still told me off if I came home late, but I just let it wash over me.

The only serious problem was I had nothing to sleep on. A bed was expensive. Mama and I put together what money we had, but it was only enough for a garden recliner – a simple metal frame with canvas stretched over it. I didn't realise how dangerous this thing was until we brought it home. I had to get on it exactly in the middle or this contraption would either catapult backwards, or, on rare occasions, fold over on me from both ends.

Mama and Willi went to bed at eight, and if I came home later, the flat was in darkness. I'd let myself in quietly, undressed in the kitchen, and crept to my bed. Now the danger was at its highest, with Mama's bed right next to mine, with only three inches in between. If her hand lay on the edge of the bed, she would wake. Should I manage this hurdle as well, sitting down with a sigh of relief, the damned contraption would collapse. I'd somersault backwards and land on the floor with a crash.

"Where have you been?" Were always Mama's first words, and whatever I said, she'd tell me off, and my brother joined in. And though we all tried to get along – especially me – under the stress of living together so closely again, our old patterns re-established themselves. But I didn't take it to heart, now that I knew my mother loved me. Even my brother must at least have wanted me here, or he would have done his best to stop Mama. It was doubtful if she could have held out against him, though recently she had surprised me.

And it was terrible for them, to be woken up after going to sleep. But I found it impossible to come home from work, eat, and get ready for bed, as Willi and Mama did.

We heard nothing from my father or Frau Hammer.

My case went back to juvenile court. Mama was given custody again, but my father retained his rights as my legal guardian.

This meant I could get no passport until I was twenty-one. He would never give his consent. We had frequently talked about it, as I would have liked to visit Christl. She had often invited me and wanted me to live with her permanently. She would have been glad of my company and help, with their second child just two years old, and a new baby on the way.

I would have loved to go, away from the confines of our flat, and from my job, which I hated as much as ever. The adventure to live in a foreign country attracted me also, but it was no use, I knew Papa would never sign a passport.

At least, I was now in the third and final year of my apprenticeship. Once I passed my exams, I had a qualification to fall back on if I couldn't find a job which suited me better. We still had high unemployment, so finding a job might be difficult, and a qualification would certainly help.

But everything to do with sewing was hard for me, and my teachers were concerned. My lack of interest had been apparent for a long time, and although theoretical subjects were no problem, in my practical work I was slow and barely scraped through. My teachers sent me for psychological testing, where I had to look at coloured ink blobs, and say what I saw in them. Then I was asked lots of questions, which I answered as best as I could, and eventually I was told my job was totally wrong for me, and my mother should come for a talk.

Mama did come; she even listened. Then she said: "My daughter is finishing her apprenticeship; she needs to earn her living." She got up, took my hand, turned, and walked out of the door. I could do nothing but say goodbye, and follow her. I felt sorry for the psychologists – so much time wasted – and I felt sorry for me. But I saw Mama's point: I just had to carry on for another nine months.

My situation, and what I'd been through, affected my health. My heart pains grew more frequent and were so strong; I couldn't always hide my condition from Mama. She made me go to the doctor, who prescribed tablets.

My throat and chest infections also increased, I developed high blood pressure and constipation. Doctor Melka said I was too young to take blood-pressure tablets for the rest of my life, and advised me to eat more brown bread and salads and fruit, which I did, and just carried on.

But though my life wasn't easy, and most of my dreams had crumbled to dust, one dream came back to life. Walking through the city, I had discovered several judo schools and watched the training. I talked with the instructors, but it was always the same: judo was a sport for men only. Only one teacher, Herr Buchelle, an impressive fourth dan, tried to help me. He said he would be happy to teach a group of girls, but there must be at least ten.

But where could I find another nine girls? None of my friends were interested, they thought I was crazy. Why should any girl want to do something unladylike as judo? Girls went out on dates; they went dancing, swimming, and perhaps even skiing – but judo? It would be as ridiculous as girls wrestling, boxing or playing football. I could not find one girl who would learn judo, not even as a favour to me.

But I continued to visit every club I discovered, and finally I was lucky. The class was in progress as I entered the dojo for the first time. I watched the boys practising. They were all between fourteen and twenty. If I were a boy, it would be so easy.

During the break, I talked with the instructor, Herr Wunsch. He was an old man, sixty-eight, I learned later. I told him how much I wanted to learn judo.

"We don't have any girls," he said. Then he fell silent for a while, his forehead wrinkled into dozens of fine lines, obviously he was thinking hard. He looked at me intensively, as if he was searching my soul. Finally, he came to a conclusion.

"If you don't mind mixing in, and training with the boys, we'll manage somehow. You can change in my office; there is a curtain to pull across. Just watch, when you go to the showers after training, the cubicles have no locks. Throw your jacket over, so the boys know you are in there, I'll let them know the score. The beginners practise three times a week – Tuesday, Wednesday and Friday, from six to seven."

I could hardly believe it! I felt elated, full of joy and excitement. My whole world was suddenly right again. My dream was about to realise itself after all.

At home, I said nothing about judo; Mama would never accept I'd do such a sport. Perhaps I could pretend to go to a gymnastic club – at least it wouldn't be a complete lie, as we did gymnastic exercises as a warm-up.

Mama didn't agree with gymnastics either, but she couldn't stop me, as I went straight from work to the club, to get there at six.

I worried throughout the journey – stupid worries went through my mind. I had to walk in on my own, go to the office and greet Herr Wunsch – what should I say? Would I look a fool? Would I look ridiculous on the mat, I was awkward and fat – well, not really fat, but I could do with losing a kilo or two.

I had never taken part in any sport – how would my heart cope with it? I had already serious problems, especially during the night, fighting for breath whilst trying to hide my condition from Mama. My heart had only got worse through the years.

The doctor had warned me that I should do everything in moderation only.

Moderation? I didn't want moderation. I needed to live fully, swim the Danube, parachute from the sky, and climb the highest mountains. I wanted to live at the edge, to the extreme, learn to control every muscle in my body, throw giants over my head with a judo throw.

Walk, had the doctor said, and don't run. But I wouldn't listen to her. I would run – I would do everything – I would really live. From now on I would forget about my heart and my fears, stop whingeing, and begin my new life. Even if everyone stared at me and thought I was crazy, I would walk into the dojo and learn judo.

The club was sponsored by the public transport system and subsidised, and if I spent no money on anything else I could afford the fee. The beginners could borrow jackets and belts, and wear their own trousers or shorts, so, for the time being, my problems were solved.

I was the only girl, but as two boys also started at the same time, at least I was not the only newcomer. I worried about the people sitting on benches to watch; they looked surprised as I entered the dojo in my borrowed gear, the only girl, among so many men and youths. It would be so embarrassing if I couldn't follow the instructions, people might laugh.

But I needn't have worried; we three newcomers were taken round the corner to a second mat where no one could see us. Here we were taught the rudiments of falling – particularly the judo roll – which was all we did on that day, and all I did for the next three months.

The boys progressed quicker. I just couldn't get the hang of the judo roll. I developed three permanent bruises: one on my elbow, one on my shoulder, and one on my back. I seemed to bump from one painful spot to the next, in my endeavour to master this new challenge.

I tried to make a joke of it, and said my problem would hold me back from making the black belt. But my lame joke only brought a smile of pity to the lips of my fellow students, who had already accomplished the tasks of falling, and were learning to throw.

But nothing would stop me, I promised myself again and again. If I had to overcome my inabilities, overcome them I would. My body would do as I wanted. And eventually it did. As the months passed, I caught up with the other beginners, and in time became better than the two boys.

One day another girl joined our club. Her name was Eva, and we became friends. We often spent time at her home, where I always found a warm welcome. Her parents made me feel part of the family. Entering their flat, I entered a different way of life, almost a different world.

Eva's parents were reporters, and their free way of life – their casual acceptance of me as their equal, delighted and fascinated me. Eva and her brother had travelled the world with their parents, yet the whole family was so natural, so unaffected and casual about themselves and all their adventures, that I loved them all, particularly Eva.

My new friend was only fourteen and still went to school, but in many ways she seemed as old, even older than me. Small and petite, with dark brown curls surrounding her pretty face so alight with the joy of living, she would call for me at my crummy flat. Not with one look did she ever betray that it was so much worse than her beautiful home.

She was the only one I ever knew, who could charm even Mama, bring a smile to her lips. Yet she talked as natural and casual with my mother, as with everyone else. But from Eva, Mama accepted whatever she said, and never criticised her.

The day I had dreaded came. I had to tell Mama about judo, admit my gymnastic class was a front, a lie really, if it came down to it.

With Tante Paula's help, I had made myself a judo suit out of cheap bedding material. It looked just like a professional suit, no one would know any different. The problem was I had to take it home with me. It was better to tell Mama the truth before she found the suit.

Mama was furious about my lies, but I knew behind her anger was worry about me. She reminded me that the doctor had said I was not to take part in any sport. I had to stop with judo at once; it had been bad enough when she thought I went to a gymnastic class.

But because I went straight from work, she couldn't stop me; only tell me off when I came home.

I was sorry to upset my mother so much, and I understood how she felt. But I had to continue, I had to learn judo, it was the last dream I had left. I just had to train my body and mind in this way. It was what I needed.

Eventually, Mama resigned, she realised that I would go to judo whatever she said. I had reached my goal; my life had taken a turn for the better. After work, I met Eva, or one of my other friends, and three times a week I went to the club, where I belonged now. Here, being a girl made no difference, we all trained alike. One of the boys became my friend, his name was Martin, and he teased me a lot – but in a nice way, and I soon learned to retaliate.

We often practised randori together, a friendly contest on the hard floor, where a throw had to be stopped before the partner would hit the floor. Once, Martin couldn't stop his throw, and I fell with full force and passed out.

"You'll have to excuse me, if I am rough, Gerti," he said, when I returned to life again. "I keep forgetting you are a girl."

I glowed with pleasure – what a compliment! I was so proud. Martin had admitted I was as good as one of the boys.

But there was another boy I noticed: Christian Such, junior champion of Austria, and the best in our club. He only attended the advanced class. I was still a beginner, but as a special favour, Herr Wunsch allowed me to train with his advanced students, as long as I took the beginners class too.

Christian had a green belt, and I often watched him in contest. With his jacket open, his body glistening with sweat, every muscle was clearly defined on his chest and his shoulders. He was handsome, with short, curly blond hair, green eyes, a cute, straight nose and a short upper lip, showing perfect white teeth when he smiled.

He was up there in the league of champions, and I still wore a white belt, though my examination for the yellow belt was only a few weeks away.

In spite of all this, it happened quite often that we practised together. But it was probably just a coincidence.

Coming home from judo one evening, the light in our flat was still on. My mother and brother were waiting in the kitchen for me. Something was very wrong, I could feel it. Mama was too upset to be coherent, she talked about a letter, but I didn't know what she was on about, until she thrust it into my hand. It was addressed to me. That she had opened and read it was clear, but although I was annoyed about it, there was no point arguing. And as soon as I started reading, I had other worries.

'Dear Gerti,' the letter began like so many others, but continued in a very different way. I was shocked as I continued to read.

'You will soon regret what you did to me, Gerti. The time has come, to pay you back for all the humiliation I suffered from you. You have to die. I watched you go by, but you took no notice of me. I suffered, because you ignored me. I even went to your judo club and tried talking to you, but you just walked away.'

Who was he? It couldn't be one of the boys from the club, I practised with them, we talked and laughed together, I didn't ignore any of them. Perhaps a visitor to the club? So many came, relatives and friends – anyone could walk in and watch.

Sometimes a man tried chatting me up, asked for a date, because I was unusual, a novelty – a girl competing with men – a challenge to some. I avoided long conversations, and refused to meet anyone, my time it the dojo was too valuable to waste.

I turned my attention back to the letter and carried on reading.

'Your time has come,' he wrote again. 'You must die.'

I could not believe it. Who hated me so much to want me dead? He described my death, the pain I'd suffer, the cemetery where I would be buried – and my grave.

'It will be soon,' the letter ended, without signature, or any indication who the sender might be.

Who could have written it? Who hated me enough? The letter was handwritten, on thick yellow paper, the envelope matched. My name and address were on the envelope, but there was no stamp. He had delivered the letter himself. It must be a man, there was no doubt. If a woman had tried talking with me, I would remember. Few women came to the dojo.

I tried to make light of it, not to frighten Mama even more. She wanted me to go to the police with her, but I refused. It must be a stupid joke – a sick joke, someone was playing. So I pretended everything was all right. But I worried, especially coming home in the dark. It was winter and dark early.

I couldn't stop thinking that someone wanted me dead. Even at work, terrible pictures appeared in my mind.

Two days later another letter arrived. This time two pills were included, large green tablets. He wrote for me to take the pills; it would be an easier death, than what he had planned for me. The letter was four pages long, covered in small disorderly writing, rambling, full of threats. And when he described how he would make me suffer, his sadistic pleasure was obvious. Some of his writing didn't make sense, but the intention behind it was clear, and was repeated over and over: he would kill me. He had drawn a window with crossed bars, like in a prison. He wrote about the agonies he had suffered behind these bars. But my pain would be ten times worse. Take the pills, Gerti, the letter ended, easier for you. Again, there was no signature.

Mama was desperate – even Willi was worried. I didn't know what to do. It was November, when I came home from work it was dark, the Pelzgasse would be deserted, and there was no light when I entered our building.

Next day was Saturday, and Eva came to collect me in the morning, her brother Harold was waiting for us in the street. He often spent time with us, and had almost become a brother to me too – a helpful and nice younger brother. I was glad he was with us, when I told my friend about the letters.

Eva looked at her brother and asked: "Have you got your pistol with you, Harold?"

He nodded. She held out her hand and to my astonishment her brother took out a pistol from his pocket and put it into her open hand. And everyone around us just walked by as if nothing was happening – no one cared, that two teenagers handed each other a pistol, on the open street in broad daylight.

Eva showed me the gun, and explained, travelling abroad, they frequently got involved in dangerous situations. Eva had even been kidnapped once. All of her family had pistols, but hers was at home.

A murder threat didn't seem unusual to Eva. She talked about my situation in the same casual way she talked about clothes, or if she could borrow my boyfriend, just to find out how he kissed. She had asked this favour a few days ago, and I had agreed – after all, he was just a boy I had met a few times. Eva had promised to return him – which she had – and the boy had not minded at all.

But this was no game – someone wanted to kill me. But though Eva and her brother discussed my situation in their easy way, they took the threat seriously. Eva wanted me to carry the pistol on me, to defend myself. And she showed me right here on the street, how to use it.

"You push the safety catch back," she said, "like this, and then you pull the trigger." She stopped short, because there were two blanks in it. "Just to frighten someone off," she explained. "But the gun can be loaded properly." She looked up, smiling at me reassuringly. "We just have to get proper ammunition, Gerti."

I shook my head, this was taking it too far, someone could get killed although the chances it would be me, decreased with a loaded gun. I would feel better about the odds, but things could go wrong. I shook my head again.

"OK, if you are worried about live ammunition, Gerti," Eva made the concession, "I'll try to get tear gas."

I definitely preferred tear gas, it would make my attacker helpless for a while, so I could get away, perhaps even overpower him.

"Anyway," Eva added, "it would be difficult to buy real bullets. We'll get tear gas, Gerti, but it could take a few days."

Later, after a pleasant day with Eva and her family, I felt better going home with a pistol in my pocket. I had stayed longer than intended, and it was getting dark as I turned into the Pelzgasse.

The street was deserted and dark. One street lamp shone weakly, and I realized even darkness has shadows. My killer could lurk behind any parked car or in the doorways of houses. He could be anywhere.

It was totally quiet. There was not a sound, no people around not a soul to be seen who could help me. Suddenly a figure came towards me out of the shadows. It could be the madman, but the man just walked past.

It had been stupid, to stay out so late but if I avoided coming home in the dark, I would be a prisoner. And I had to go to work. Even if I came straight home, it would already be dark. And there was judo.

Better to stop thinking altogether, until I was home, in the safety of the flat, with my mother and brother. Then I could relax. But first I had to get there. I felt like running – but knew I mustn't. He could be watching; I must show no fear. And I had to be aware of what happened around me, or he'd catch me unawares. So I made myself walk slowly, looking round all the time. 'Stay away from the cars,' I told myself, 'but don't get too close to the doorways, in case he is hiding, and ready to jump out.'

Finally, l reached my house. The entrance was in total darkness. I had to enter into this darkness, walk through the hallway, and up the staircase to our flat.

With my right hand I turned the key in the lock; my left hand grasped the cold metal of the gun, still in my pocket. It felt reassuringly solid, in spite of being loaded only with blanks.

Pushing open the door, I stood listening: all was silent. I could see nothing, except shades of black. Usually this was no problem, I knew my way, and every step was familiar. Along the corridor, past the stairs leading off to the left, then past a passage to the right, until I came to our stairway. Next came the entrance to the cellar. If he dragged me there, no one would hear me. Various rooms were down there, it was two storeys deep.

I walked on through the dark. Up the stairs, round the corner to our flat. Nothing had happened.

I was safe now.

Mama was still up; she insisted I should go to the police. But what could the police do? They would say it was a sick joke. And perhaps it was.

As I showed my brother the gun, Mama got really upset. But I stayed calm and showed Willi how the pistol worked.

"And then you pull the trigger," I said. I barely touched it when there was a terrific bang.

Mama screamed, her voice full of fear. When she had calmed down a bit, she said: "This gun is more dangerous than anything."

Then we worried about the neighbours, they must have heard the shot. Soon they would be banging on our door, to see what had happened, to check we were safe.

But no one came. The whole house remained silent. It seemed even quieter than before, all the usual noises, had stopped. There was absolute silence.

"You could be shot in this house, without anyone raising a finger. No one would care," Mama complained. "No one is coming now, to see if we are still alive. I will not have this gun in my flat, Gerti."

"Do you want me to get killed?" I countered.

"No, Gerti," Mama said. "I want you to come to the police with me, and you can take this weapon with you and leave it there."

But I still believed the police wouldn't take the letters seriously, and I was afraid to be ridiculed. Apart from two letters, nothing else had happened yet.

Not yet – this was the point.

A few days later the next letter arrived. Mama didn't wait until I came home; Willi told me, she took all the letters to the police.

"What was in the new letter?" I asked, full of apprehension.

"He wrote that it was your last chance to pray, and to go to your final confession." Willi seemed reluctant to go on. In spite of having tormented me so much in the past, now he was on my side. He didn't want to tell me the horrible details.

But I had to know, and asked him to tell me the truth.

"He urged you to kill yourself, because it would be much worse for you, if he had to do it. And then he described how he would torture you."

We heard Mama's footsteps on the landing, and she opened the door. My mother looked terrible; she had suddenly aged twenty years. I felt so awful, so guilty of having brought this trouble upon her.

We waited for her to speak, but she wasn't able to, and just sat down, breathing heavily, shaking her head now and again, as if she couldn't believe what had happened.

"They are not going to do anything," she said eventually, having recovered a little. "The police can't help us, until he does something. They said writing letters is not a crime, irrespective of what is in the letter."

For a while we sat in silence, even Mama had nothing to say anymore. Later, when she felt better, she told us, after reading the letters, the police had taken the threats seriously. But they were powerless, until he attempted to realize his threats. After stopping to regain her breath, she added: "And then it may be too late."

We sat in silence once more. Eventually Mama began with her usual litany: why was it always me causing her trouble, jumping from one danger or problem to the next? All her three children together hadn't caused her as much worry, as I, all by myself. And now the rest of my misdeeds were pulled out to see the light of the day.

I was even glad Mama was telling me off, it was much easier to listen to her usual accusations, than to see the fear and worry in her eyes, and to know I had caused it.

Although I pretended not to take the letters seriously, Mama knew I was frightened. At times I was petrified.

But nothing happened in the next few days. Instead of alleviating my fears, this made it worse, because all the time I waited for something terrible to happen. At work, sewing away at whatever was in my hands, my mind would conjure up the worst scenes: how this madman would suddenly jump out at me with an axe or a knife. Or he tried to abduct me, dragging me down the steps to the cellar, to perform all the horrors he had written about.

How could I ever have been so stupid, to crave adventure and excitement? All I wanted was my old life back, without any threat hanging over me, like the sword of Damocles. To live without worry, the highlight of the week a visit to the pictures on a Saturday afternoon with Mama. And judo, of course; I was determined this madman would not stop me from judo.

Eva had not yet managed to get any tear gas. But in spite of having only a blank in the gun, I felt better, walking home from work through the deserted dark streets. Holding the gun with my left hand in my coat pocket, I felt less helpless. The right hand I needed when I reached our building to open the door. This was always the worst moment, in case he was hiding inside.

I had thought of carrying a torch, but was afraid I would provide a better target. No, it was better just to hold the pistol. The loud bang might frighten him off; perhaps bring someone on the scene to help me – although the last time the blank went off, no one had come to inquire even later.

Four or five days passed, then one evening, as I opened the door to our flat, the light was still on, and my mother and brother were waiting for me. "Where have you been?" Mama shouted. She was very agitated.

"In judo, as usual," I said. She knew where I had been. I had gone straight from work, as always.

"He was here, Gerti," Mama took a big breath. "I knew at once it was him, from his wild look."

Now Willi joined in, and with both talking at the same time, it took a while until I made sense of it all.

Around six in the evening, they heard a knock on the door, and saw a young man standing outside. "Where is she?" he had shouted, pushing his way past Mama into our flat. She said I was out, but he didn't believe her, and tried to ransack the flat.

Willi then took the initiative. He recognised the intruder, who had gone to school with him.

"Get out of my flat," my brother had said. "And stop writing stupid letters."

But this had angered the intruder, and he attacked Willi. My brother had grabbed him, pushed him out of the door and bolted it.

The man had tried bashing the door in, without any success, but he kept shouting, threatening he would have his revenge; we'd all have to pay for it now.

Then it got quiet. He seemed to have left, but Mama suspected a trap. He might wait on the landing for me, or on the staircase. She wanted to call the police, but Willi would have to go to a phone box, and this man could attack him in the dark.

They were still debating what to do when they heard the sirens of emergency vehicles.

Fire engines, police, and an ambulance arrived. Our house was lit up with their lights, and police swarmed all over.

They'd had a phone call, informing them I had planted a bomb in our house. The caller had given my name and address.

Once our building had been searched and no bomb was found, two plain clothes officers came to our flat. Mama was glad she had been to the police station, because now she was believed that we were not responsible for bringing such huge costs to the emergency services.

Now they had a good reason to look for the man, the police found him easily, as Willi could tell them where he lived, remembering the building from his schooldays.

The next morning the same officers came to tell us they had apprehended the man. He had psychiatric problems, and was released from a mental institution only six months ago. He lived round the corner from us, and from the window of his flat saw me going past every day. He had followed me a few times, and in the judo club tried chatting me up, trying to make a date with me. I had ignored him, and he had wanted to take his revenge.

It was as simple as that.

For us, this trouble had found its end. The man was taken back to the mental institution, and we heard no more of him.

CHAPTER 25

MY JUDO DREAM COMES TRUE

It was strange, how quickly everything could go back to its old patterns. When my life was in danger, I was sure if this threat was lifted off me, I'd be the happiest girl on earth. And for a time I felt really like that – happy and so relieved. Everything glowed in beautiful colours, a new special light seemed to shine. My life was a wonder, it was marvellous. It was enough, just to live without constantly being on guard, without worrying someone might jump out of the shadows, without someone wanting to kill me.

This danger was over. The man was behind bars once more, and could do nothing to hurt me. I was safe again – at least as safe as I had been before all this started. I could forget him, and enjoy life again, even more than before because now I valued what I had much more.

But as the weeks went by, my intensive feelings of happiness. awareness and appreciation, slowly dimmed and faded away, and life at home moved gradually into its old ways and routines. Soon it was back to 'normal' again. But it still surprised me, how supportive my mother had been during this terrible time. Our relationship had remained much better than ever before. Mama still nagged, and called me bad names at times, but her language was milder and her outbursts didn't last quite as long.

But perhaps I didn't give her as much reason to be angry with me. I tried to be more co-operative and helpful. Knowing Mama loved me – that she cared enough to have gone to see me when I lived with the Hammers – and that she'd wanted me back, and had supported me when my life was in danger made a big difference.

Only judo I would not give up, even for Mama and for more peace at home. I understood why she was so against it. She was concerned about my health, because of my heart. But she didn't understand what judo meant to me.

Willi too had changed towards me for the better. He must have wanted me back, or at least had not objected. Even his tormenting had lost some of its edge. And when this madman had come to our flat, Willi had thrown him out. I was proud of my brother; he had protected me. What was more, he didn't put all the blame on me.

The gun was safely back with Eva, and we were all glad it was gone.

My life at home remained better than it ever had been, and this trend seemed set to continue. Only another eight months and my apprenticeship would end, and perhaps I could find a job which didn't involve any sewing. But whatever happened, I enjoyed my life again, in my free time I could do as I pleased. I met my friends when I could, especially Eva. We were still the closest of friends, especially as we shared our enthusiasm for judo.

My real life continued to revolve around judo. But even here problems arose. The yearly championship for newcomers was approaching, and the five best beginners would be sent to compete. It was a big event, every club in Austria would send their best new judokas, and I would be among them. I worked even harder, knowing I was as good or better than any of the new boys.

I looked forward so much to the championships, until Herr Wunsch took me aside one day telling me we needed to talk.

"I am sorry, Gerti," he said, kindness and understanding in his eyes. I knew something was very wrong, even before he said:

"You cannot go to the championships. I know you are as good as any of the new boys, but women don't fight. I've enquired if we can make an exception, but the judo federation turned me down flat. It can't be done. I am sorry, Gerti, but my hands are tied."

"But," I began, and didn't know how to continue, my dreams had turned to ashes under his kind, but firm words. He was still looking at me with sympathy and concern in his eyes.

"Here in the club, I can make the rules," he said eventually. "And here you practise and fight like everyone, boy or girl – and you are better than many. Outside the club, I have to stick to the rules." He put his arm around my shoulders, as he continued: "I am sorry, Gerti."

Listening to his words, my world collapsed around me – my judo-world, which I had so carefully created. It was so unfair. Just because I was a girl, I was treated worse than the boys.

But what could I do? Of course I continued with judo, but something was missing, something vital. It didn't matter anymore if I won in a contest, or lost – it did not matter if I was the best.

My friend Martin won the championships, and I was pleased for him. But I was as good as he was – but such thoughts were pointless now.

Our club was very successful that year. Christian Such, the boy I had noticed for a long time, won the Austrian junior championships at lightweight. He had succeeded in keeping his weight just below sixty-eight kilos. This was my weight too now.

I had lost two kilos without even trying, but wanted to lose a little more. But it was difficult. I left for work at six thirty in the morning, still half asleep and too tired to eat breakfast. And so early I wasn't hungry, and had no time anyway.

Mama packed me sandwiches for lunch, but by ten, I was always so hungry I ate them. Which meant I had nothing left for lunch, and by the afternoon I was ravenous. Three days per week I went directly from work to judo. I had to go by tram, it was too far to walk, but this meant I had no money left at all, not even to buy a bread roll. In the excitement of judo I forgot my empty stomach. I took the advanced class now as well as the beginners, which meant three hours of non-stop training. I was famished when I came home.

Somewhere I had read that eating late would cause me to put on more weight, so I tried not to eat when I came home.

"I must not eat," I'd tell myself, trying to conjure up a slim me – how I would look if I lost a few kilos. Mama and Willi were already in bed – the flat was in darkness. I'd undress quietly in the kitchen, not to wake them, ignoring the enticing smell of food coming from the table.

"I've left you some of your favourite sausage, already in a roll, and potato salad," Mama's voice would emerge from the dark. She rarely shouted at me now if I came home late, she had given up. Instead, she would tempt me to eat – and usually she succeeded.

My food lay enticingly on a plate. A small shaft of light shining through from our neighbour's window would illuminate the contours of the delicacies on the table which always smelled delicious. My mother wanted to tempt me, and tempt me she did.

'I'll just have one bite,' I would tell myself – only half a Knackwurst, or just one roll, or half a sandwich – but then I would eat the other half too, or the next bread roll. Suddenly the slim Gerti didn't seem to matter anymore, so I enjoyed the potato salad as well. I'll start tomorrow with losing weight, I'd tell myself sleepily, as I crept into bed, satisfied, and forgot the slim Gerti.

CHAPTER 26

IN LOVE

Although my life on the whole had improved, it more and more split into separate parts which had little to do with each other. I seemed to live in different compartments, different boxes, the small ones more interesting, and important to me.

In my largest compartment was my work with Tante Paula, because I spent most of my time in her shop. Although I still hated sewing, I coped quite well; I liked Tante Paula, she was kind on the whole. But my employment would cease when my apprenticeship ended, because my aunt couldn't afford to pay a 'proper' wage.

My home life was in my second compartment, where everything to do with Mama and Willi had its place, and with the Pelzgasse. Although this part of my life was better since coming back from my father, it was still difficult. I longed to be independent, have a room to myself, or at least more space.

And although my relationship with my mother remained better, at times she still nagged for hours, and, if I provoked her, she might slap my face. Until the day, I just stood in front of her, and said calmly: "Do you feel better now, Mama?" It must have done something, because she never hit me again.

If my life was not easy, at least it was bearable now.

Mama still tried to stop me going out in the evening, particularly to judo. But her attempts were half-hearted and she didn't expect me to heed her words any more. And she still disapproved of my friends, with the exception of Eva. In spite of having lent me her pistol, Mama liked her, and always enjoyed a long conversation with her.

One serious problem was that if I came home from a café, my clothes smelled of smoke. Mama would get up and put the chair with my clothes outside on the landing. Anyone might go past, and I was afraid my belongings could be taken. So I'd get up again, and bring the chair back in. Then Mama got up a second time, to take the chair out. I took it back in and after two further repetitions I gave in, leaving the chair with my clothes outside our flat, in full view of our neighbours walking past in the morning.

Mama definitely had more staying-power than me.

Facing our neighbours and saying hallo when we met, was very embarrassing, though no one said anything.

I just had to accept the situation, at least until I was eighteen, and earned enough money to live on my own. And my life was a paradise now, compared to my life with Frau Hammer. So, on balance, life in my second compartment was better, than it ever had been.

My friends had their place in my third compartment, together with entertainment. Here were the books I read, and a new boyfriend now and again. But nothing serious developed, and it always ended, when a goodnight kiss wasn't enough for him anymore. But I didn't mind, I rarely went on a date, because I needed my energy and time for judo.

Judo deserved a whole compartment, as the most important part of my life. When I entered the dojo I could be who I was, and do what I liked most. I didn't have to please anyone, did not have to be nice. I could be aggressive, because if tempered with skill it was a plus in a fight, which was called a contest in judo. I could be as good a fighter, as I was able to be – fighting was a sport now.

But just lately, my attention wandered away from fighting, if my partner was Christian Such.

After teaching us a new technique, our trainer would say: "all right, partner up." And increasingly often Christian happened to stand next to me, and we would practise together. Usually, it wasn't for long, because Herr Wunsch would clap his hands, and call: OK, change partners, and gave Christian a more advanced boy to practice with. Though I belonged to the advanced class now and had a yellow belt, Christian wore a blue belt, and during the last year had won several championships.

But still, increasingly often we practised together.

Perhaps he liked me too, I sometimes thought, but always pushed the thought quickly away. Christian was not only the best in our judo club, he was really attractive – he could have any girl – the most beautiful one. Why should he be interested in me?

One night we left the club at the same time. Christian walked by my side, and we kept talking until I was home. From then on he waited for me after training, to walk me home. He pretended to live near, and it took a few weeks before he admitted he lived in the opposite direction. But by then we were in love. I knew it for certain when he kissed me. I had the key in my hand to open the door to my building, as I turned around to look at Christian for one last time. Our eyes met, he put his arms around me and kissed me. It was a tender, gentle kiss, but it lasted a long time, and I almost drowned in my feelings of pure happiness and bliss.

Now we belonged together, he was my boyfriend, and a new and special compartment opened itself up, a different, secret compartment, which contained our love.

Just as the trees opened their buds, presenting their blossoms and leaves to the sun, so our love grew, showing its beautiful flowers. We lived in an enchanted world. My whole life had been a build-up, leading to now, so I could fully experience this total absorption, the bliss of being in love. Nothing else mattered – at least not much, except judo of course.

I knew Christian felt exactly like me, because we shared each step of the way, walking hand in hand.

Although I had been out with many boys, what I experienced now was very different. With Rolf, I had experienced magic too but fairy tale magic. Christian and I were reality – here and now.

Not that I ever thought about Rolf, or the past – at least not a past before Christian. Only the moment counted, the moment I was with him. If he was not with me, I relived what had happened, thought of our next meeting, and talked about him with my friends, sometimes with Tante Paula. I rarely mentioned him at home, because my brother would tease me. And though Mama had never met Christian, she disapproved of him – partly because she disapproved of all my friends except Eva. But the greatest obstacle was because I knew him from judo, and anything to do with judo was still like a red rag to a bull.

Judo remained a priority for me, but that was good, because we shared judo, too. Now I had another reason to look forward to training, we were together even there. And afterwards Christian would walk me home. We'd sit on a bench in one of the parks on the Guertel, watch the flowers and trees, watch people hurrying or strolling by and the cars on the road. But we only had eyes for each other.

After work, if there was no judo, we'd sit in a café and talk, or go for a walk, or to the cinema on occasion. At the weekend, we'd take a trip into the country if the weather was nice, or go swimming.

When Christian went to championships outside Vienna, I had time to catch up with my friends. They knew him, because sometimes we met in a group, so we all could stay in touch.

Christian wanted to pick me up from home, meet my mother and brother. He had asked me a few times now. But I'd always refused, ashamed of our small flat with the worn lino, and the peeling walls which should have been painted years ago. But this wasn't the only reason. I was afraid of Mama's reaction if a boy came to collect me. And how would Christian react to her?

It was far safer not to take any risks and keep my boyfriend away from my mother. But one day I was in bed with the flu, and couldn't let Christian know. I was too ill to worry about anything, when a knock came on our door. Mama opened it, and I heard Christian's voice. He introduced himself and asked for me. To my surprise, Mama asked him in, and even let him sit on my bed. But she stood right next to him, using this opportunity to question Christian about his parents, and if he was a Catholic.

Christian didn't have any kind of a religious upbringing, and though I looked at him imploringly, he wouldn't lie to my mother. He said no, when she asked if he went to Mass on a Sunday.

"And what about Gerti?" Mama asked. I had to do something quickly, to prevent a catastrophe. But my mother was not to be diverted, and looked at Christian with a challenge in her eyes.

"What about Gerti on a Sunday?" Mama repeated. I was so embarrassed, but she would not let go of the subject. "If you meet so early to spend a day in the countryside, Gerti has no time to go to Mass."

"I can go to early Mass before catching the train," I lied quickly, hoping to avoid a disaster. "Or go to Mass in the country."

Christian didn't contradict me, and I breathed a sigh of relief as Mama dropped the subject – but only to interrogate him about his job. Christian had an apprenticeship in telephone–communication with the post office, and his long-term prospects were excellent. But his apprenticeship lasted five years, two years longer than mine.

Mama found no fault with this and wanted to know more about his family.

But I'd had enough of this interrogation, and Christian must have felt the same, because after answering Mama's first question politely, he quickly stood up and said he had to go now. After wishing me a speedy recovery, he assured Mama how glad he was they had finally met. He even managed to sound sincere.

And he made his escape.

Even this visit changed nothing between us, perhaps Christian was even more understanding. And now, after he had seen our flat and met Mama, I could finally talk to him about my whole life. Whatever happened seemed to bring us closer together.

Only one problem remained, which concerned Christian's parents.

In a vague sort of way, I had known them, since I'd started judo, because they were often in the dojo, watching their son with pride. An elderly couple, Christian was their only child, conceived late in life. His father had been in an acrobat in the circus, until he was getting too old and wanted to settle with a family. So he had married and joined the police.

Mr and Mrs Such were so proud of their son, and they made it obvious. They also made their disapproval of me obvious. Christian said they didn't disapprove of me personally – they did not really know me – they would have disapproved of any girl he went out with. In their opinion, at seventeen, he was too young for a serious relationship.

He must have convinced them otherwise, because after a few months, I was invited to dinner. I didn't want to go, but Christian convinced me this visit was necessary for our future together.

Their flat was so different from ours. It was sunny, large and well kept, with beautiful furniture and strategically-placed flowers and plants. Everything looked perfect. But although Herr and Frau Such were polite and we talked, the atmosphere remained rather cool. The meal was delicious, but I was too nervous to enjoy it. Christian did his best to keep the conversation flowing, and when I said my goodbyes, Frau Such invited me to visit again. I was accepted as Christian's girlfriend.

Summer arrived, and we lived in an enchanted world, a world of magic, only shared by my boyfriend and me. Our kisses grew longer and deeper, and soon our kisses seemed not enough. Christian respected my boundaries, but I asked myself, were they still necessary? So much had changed – I had changed. In the past I could not imagine to give all of myself – but now, I imagined it only too well. And my body did too.

But my mind stayed in control. Christian did not try to rush me – but our bodies pushed against my boundaries, as if they had a life of their own. But we kept in control, until the morning we took the early train to Baden.

Walking out of the town past the vineyards, we stopped at the castle a while, and then took a path into the wood. It was an ancient, enchanted forest, with giant trees, centuries old. Our path led us ever deeper and further into this fairy tale forest.

Quite suddenly it started to rain, thick heavy drops, promising a deluge. No shelter anywhere, just woodland around.

"Look Christian," I said, pointing to a large beech. "This tree is like a huge umbrella."

We walked off the path and took shelter. Like a magic circle, giant bushes grew around the tree, opening just wide enough to let us through, to close behind us again. It was completely dry and sheltered here, and private, like in a hut made of branches and twigs and of leaves. Christian took off his jacket, spread it on the ground, and we sat down. I opened my bag to take our sandwiches out, but we didn't get to eat them, because Christian kissed me. Time seemed to stand still, nothing existed only Christian and I, and our love.

At some time, I became dimly aware of the sound of the rain, but it was a comforting, familiar sound – it was outside our den. In here we were warm and protected, safe under our tree. Our kisses grew longer and ever deeper, he was touching my body, and we both were on fire and forgot everything. Perhaps my no was not firm enough, or perhaps I never said it, as waves of excitement took us into new worlds. I was drowning in love – becoming one with my lover – until a sharp pain brought me back to reality.

My wonderful feelings were gone, and I felt only pain. And then that was over too.

Is this it? I asked myself. I was furious, too furious to speak with Christian. But I was even more furious with myself. I was so angry, I pushed Christian away, jumped up, pulled my clothes into order, and, grabbing my jacket, I turned from Christian and I ran.

I ran through the forest, past the castle and all the way back to the town. I did not stop once, did not look back, I just ran – as if I could run away from what had just happened.

The train was just pulling into the station, I got on and found a place to sit down. As we started to move, Christian slid into the seat next to mine. Neither of us spoke. He put his arm round my shoulders. I almost shrugged him off; I was stiff with anger. But the familiar feel of Christian next to me eased my feelings; his faint scent, the way I always felt when he was close to me. I sighed, and snuggled into his shoulder. It had happened, there was no going back.

As Christian whispered how much he loved me, and that we would always be together, my anger melted away. And as he said he would never again make love to me, unless I clearly said that I wanted him to, I had to smile. I had not intended it, and it had hurt, but it had to happen at some time. And perhaps it would be different next time – as beautiful all the way, as it had begun.

It really did become beautiful, and even better and more wonderful than I could have imagined. I was Christian's first lover, just as he was mine, but this wasn't a problem – quite the opposite. It was exciting to experiment, to discover new ways to express our love. To know each step we took was the first for both of us, gave our love and the sex which belonged to it now, a new dimension.

Our love kept growing, filling both our lives. Everything we did just filled in the time until we were together again. Then our real life began – our love – although this love was always with us, even if we were apart.

As winter approached we enrolled in a dancing course, so Christian would learn to dance too. I liked dancing, and now we could share this pleasure as well.

I still met my friends, and occasionally I went to the cinema with my mother. We enjoyed going to the pictures together, or to the market, shopping for food, and we cooked together. Although Mama still nagged, and complained when I came home late, it didn't matter so much anymore. In a few years I would no longer live here, but together with Christian.

Winter came, and we decided to go away for a few days after Christmas. We both lied at home, pretending we were going with friends, but I was sure, Mama suspected the truth.

Christian knew of a small inn right in the country – it was secluded and quiet – most people preferred the big ski resorts.

As Christian signed us in as Herr and Frau Such, I felt very apprehensive. We were both only seventeen. But no one questioned us, and soon we relaxed in the privacy of the small room we shared. Now we could be together for days, and alone. We took long walks in the wood, and on New Year's Eve we celebrated in our room with a bottle of champagne.

Of course we made love – we always made love, at every opportunity, and again and again. But in between we talked, and I told my lover about my childhood, and the 'false' confessions. And how terrible I had felt – afraid to die, being destined for hell.

Christian had no religious upbringing at all, and had no fear of hell – he didn't even know what a sin was. But after I had explained the basics about sinning and hell, and we talked how it had been for me, he understood and sympathised.

"Why don't you go to confession now, Gerti?" he asked. "Surely you could explain to the priest how it all happened, and make a real confession, if it would make you feel good."

I thought about his words for a while. But I felt good anyway – well, at least when I was with Christian – or when I knew I would see him soon. But on some nights, I still lay in bed with pains in my chest, and fear in my heart. Even if I didn't want to admit it to myself – I was still afraid of dying and going to hell – I just didn't think about it so often.

But yes, I would have the courage to make a real confession. But there was a new problem.

"Making love is a sin," I felt stupid as I said it, because it didn't feel like a sin.

Christian looked puzzled. I felt like an idiot, sex was part of our love for each other, and it felt right, it was the most wonderful aspect of our lives. Sex must surely have been created for everyone to enjoy – and not just for married Catholics. But these thoughts were almost certainly sins again. I couldn't get away from sinning.

"The problem is," I started again – it wasn't easy to explain my problems to Christian, who knew nothing about the complications of a confession. "The problem is," I repeated, "I would have to intend, not to make love again. And I must to mean it, otherwise my confession is false again, and another sin."

My lover pondered on this new information. "If this really is such a problem for you, Gerti," he finally said, "we could wait until we are married. Then, it surely couldn't be a sin anymore."

We were silent for a while, as I got lost in my thoughts. That Christian would wait – two, maybe even three years, until we could afford to pay for a flat so we could get married, made me feel very special. He loved me so much that he would do anything to make me happy. But I was happy. And it would be wrong – and very difficult if not impossible – not to express this part of our love, now we had started.

I shook my head. "No, Christian," I said, and had to smile, as I saw the relief in his eyes. "It's too late, sex has already become too much part of us now."

We made love again, slowly and tenderly this time.

With my lover I was already in heaven – in our heaven – and the other heaven could wait.

CHAPTER 27

WALES 2021
THE CIRCLE CLOSES

Nearly three decades went by since I had finished writing.

Now, as I looked at my story again, I realized that by reliving it all, in my mind I had been Gerti the child, seeing things through her eyes, with her changing viewpoint throughout the years.

As my perception expanded and I saw things from different angles and sides, some bits about later years had to be added. During this process, so much happened on a deeper level I have no words for. And it wasn't just about me, but my family too, and the wonderful people who helped me out on the way. Once I started, more stuff came up asking to be revisited. And old journals, diaries with scraps of paper inside, also triggered clear pictures of the past.

I didn't rush, didn't have to consider anyone else or how long it would take. This was my story, it was about facing myself, about healing – which carried on, in dribs and drabs, and hopefully will continue.

After the accident, my body repaired itself as best as it could, but some damage is left, even now, and pain too. Being close to the sea was a bonus, and the solitude, which I'd always needed, helped too.

When I had finally finished with writing, I put the pages into a drawer, where they stayed until now, a time, when the circle of my life is beginning to close. I am nearing eighty, and it is time to put order into my life. What is of no use anymore, has to go. But there is still time. Even more time, as we are in lockdown because of the corona crisis. I had to stop going to places, meeting friends, even my son. But if the outward journeys are closed, all the more reason for travelling inwards. So I looked at the manuscript and read it through, trying to decide what to do with it. Should I publish this story? Would it be of any interest, any use to anyone? Or perhaps I should just bind it and leave to my family, for later generations, not just to find out about my life, but as a window into a time long past. Perhaps reading my story, they'd be more aware of the changes which happen through ordinary people, through people like all of us – just as our descendants will leave their mark behind for future generations.

Everything has changed so much and is changing so quickly – more so now, seemingly speeding up every day: our conceptions and ideas, and opportunities, especially for girls. Today, if I were young, I would have no problem in finding a judo club – at least once the pandemic is over, and contact between people is allowed again.

In judo, I was one of the forerunners, smoothing the path for the next generation, and those yet to come. I wonder, if any of the young girl athletes, playing football, boxing or judo, ever think how hard it was to make a beginning, many years ago.

Reading through my book, I had a big surprise in store for me. Only now did I realize, how many of my childhood dreams came true – dreams, which at the time I couldn't admit even to myself, because I thought they never could happen. Yet nearly all of them did. Some in a slightly different fashion, but containing the same core.

My judo dream materialized first. After four years of training, I made my first dan, though the black belt was no longer important to me. I just wanted to fight and win championships. And as many things changed rapidly during these years, I was given the chance.

In 1964, the Judo Federation of Czechoslovakia invited all European countries to ladies championships. Behind the Iron Curtain the attitude towards women and sport was very different. Men and women trained alike, at least in judo, but probably in other sports too. Sport was important, bringing advantages not only for men who excelled, but even more so for women. Judo was a sport for men and women alike in their world.

Most countries declined the invitation, including Great Britain. Their women were not ready for championships, so they wrote. East Germany accepted and sent their judokas, and the third country taking part was Austria. But though quite a few girls were learning judo by then, I was still the only girl used to fighting. With the championships coming, this changed overnight. But although our girls were willing and worked hard, with just a few weeks preparation, their chances were small.

It was quite an adventure, and a privilege, to travel behind the Iron Curtain, which was closed to nearly everyone. Just over an hour's ride by car, we entered a different world. In Bratislava, empty spaces were plastered with huge placards, announcing: 'through sport to peace and unity between countries'. Our championships were meant by this, as the coming events were announced in big letters. Not only women's championships were held, men had their own events too, and team contests also took place. The events lasted several days.

The Czechoslovakian state paid for it all: our stay in a top class hotel, where everything was provided, from food to champagne. We even had our own political advisor, so we wouldn't put a foot wrong, or rather say a wrong word and get into trouble. We were invited to the Austrian Consul where I saw my first butler, and a banquet was given in our honour.

The girls from East Germany and Czechoslovakia were brilliant fighters, they had always trained the same as their male counterparts. But so had I, and I won the championships in my weight class.

A year later, at the next championships, I won again.

Then I came on holiday to England, and fell in love with a Welshman. We got married, and I came to South Wales. I trained with the Dockers club in Newport, and took part in the Welsh championships in1968, which I also won.

Judo remained a big part of my life, but my family, and especially my son, had priority now. These years were not always easy, and often quite challenging, as my marriage didn't work out and ended in divorce, and I brought up my son by myself.

Just as my mother had prophesied, my sewing skills came in handy during these years. I didn't only make most of our clothes, I also made all the uniforms and some equipment for my son's action men. His friends pestered their mothers for similar things, so I made their stuff too, and even got paid for it. It seems, not much in my life was totally wasted.

I kept the promise I'd made myself as a child: I never spoke negatively about Sean's father. Our son could see him, and, as he got older, could stay with him if he wanted to. He had a happy childhood. I enjoyed these years too, reliving my childhood, but in a way I would have liked it to be. We built wigwams in the wood, fished with small nets for sticklebacks and tadpoles, releasing them back to their environment at the end of the day. I taught him to swim, and we soon swam in the sea. And we swung from trees on my climbing rope, which I still had from Austria.

Mountaineering and rock climbing were also dreams which came true, and of course, I swam across the Danube and back, which was a bit unnerving because of the strong current and the noise the water made, rushing over the big boulders and stones.

During the early years of my son's childhood, I worked only part time. My sisters-in-law would look after Sean. All my ex-husband's family were supportive, and Sean grew up with quite a few aunties and uncles and cousins around, as well as his grandmother.

Some years later, at the local leisure centre I took oil painting classes. This medium was the right one for me, and I continued painting until recently, and even sold a few paintings. Clare, my painting instructor, encouraged me to study fine art. I was accepted for the foundation course, but changed my mind. I needed a career which would give me more security than a degree in fine arts, and I needed a job with a good salary, which would support us both – my son was about fourteen at the time. But in this, fate, or spirit, or whatever it was, came to my assistance. Clare was a social worker in her daytime job, she had become my friend, and we frequently painted together. Through her I learned, that although academic qualifications were necessary to qualify for social work training, exceptions were made for people with the right life experience and special abilities. So, eventually I decided on social work, which had interested me for a long time, especially working with children and families, and of course, mental health.

Initially, I took a few courses, including English O level, thinking as I was not a native speaker, this would be a good beginning. I passed with an A, at the same time as my son, who had a B. But perhaps the examiner felt sorry for me and gave me additional points, because of my sad story about my sixth birthday, with the sausage as a present. However, my courses were irrelevant, as I was told at university that O-levels didn't count.

Filling in application forms for social work courses, meant writing relevant essays too. It was a lengthy procedure, with a lot of writing and long interviews, but eventually I was accepted everywhere I applied, and chose the post graduate course for social work at Cardiff University, simply because of how I had felt in my childhood, with higher education out of my reach. And perhaps I wanted to prove something to myself by passing a postgraduate course, with only eight years of basic education.

Another dream had come true: I was a university student. I was even given a discretionary grant from my local authority, for both my son and me.

Perhaps this was one of the reasons I had to come to this country. In Austria, I would never have been accepted at university without higher education. And a postgraduate course without a degree, would have been unthinkable.

Once I had found out about bibliography and references, I adapted quite easily to academic essays and the other course work, and made the CQSW, and the Diploma for Social Work, which were the best qualifications. At the age of thirty-nine I became a social worker, specialising in working with families and children. With my life experience, it came natural to me. I enjoyed my work, and was good at it, though our team was very pressurised, because of limited staff and resources.

Quite obviously, I didn't die before I was thirty, as I had always expected. To my astonishment and delight my heart healed itself. Even now, it is well and healthy. How it happened, I have no idea.

At twenty, I still had my heart problem, as I knew from examinations in Vienna, and electrocardiograms. Ten years later my heart was healed, as I was to find out.

Bringing up my son alone and still having chest pains, I thought it better to check on my heart, to better prepare for the future.

I had kept all my electrocardiograms and other relevant medical papers – in Austria you keep these yourself. And after a referral from my doctor, l went to see the heart specialist.

After extensive examinations and a new ECG, I sat in his office. The consultant smiled at me. "Everything is fine with your heart, Mrs Baldwin," he informed me. "You are fit to live to the ripe age of ninety-five."

"But," I nearly stammered, finding it difficult to take this news in. "I have always been told, my heart would never get better."

And I put the evidence on his desk.

He looked through the pictures of the beat of my heart. I offered to translate the reports, but he shook his head. "I don't need to know, I have more than enough evidence, that your heart has healed itself. The best you can do with these papers, is to throw them away."

"But," I started again, still having problems to accept this new situation. "What about the pains in my chest?"

He wrinkled his brow, was silent for a while, then looked at me over the rims of his glasses, with an expression of great interest.

"If you have chest pains, does it worry you?" he finally asked.

"Yes," I just said.

"Worrying makes the pains stronger."

Then he sat in silence again, looking at me, as if he was considering something, until he finally asked: "If you had pains in your big toe, would it worry you?"

"No," I said, thinking about his words, which made no sense at all.

"If I had pains in my toe, I could still breathe," I finally said, because he remained silent and seemed to wait for me to go on. "But the pains in my chest affect my breathing, especially during the night. I can't even lie down."

"Fear makes everything worse," he said, "especially panic. The heart is a muscle, and every muscle can hurt. Through fear, we make everything worse. Next time you have chest pains, pretend they are in your big toe."

Could this method really work? Could it be the solution? Throughout my childhood and youth, I had always been told to take things easy, and not to exert myself. I had not followed this advice, and lived my life to the extreme. Now, only ten years later, this medical expert told me my heart was healthy. And then he even said that sport was good for the heart.

He pushed my papers towards me, and I took them, to put them into my handbag.

"What shall I do with them?" I wondered.

"The best you can do," he advised me, "is to put them in the bin." And he pointed to the waste paper basket beside his desk.

I really put all my old documents in. And this was the end of this problem.

If my chest pains returned, I practised his method of transferring my pains to my toe. It really helped, though it didn't totally work. Through the years, my pains diminished, though even now they return occasionally for a visit. I either ignore them, or take a remedy from my homeopath, which also helps.

More recently, getting older, my heart has been examined with all the new methods which have been developed throughout the years. But even now I am told that my heart is healthy.

But the biggest and best change in my life is that I am no longer afraid of hell, or of dying. It took a long time and was a slow journey, which started, when I finally made a proper, valid confession.

I was twenty at the time. My relationship with Christian had ended a few months earlier. It had been my doing, my own fault. I was not ready for marriage and children, still needing adventure, wanting more out of life. Christian was far more stable and responsible, he was ready to settle down, and couldn't understand why I wanted to travel, to explore life. So in the end our relationship broke up.

Now I was in hospital with hepatitis, and on the way to recovery. A young priest came to visit. He popped his head around the door to ask if anyone wanted to make a confession. I took this opportunity. I wasn't afraid any more of telling a priest about my past and my sins. And without Christian, or another man in my life, I had no problem intending to remain chaste.

So I told the priest everything, and made a full and valid confession.

Afterwards he stayed for a while and we talked. He claimed that each individual has a different kind of conscience, varying greatly from one person to another. He couldn't think of a better way, so he said, but compare a conscience to a sieve, a strainer used for cooking, straining the water from vegetables or pasta, or even tea.

You could get sieves with small holes, he said, getting quite into this theory now. Some people had very big holes in their sieves, so he said, and many varieties existed in between. My problem was, that the holes in my sieve – or in my conscience – were too small. They hardly let anything through. Some people could commit serious crimes, even harm people, yet their conscience let everything through, like a sieve with big holes. And because of this, they hardly felt any guilt. In future, so this young priest advised me, I should remind myself, that my conscience was a sieve, where the holes were too small.

This made sense to me, and it did bring relief. And having made a full and valid confession for the first time in my life, a burden was lifted from my shoulders. I took Holy Communion, receiving the body of Christ. My fear of hell had diminished, but my fear of death had not disappeared. And I didn't feel any closer to God.

After being discharged from hospital and recovering for a few days, I climbed up the Hochschwab, a mountain about 2,000 meters high, where I frequently went for a week end. It was only a few hours travel from Vienna.

After climbing for many hours I was totally exhausted. But I reached the summit, and stood where a cross marked the highest spot. Here, with the wind in my hair, and looking down at the lower peaks and the valleys, I could feel God. Though I didn't know it then, the deep connection I felt was my connection with a higher power. And my longing, was a longing for God.

So I walked back down the next morning, and took my old life up again. As I had to work hard to earn a living, spending my weekends in the mountains and most evenings in the dojo, I had little time to think about the more spiritual aspects of life, and what would happen after I left this earth.

But again and again something would happen, forcing me to think on a deeper level. When my mother died, over a decade later, I was no longer able to push death away. Wherever I was, suddenly a picture about death would appear in my mind – my own death – my body, lying in its grave, with worms busily eating my flesh.

During the day, I could distract myself somehow, but not at night. I couldn't control my dreams – they were nightmares, and I woke up in terror. Suspecting there might still be some remnants of my old fears lurking inside me, I told myself, that I was safe, and would not go to hell. But it made no difference. Heaven was too nebulous a place to bring any comfort, and praying didn't help either. Death continued stalking me.

Finally I realized I had no other choice but to face whatever it was. So rather than push away my thoughts about death, I let them meander on, wherever they wanted to go. I would look at them, ask them why they were here, and what was behind my fear. So my search began. What I was searching for, I didn't know. But I knew it had to do with the reason of life, with death, and what would come after.

I had always been interested in yoga and Buddhism, even took a few classes in my youth, when I was still in Vienna. Now I went to courses and workshops on various related subjects, including reincarnation and karma. I read books about different religions and methods of self-development, joined a Gurdjieff group, learning about the different parts of myself, of self-remembering, and observing my emotions. But after a few years, I felt this path wasn't taking me far enough, and it was too slow for me.

I looked closer at the different paths of psychology – especially Jung I liked. I read more books on self-development, trying this or that method, going to more workshops, and collected crystals.

It seemed there were as many different paths as there were people, and I just had to choose the most suitable, at any given time.

When I discovered Shamanism, it was like coming home. The shamanic journey was so familiar. As a child I had taken similar journeys, often with my black panther, who still on occasion visited me. For a few years I worked with shamanic methods, taking courses with Kenneth Meadows, who became a friend. But even this path wasn't enough as my consciousness expanded.

Then, fifteen years ago, I found the right path for the rest of my life and beyond: Eckankar. Dreaming, and travelling into other worlds, took on new dimensions. Everything I had struggled to learn, to find out, and to develop in myself, finally found its home. Karma and reincarnation had long become facts for me. Now, as I explored my past lives, I was on a path which was leading me ever further. I experienced, that I am soul. A soul with many energy bodies, and a physical body to live here on earth. And when I leave this body behind, I go on to a different plane – or dimension – perhaps another life here on earth again after a spell elsewhere. What seems certain, learning continues in some form.

My understanding has changed, and is still changing, but life remains my biggest, my most important teacher, with challenges bringing new possibilities, new opportunities for learning. My car accident was an opportunity for further growth. It brought change, I had to adapt to a different way of life – needed to develop new strength, and accept my weaknesses, which was for me a most difficult task.

At sixty, I returned to Vienna, and stayed seven years. Lilly was no longer alive, and I missed her. But I spent much time with Christl, and with my nephews and nieces, their children, old friends, and the new friends I made.

Then I came back to Wales, because this is also my home, and my son is here, a wonderful man, who was able to develop freely, and never feared death. I did not pass my problems on. As a child, when he asked about God, I simply said, God is love – at least this I already knew even then.

My fear of hell disappeared decades ago, and a few times I looked deeply into the eyes of death, who is no longer the enemy but a friend. I am ready to die, to step through the door to a new life.

I have always loved God, but just didn't know. It took me so long to realize, that the wonders of nature, the love of animals and the many wonderful people I met, are all expressions of God's love.

When my body dies, my life continues, because I am soul, a spark of God, and I will go on to new worlds, and to new wonders.

The author

Gerti Baldwin was born in Vienna in 1941. Spending her earlier years in poverty with her mother and siblings, after formal education she had various jobs including tailoring and office work.

From childhood on she liked to read and write. Her first title, Nico and sein Drache was written in German and published in 2007 in Vienna. She wrote an English version of this book in 2017, coupled with the book In Mysterious Way, both under the pen name Geri Stone. There is also a German version of her current book, The Other Heaven Can Wait.

Growing up, Gerti loved climbing, swimming and her favourite, judo. She was the first girl to join a judo club and won several championships.

After taking a postgraduate course in social work, she worked mainly with children until retirement. She lives in Wales with her partner and has an adult son. She loves the sea, enjoys swimming and tai chi, pursuing interest in art, psychology and alternative healing methods.

The publisher

He who stops getting better stops being good.

This is the motto of novum publishing, and our focus is on finding new manuscripts, publishing them and offering long-term support to the authors.
Our publishing house was founded in 1997, and since then it has become THE expert for new authors and has won numerous awards.

Our editorial team will peruse each manuscript within a few weeks free of charge and without obligation.

You will find more information about novum publishing and our books on the internet:

www.novum-publishing.co.uk